D0952191

MANAGING THE RISK OF FRAUD AND MISCONDUCT

MEETING THE CHALLENGES OF A GLOBAL, REGULATED, AND DIGITAL ENVIRONMENT

RICHARD H. GIRGENTI, J.D.
AND TIMOTHY P. HEDLEY, Ph.D.

McGraw Hill

New York   Chicago   San Francisco   Lisbon   London   Madrid   Mexico City
Milan   New Delhi   San Juan   Seoul   Singapore   Sydney   Toronto

2 3 4 5 6 7 8 9 0   DOC/DOC   1 6 5 4 3 2 1

ISBN 978-0-07-162129-8

MHID 0-07-162129-6

This publication is designed to provide accurate and authoritative information in regard to the subject matter covered. It is sold with the understanding that neither the author nor the publisher is engaged in rendering legal, accounting, securities trading, or other professional services. If legal advice or other expert assistance is required, the services of a competent professional person should be sought.

—From a Declaration of Principles Jointly Adopted
by a Committee of the American Bar Association and
a Committee of Publishers and Associations

This book represents the views of the authors only and does not necessarily represent the views or professional advice of KPMG LLP.

McGraw-Hill books are available at special quantity discounts to use as premiums and sales promotions or for use in corporate training programs. To contact a representative, please e-mail us at bulksales@mcgraw-hill.com.

This book is printed on acid-free paper.

Contents

About the Editors/Authors

Richard H. Girgenti, Principal, KPMG

Rich Girgenti is the National and Americas leader for KPMG LLP's Forensic Advisory Services, global lead for the firm's Compliance and Monitoring network, and a member of the firm's International Forensic Steering Group. He has more than 35 years of experience both nationally and globally conducting investigations and providing fraud risk management advisory services to public and private corporations, as well as federal and state government entities and not-for-profit organizations.

Rich has served as a member of the board of directors for KPMG LLP and the Americas region. He has chaired the board's Governance Task Force, as well as the Professional Practice, Ethics and Compliance and the Nominating committees. He has also served as a member of the Audit and Finance and the Pension committees.

Prior to joining KPMG, Rich held a number of high-level legal and law enforcement positions. He served as New York State Director of Criminal Justice and Commissioner of the Division of Criminal Justice Services, where he oversaw and coordinated the policies and initiatives of all the state's criminal justice agencies and worked closely with all federal and state law enforcement agencies. He is a former veteran state prosecutor in the Office of the Manhattan District Attorney, where he handled investigations, trials, and appeals in both the state and federal courts, including investigations and prosecutions of white-collar, violent, and major narcotics organized crime cases.

Rich holds a bachelor's degree from Seton Hall University and a J.D. from Georgetown University Law Center. He is a Certified Fraud Examiner.

Rich publishes extensively on a wide range of criminal justice, white-collar, and fraud-related topics. He lectures frequently and conducts training programs and workshops on all aspects of fraud investigations and on the evaluation, development, and implementation of integrity programs.

Timothy P. Hedley, Partner, KPMG

Tim Hedley is a partner in KPMG's Forensic practice where he serves as global lead for the firm's Fraud Risk Management network. He provides clients with a wide range of forensic services by assisting with the prevention of, detection of, and response to fraud and misconduct. Tim also directs the development of methodologies and tools to assess the effectiveness of anti-fraud, corporate compliance, and integrity programs for multinational business organizations.

Tim has significant experience working with both public and private companies across a broad range of industries to respond to allegations of fraud or misconduct, including, among others, allegations involving earnings management, counterfeiting, bribery and kickbacks, construction, potential Ponzi schemes, and employee theft. He conducts fraud and compliance risk assessment and designs and conducts fraud awareness and compliance training programs. Tim assists clients with benchmarking their anti-fraud and compliance efforts against recognized industry practices and with designing, implementing, and evaluating corporate fraud investigative units. He also coordinates detailed internal audit testing of identified fraud, compliance, and integrity risk areas, including, among other areas, cash, FCPA, conflicts of interest, equal treatment, and antitrust.

Tim has served on KPMG's Legal and Compliance Committee, chairing the Code of Conduct task force and the Investigative Process Enhancement task force.

Tim is a Certified Public Accountant and a Certified Fraud Examiner and is certified in financial forensics. He holds a bachelor's degree from Siena College and a master's degree from the State University of New York at Albany, both in accounting. He completed his Ph.D. in public management (accounting and control) from Rockefeller College, State University of New York at Albany.

Tim is an adjunct associate professor at Fordham University. He publishes and lectures extensively on fraud, misconduct, and compliance-related topics.

Contributors

The editors would like to thank the following individuals for their invaluable contributions:

Scott Avelino
Sandra L. Beedle
Ori Ben-Chorin
Adam M. Beschloss
Laurence Birnbaum-Sarcy
Bernard A. Boit
Adam K. Bowen
Peter J. Bradford
Kelli J. Brooks
Cassandra C. Cohen
Joy Cohen
Marikay A. Corcoran
Andrew J. Curtin
Joseph P. Dooley
James Dowling
Laura E. Durkin
Douglas E. Farrow
Nina K. D'Arcangelo
Colleen M. Doyle
Jamie M. Faulkner
Edward L. Goings
Aaron Grieser
Christopher D. Hunt
Jaime G. Jue
Thomas P. Keegan
Kenneth C. Koch

James R. Littley
Kate Lyden
Carrie A. Malachowski
Stephen D. Marshall
Brent D. McDaniel
Charles S. Meier
Marc L. Miller
Glenn E. Moyers
Graham J. Murphy
Philip D. Ostwalt
Chris H. Paskach
Nancy Pasternack
Teresa A. Pesce
Barbara M. Porco
Charles H. Reid
Amanda Rigby
Joshua Riley
William W. Rudolph
Michael B. Schwartz
Carla F. Sheinkopf
Justin H. Snell
Nicole Stryker
Nimna Varghese
Alan Williamson
Brian Wilson

Acknowledgments

No effort of the magnitude of writing and editing this book could ever succeed without the encouragement, work, and support of many others. We have listed the names of all those who participated in this effort in the list of contributors and wish to express our gratitude to them. We would also like to underscore here the special efforts of those whose additional support and contributions helped shape the book.

We would like to acknowledge Scott Avelino, Casey Cohen, and Nimna Varghese who throughout this process worked tirelessly researching, writing, and editing much of the content for this book. A special thanks to Chris Hunt and Peter Bradford for their work on the early drafts of the Auditing and Monitoring chapter, to Justin Snell for the chapter on Risk Assessment, and to Doug Farrow, Marc Miller, and Chuck Reid for their contribution to the chapter on Financial Reporting Fraud.

We are grateful for the editing and feedback provided by Phil Ostwalt on the Investigations chapter and by Kelli Brooks on the chapter on Recovery, Presentation, and Analysis of Electronically Stored Information. We also want to thank Tom Keegan for his work on the use of forensic technology in conducting investigations and Kate Lyden for her work on Anti-Bribery and Corruption. We also wish to recognize Tim Dougherty, who played a key role in the early days of this effort in helping shape the vision for this book and helping plan its direction.

A special note of appreciation is due to Ori Ben-Chorin. In addition to coauthoring some of the chapters of this book, Ori played an indispensable role in editing, reviewing, and helping with the management of the overall effort.

In addition, we wish to express our appreciation to Joy Cohen, who has worked assiduously from the beginning of our efforts more than two years ago to the very end. Joy coordinated all of the brainstorming sessions that resulted in the development of the book. She project managed all of the writing, rewriting, and editing of the book. She ensured that we met our deadlines and coordinated all of our interactions with our publisher.

We especially want to acknowledge our appreciation for the support of our families who tolerated our absence on frequent weekends, late nights, and holidays so that we could complete the book. A special thanks to Catherine, Matthew and Christopher Girgenti and to Grant and Mason Hedley for their inspiration and support.

Introduction

As we witness the end of the first decade of the twenty-first century, we find that the issues of fraud and misconduct remain front and center. This is so, despite a decade that saw major reforms, including, among other initiatives, the Sarbanes-Oxley Act, new Federal Sentencing Guidelines, and the USA PATRIOT Act. These reforms were in large measure a response to the financial reporting scandals of the early 2000s of Enron, WorldCom, HealthSouth, and others, as well as an effort to combat terrorist financing in the wake of the terrorist attacks of September 11, 2001.

The corporate financial reporting fraud scandals of the early 2000s were a wake-up call that corporations and those responsible for the integrity of the capital markets were not getting the job done and that more needed to be done. In the aftermath, we saw a renewed focus on risk management, compliance, and governance. Sarbanes-Oxley was a unique piece of legislation that put together, at a single point in time, a number of practical ideas that incorporated fundamental governance principles and best practices about financial reporting. Among its most important aspects, Sarbanes-Oxley included the recognition of the importance of the "tone at the top" of the corporate environment, the vesting in an independent audit committee of direct oversight responsibility for financial reporting, a new system of executive certification and responsibility for the integrity of a company's financial reporting, and a code of ethics for senior financial executives. It also mandated the communication and upward flow of bad news by requiring audit committees to put in place a system for the confidential, anonymous submission by employees of suspicions of misconduct.

As Sarbanes-Oxley did in the area of financial reporting, the Sentencing Guidelines—as enhanced in 2004 and again in 2010—not only fundamentally changed the corporate focus on governance, risk management, and compliance, but also reshaped and drove executive and board behaviors and accountability. The original Sentencing Guidelines were intended to drive the behavior of organizations by "rewarding," with more lenient sentences, the corporate offenders who, at the time of an offense, had implemented an "effective compliance and ethics program." The thinking was that organizations, fearing harsher penalties, would adopt such programs as a precautionary measure. This led to many companies implementing compliance programs for the first time, but left open the question of whether these programs were making a difference. The revised Sentencing Guidelines placed the responsibility for ensuring that programs were designed and operating effectively squarely on the shoulders of executives and boards, and the Sentencing Guidelines were tailored based on the most significant risks to a company.[1]

In light of these reforms, the story for the first decade of the twenty-first century might have been one of getting through a period of financial reporting scandals with stern, but effective, reforms and improvements in corporate governance, risk, and compliance. However, much of the progress that was made was quickly overshadowed by the worst economic downturn in 75 years, the meltdown within the financial sector and the sense that the risks that brought about this crisis went either unnoticed or unmanaged, or perhaps both.

As our current economic downturn was reaching "Great Recession" proportions in the fall of 2008, KPMG LLP sponsored an independent survey of a cross section of over 200 executives from all major industry and government sectors. KPMG asked about their perceptions of fraud within their organizations and across their industries. What nearly two-thirds of these executives reported was that fraud and misconduct remained a significant risk factor in their industries. And if wrongdoing occurred, 71 percent feared a potential loss of public trust at a time when market confidence was at a premium. Most significantly, a third of these executives expected some form of fraud or misconduct to rise in their organizations in the upcoming months and year.

A confluence of circumstances at the close of the first decade resulted in a toxic brew, which made the concerns of these executives none too surprising. Giant and storied financial institutions such as Bear Stearns, Lehman Brothers, AIG, Merrill Lynch, Wachovia, and others were gone—sold to competitors or thrown into the arms of the government for their very survival. Massive and well-publicized Ponzi schemes, such as those perpetrated by Madoff and Stanford, could no longer be sustained in a down economy and were uncovered, further shaking the confidence of investors in the financial sector and in its regulators. In response to the global financial crisis, U.S. and international regulators and law enforcement agencies upped the ante with increased focus and resources and greater cooperation.

At the same time, Congress passed the Emergency Economic Stabilization Act of 2008 (EESA) authorizing trillions of dollars for the purpose, among other things, of stabilizing weakened financial institutions and purchasing troubled assets. To serve as the watchdog for this new program and spending, EESA also created—with broad powers—the Office of the Special Inspector General for the Troubled Asset Relief Program. Not long after, Congress passed the American Recovery and Reinvestment Act of 2009, which created new federal programs and authorized hundreds of billions in new federal funding, and the Fraud Enforcement and Recovery Act of 2009 to strengthen regulatory controls to help prevent and detect potential fraud, waste, and abuse.

In March 2010, Congress completed the passage of legislation and the president signed into law massive health-care reform—the Patient Protection and Affordable Care Act (which included provisions designed to combat Medicare and Medicaid fraud)—and the Dodd-Frank Wall Street Reform and Consumer Protection Act that, among other sweeping reforms in the financial services industry, created new enforcement powers for the Securities and Exchange Commission and enhanced incentives and protection for corporate whistleblowers.

The good news over the past decade has been that more and more companies have recognized the importance of a robust and effective compliance program. Over the last 10 years, in the wake of corporate fraud scandals and related regulatory reforms, effective compliance programs have become recognized as essential to combating corporate fraud and misconduct. According to a recent survey of 386 compliance, legal, and audit executives conducted by *Compliance Week* and Paisley, 93 percent of those surveyed indicated that their companies' compliance functions were developed over the last 10 years. And of those surveyed, 82 percent were 5 years old or less.[2]

Despite this positive development, the maturity of these programs varied widely, and the same study strongly suggested that a great deal more work needed to be done "to turn [these] compliance efforts into strong, mature programs that can handle the broad range of risks corporations face." More specifically, the *Compliance Week* survey found that "a plurality of respondents (44 percent) described their compliance functions as 'organized but reactive'—that is, compliance exists as its own function and has visibility throughout the company, but it is still mostly reacting to problems as they occur rather than preventing them in the first place." Other compliance programs (20.2 percent) fared worse and were described as "siloed and inconsistent" or, put in other terms, "largely isolated from the company's daily operations."[3]

Not surprisingly, the survey also found that in those areas where there had been strong consistent regulatory enforcement over a longer period of time (e.g., Foreign Corrupt Practices Act, securities law, and insider trading), compliance programs designed to address these specific issues "had much higher levels of maturity." Other compliance risk areas, however, such as antitrust, money laundering, and import-export law, lagged. Of particular note was that in areas of recent government scrutiny, such as antitrust and import-export laws, "companies not in highly regulated industries could be particularly vulnerable since compliance efforts there typically struggle to win support from top management until something bad happens."[4]

As we enter the next decade of the twenty-first century, issues of fraud and misconduct will inevitably play a central role in both the public and private sector. Recovery from the economic downturn, postrecession performance, and effective and sustainable management of risk, especially the risk of fraud and misconduct, will distinguish the winners from the losers.

In its *Executive Guidance for 2010*, the Corporate Executive Board identified the rising losses and steeper penalties due to high levels of employee misconduct as one of the six enemies of postrecession performance. The report explained the reason behind its finding in noting, "The steady flow of bad economic news over the past year has altered the psychology of the workforce—there is an increased state of distrust and anxiety among employees. Worse yet, as organizations have restructured or downsized to address the economy, the effect of these changes on employees has been underestimated. Employees who have seen and experienced these changes have become cynical about their companies' ethics and the integrity of their coworkers. This cynicism has translated directly into a rise of fraud and misconduct."[5]

The new world order that will emerge in this decade and beyond will likely include further globalization with increased shifts of economic power from traditional Western markets such as the United States and Europe to emerging economies such as China, India, and Brazil. In this shifting global economy, managing the risks of fraud, corruption, money laundering, and violation of import and export laws will likely become increasingly complex and difficult, but a necessary core competency for success.

As we move out of the economic downturn, organizations will find themselves in an environment of increased regulation, enforcement, and global cooperation among regulatory authorities. As the Corporate Executive Board observed, "Legal tolerance for bad behavior is at an all-time low. Governments of most industrial nations are responding to public scrutiny over the cause of the economic downturn and general anti-corruption sentiment with a wave of new regulation . . . and perhaps most importantly—an increased zeal for enforcement."[6] An example of this increased zeal can be found most noticeably in the announcements by the SEC in January 2010 of new enforcement initiatives designed to encourage greater cooperation from individuals and companies. These initiatives included new tools and guidance for cooperation agreements and for the evaluation of cooperation normally associated in the past with criminal investigations and prosecutions. The announcement of these new tools followed previous initiatives creating new enforcement units dedicated to highly specialized and complex areas of securities law.

Those companies that can harness and leverage the power of technological innovation to enhance market competitiveness, better understand and manage their own organizational data and intellectual property, and at the same time continuously monitor their own risks, will have a decided advantage over their competitors. Speed in detecting and preventing misconduct, reducing the costs of litigation, effectively responding to government and regulatory inquiries, and effectively monitoring relationships with third parties will make information management one of the most critical operational and risk avoidance priorities for organizations.

Finally, the governance, risk, and compliance of leading organizations will likely evolve and mature to create a vibrant and effective risk and integrity culture that will become an integral part of its overall business strategy, operations, and management. Those organizations with the most evolved and mature compliance programs will have embraced the concept of integrity as a business imperative. Ben W. Heinenman, former general counsel for General Electric and current senior fellow for corporate governance at Harvard Law School and the John F. Kennedy School of Government, captured this concept in the title of his book *High Performance with High Integrity*, where a value-based culture is fused with how the organization operates. Leading high-performing companies not only will adhere to the letter of the law and adopt appropriate risk controls and ethical standards but, just as importantly, will also create a corporate culture of integrity where there is mutual trust among employees and management that each will do the right thing in the right way, that employees will feel free to raise concerns, and that management will be responsive to those concerns. In this environment, other stakeholders, whether shareholders, consumers, business partners, the capital markets, regulators, or others, will have confidence in the organization's integrity, which will enhance brand and help ensure sustainable business success.

Richard H. Girgenti

Part I

Understanding Fraud

Timothy P. Hedley

In Part I, you will be introduced to the nature of fraud and misconduct. Chapter 1 covers asset misappropriation—the embezzlement of cash, the theft of cash or other assets, the misuse of company assets, and, in particular, Ponzi schemes. Chapter 2 discusses the nature of fraudulent financial reporting—the misrepresentation of financial information required for managerial decision making and external reporting purposes. Each chapter provides specific examples of the major fraud schemes, insight into some of the factors that contribute to such integrity breakdowns, and a discussion of fundamental mitigation strategies.

Before diving deeper into the major fraud types, it makes sense to first answer a simple question: What is fraud? Simply put, there is no one widely accepted definition of fraud; it may be defined as a misrepresentation properly relied upon by someone to that person's detriment or to the unfair advantage of the fraudster. For frauds perpetrated against individuals, this is a perfectly acceptable definition. However, for frauds committed by and against organizations, this definition may not be appropriate since it is often difficult to measure the loss inflicted or the gain achieved. As such, for purposes of this book, fraud is defined as an intentional deception that drains value from an organization. It is the "intentional deception" that is the core of what defines an act as fraud.

The Fraud Triangle

There are typically three conditions present when a fraud occurs: opportunity, pressure or incentive, and rationalization. Together these conditions form something commonly referred to as the "fraud triangle," a theory credited to Donald Cressey which is shown in Figure PI.1.

Figure PI.I. The fraud triangle
Source: American Institute of Certified Public Accounts, "Consideration of Fraud in a Financial Statement Audit," Statement on Auditing Standards No. 99, October 2002, p. 8.

How does the fraud triangle work? First, conditions must exist to allow fraud to occur. Specifically, there must be opportunities created by internal control deficiencies. The next side of the triangle is incentive or pressure. Generally, there is some pressure or incentive that provides the reason for people to commit a fraud. Lastly, there is attitude or rationalization—often the most difficult part of the fraud triangle for people to understand. Simply put, most people do not have a moral compass that allows them to commit fraud without being able to justify their actions to themselves or to others. Of course, this excludes the serial fraudster or the very small proportion of the population that has no moral compass.

The Fraud Triangle and Fraudulent Financial Reporting

Fraudulent financial reporting typically starts with pressure or incentives. It is very unusual for people to engage in fraudulent financial reporting simply because conditions existed that would allow them to do so. Typically, people engage in fraudulent financial reporting because of pressure.

There are two commonly recognized overarching pressures. The first is arguably third-party pressures. For example, Alex Berenson, in his book *The Number,* argues that the drive for quarterly earnings is a common thread for all the large reported frauds.[1] This may be an overstatement, but it is illustrative of the degree to which pressure can stem from third-party analyst expectations.

Other third-party pressures may come from a host of directions, including meeting debt covenants, maintaining exchange listing requirements, or even keeping up with competitor performance. Another significant pressure for fraudulent financial reporting is the threat to personal financial position—namely, performance-based compensation. The linkage between compensation and performance can drive extremely dysfunctional behaviors.

With respect to opportunities for fraudulent financial reporting, a significant concern is management override of controls. The American Institute of Certified Public Accountants has labeled management override of controls the "Achilles' heel of fraud prevention."[2] Additionally, many of the frauds seen in newspaper headlines were effected through management—specifically, senior management overriding internal control systems through the use of manual or topside journal entries.

The recent economic downturn has provided new opportunities for fraudulent financial reporting. First, many companies have gutted their fraud risk management infrastructure as a result of reductions in force as well as reductions in discretionary spending. Essentially, such companies either have laid off too many employees in control functions or no longer have the funds to support this infrastructure. Also, as a result of the reductions in force, there has been a move toward matrix management, which leads to issues of accountability and further weakens the ability of the company to effectively manage fraud risk.

Rationalizations associated with fraudulent financial reporting are those statements or beliefs that people use to justify their behavior to themselves or to others. This may include such beliefs or statements to the effect that the fraudster will "make up for it next quarter" or at some other point. Unfortunately, particularly in bad economic times, that next quarter or other point never seems to come. Another common rationalization may be the sincere belief that the fraudulent activity was good for the company, the fraudster believing he or she was helping the company maintain what appeared to be healthy metrics. Finally, there is the common rationalization that "everybody is doing it, so I might as well be doing it, too."

The Fraud Triangle and Asset Misappropriation

When analyzing the fraud triangle and asset misappropriation, there are a couple of key considerations. First, most asset misappropriations are driven by opportunity. In other words, people will steal when the conditions that allow them to steal are present. Second, the proximate goal of the majority of these schemes is conversion to cash. Therefore, the more cash movement there is and the more fungible and marketable an asset is, the greater the risk to the organization. Third, with respect to incentives, people will often misappropriate assets to support a vice, such as gambling or drugs, or to support a lifestyle that is beyond one's means (including inappropriate relationships).

The rationalizations for asset misappropriation and fraudulent financial reporting often differ in focus. Fraudulent financial reporting rationalizations are frequently directed toward the organization, while asset misappropriation rationalizations are commonly internalized. For example, often one will hear rationalizations for the theft of assets such as "I am not paid enough," "The company owes me something," or "I deserve a better station in life." These are very different from the fraudulent reporting rationalizations described earlier, which were about the company and the benefits a fraudster might believe are being delivered to the company with that behavior.

Chapter 1

Asset Misappropriation

Timothy P. Hedley

Introduction

The Association of Certified Fraud Examiners estimates that organizations lose billions of dollars—approximately 7 percent of annual revenue—to fraud each year. The misappropriation of assets by employees constitutes about 90 percent of all reported frauds.[1] In dollar terms, studies estimate that losses resulting from the theft or misuse of assets add approximately $120 billion each year to the costs of doing business.[2] Since many frauds, if not most, go undetected, the actual dollar loss may be significantly higher.

For the purposes of this chapter, asset misappropriation involves more than just theft or embezzlement—it includes any misuse of an entity's assets for personal gain. This chapter also provides an overview of asset misappropriation fraud schemes.

Theft of Cash

Roughly 85 percent of asset misappropriations involve cash.[3] Cash schemes can involve a single incident or can occur repeatedly over time, sometimes lasting for months or even years. Unfortunately, victim organizations often believe they had robust internal controls to help prevent these schemes. Upon closer examination or in the wake of an investigation, organizations understand that they often missed opportunities to discover the fraud or fostered an environment that allowed collusion among employees and circumvention of controls to go undetected.

Additional contributors are Cassandra C. Cohen, Nancy Pasternack, and William W. Rudolph.

Cash misappropriation often starts with small amounts taken to test the system's controls. Once the perpetrator determines that controls are nonexistent or ineffective, the amount of the fraud can skyrocket. The heart of these frauds involves the physical removal of cash from the organization as outright cash theft or as fraudulent disbursements of cash. Common specific schemes, which include skimming, larceny, lapping, fraudulent billing, payroll fraud, expense reimbursement, check fraud, and wire fraud, are discussed below.

Cash Receipts

The simplest of cash theft schemes is skimming, which involves the misappropriation of cash from an organization prior to being recorded in the financial system. Typically, skimming involves those who are in positions to receive cash, such as cashiers and tellers, or those whose responsibilities include recording payments. When the funds are received, the fraudsters typically divert the payment or part of the payment to themselves while providing a product or service at no charge.

A long-running skimming scheme from a chain of franchised fast-food restaurants in Cincinnati, Ohio, provides an example of how collusion and cash can equal an enormous loss. Two men at the organization, a managing director and a district manager, instructed restaurant managers to skim as much as $150 a day in cash receipts from the restaurants. The group netted $882,000 over a five-year period by taking cash from a customer, ringing up the sale, and then subsequently voiding the transaction in the register. The district manager collected the cash from the restaurant manager and then passed the funds to the managing director, who would kick back a proportion of the skimmed funds to the others involved in this scheme.[4] As evidenced in this example, any employee with responsibilities for incoming receipts can potentially skim cash, regardless of the industry, and the scheme can take an almost endless variety of forms, especially in cash-intensive industries such as food and beverage, entertainment, and not-for-profit.

While skimming occurs before cash is recorded in the financial system, in instances where cash is misappropriated after it has been recorded, the crime is one of larceny. This type of scheme is more risky on the part of the perpetrator because a fraudulent accounting entry or adjustment is necessary to record the theft. In 2005, a former accounts receivable clerk was found guilty in a scheme to misappropriate customer checks received by her against outstanding customer orders. For nearly three years, the employee received payments from customers and was tasked with entering the payments against outstanding invoices into the business's computerized accounting system. On numerous occasions, the employee diverted the checks to her brother and created false entries in the system to cover up the missing payments. Her brother set up a bank account using a name very similar to that of the company for which the A/R clerk worked. This enabled the checks to be deposited in the sibling's bank account. During the course of the fraud, it was estimated that over $380,000 was stolen.[5]

To avoid detection, at least in the short term, many perpetrators attempt to conceal the misappropriation through an artifice known as lapping. This is usually accomplished by crediting one account with the receipts intended for a different account. To illustrate this concept, consider an employee in the accounts receivable function at a telecommunications company. The employee receives payment for the outstanding invoice of Customer A. The employee pockets the funds, perhaps by using a bank account set up by the employee under a fictitious name. Customer A's account is thus not credited for the payment. It can be assumed that when the deficiency of this account grows, the customer will likely be contacted regarding the alleged overdue payments. To prevent this, the fraudster laps payments made by other customers by applying another customer's payment to Customer A.

As evidenced from the above example, lapping can be time-intensive and requires a high degree of maintenance. Often, these frauds start small, with the fraudsters believing they will pay the money back some time in the future. As the size of the misappropriated funds grows or the frequency of the acts of misappropriation increases, the shortfall becomes increasingly difficult to disguise, and the fiction that the fraudsters will repay the stolen funds evaporates. Often, the employees keep a separate set of accounting records to keep track of the machinations required to keep the scheme balanced. It is not unusual for employees engaged in this scheme to work late hours, rarely take vacations, and be fanatical about retaining control and secrecy over their areas of the business. Many times, these frauds are only revealed when unplanned or unforeseen events force the employees away from work and result in other parties stepping in to perform or review the activity.

Fortunately, many basic detective and monitoring controls can uncover such activity early, preventing schemes from growing to significant amounts. For example, such controls may simply take the form of segregating duties and ensuring that no one individual has sole responsibility for managing the end-to-end task of receiving and recording cash and receivables. In situations where segregating duties is not feasible due to resource constraints, management must ensure supervision of employees and regular reconciliation of bank and ledger accounts. In addition, any unexplained or unusual entries should be flagged and marked for review by managers (e.g., entries that represent the reclassification of receivables in the subsidiary ledger). Analytic review may also be employed to detect large cases of cash receipt theft. For example, an increase in accounts receivable in proportion to sales without a change in the organization's credit terms may be indicative of such schemes. Additionally, customer complaints regarding incorrect or lack of payments should be investigated, as they potentially could lead to uncovering a scheme.

Cash Disbursements

The second major category of cash theft is fraudulent cash disbursements, which involves the unauthorized release of company funds. Although there are many variations, those that tend to represent larger-dollar amounts and higher overall risks include fraudulent billing, check fraud, payroll schemes, fraudulent expense reimbursements, and wire fraud. These schemes frequently involve collusion, as the perpetrators are often company insiders who must commit multiple acts of fraud in an attempt to cover up their original fraud. Because disbursement schemes are often simple in nature, they are relatively easy to conceal and may go undetected for long periods or until they become a significant amount.

Fraudulent Billing. Fraudulent billing is a disbursement scheme that is most often, although not exclusively, carried out by an employee with some level of authorization to issue payments. This scheme occurs when funds are distributed under the guise of a legitimate payment for invoiced goods or services. A perpetrator in these situations may misappropriate company cash without ever touching the cash. Common types of fraudulent billing are personal purchase schemes, nonaccomplice vendor schemes, and schemes involving shell companies or fictitious vendors.

The simplest variant of fraudulent billing is using the organization's funds to pay for personal expenditures. In June 2006, the former director of supply chain management at Boeing was sent to prison for purchasing personal items, including artwork, jewelry, and vacations, with a company credit card. By the time the fraud was discovered, purchases totaled almost $300,000. The fraud was made possible through the director's authority to approve employee discretionary expenditures along with the collusion of another employee.[6]

A more sophisticated type of scheme is known as nonaccomplice vendor fraud. In this scheme, an individual capitalizes on the well-known name or relationship of a particular vendor to add legitimacy to a fraudulent invoice or charge without the knowledge, consent, or complicity of the vendor. Several means to implement this scheme have emerged.

One nonaccomplice vendor fraud scheme involves an employee overpaying a particular vendor invoice on behalf of the organization. For example, an employee may send two wire transfers or issue two identical company checks. Once issued, the employee will subsequently request a refund and divert the returned funds to a personal account.

Another means to execute a nonaccomplice vendor fraud scheme would be for the fraudster to create a false invoice that purports to be from a legitimate vendor but that, in fact, contains remittance details that effectively divert funds to the fraudster's account and not to the legitimate vendor. This scheme is more sophisticated, because it requires the creation of forged invoices and, in some cases, the creation of bank accounts with names almost identical to those of a legitimate vendor. A former accounting supervisor at a chemicals company pleaded guilty in 2009 for misappropriating more than $3.6 million using this type of scheme. The supervisor created falsified vendor invoices that her employer paid via wire payments to the employee's personal account from 2006 through 2008. The perpetrator faced up to 20 years in prison and a fine of $250,000.[7]

Another fairly sophisticated billing scheme occurs when a fraudster creates an entirely false entity specifically for the purpose of issuing false invoices and receiving payments. The entity may have, to a greater or lesser extent, the external appearance of an established company. It can be registered with the state and have authentic-looking company documentation and correspondence. The fraudster may even establish working contact information for the entity, such as a Web site, phone numbers, or personnel e-mail addresses. The fraudster can use this façade to purchase materials for which the entity never pays or sell materials the entity never delivers. However, behind the façade, the entity exists only on paper and lacks the internal organs of operation, production, and delivery; therefore, such entities are known as shell companies.

In one instance of using this type of billing scheme, a man stole over $500,000 from a public school district. The fraudster created a shell company and, over a period of years, billed the school for repair and renovation work that was either not performed or, in some cases, performed by school staffers under his supervision.[8]

These shell companies can also be used to conduct "pass-through" frauds as well. For example, employees responsible for procurement or vendor selection may establish a shell company as an intermediary between the employer and its legitimate vendors. The perpetrator uses the shell company to purchase items on behalf of the employer at market rates and then resells the items to the organization at an inflated price. The employee then misappropriates the difference between the market price and the inflated price. The result is always the same: the organization pays an inflated price to receive the same items that could have been purchased directly from the vendor at a discount. In its most advanced form, the use of shell companies can extend to elaborate networks of multiple shell companies set up to give the illusion of legitimate trade and industry.

To protect against these billing schemes, an organization should pay particular attention to the internal controls it has established for soliciting and purchasing goods and services. Such controls could include ensuring the appropriate segregation of duties of the organization's accounts payable, accounting, purchasing, and receiving functions, as well as maintaining and reviewing an approved vendor list. Controls should also be instituted to prevent unapproved vendors from receiving payments without appropriate authorizations and confirmations. In addition, authorization mechanisms and the retention of all necessary supporting documentation, such as invoices, purchase orders, and receiving reports, would mitigate the risk of fraudulent activity being perpetrated against the organization.

Payroll. Payroll schemes are another form of fraudulent disbursements that are perpetrated through the creation of false documentation. At the Massachusetts Port Authority in Boston, 20 people conspired in a payroll and benefits fraud scheme that involved union managers at the Port of Boston, union officials from the International Longshoremen's Association, a union timekeeper, and the manager. The scheme involved ghost employees, overstated payroll amounts, and inflated hours for the dockworkers, netting the fraudsters in excess of $250,000. Managers listed their young children on the payroll. Another manager paid a dockworker for 28 hours during an 8-hour shift.[9] While payroll schemes can take on many different forms, the most common are overstated payroll, incentive compensation schemes, and the establishment of ghost employees.

An overstated payroll scheme occurs when any aspect of a person's compensation is manipulated (e.g., base salary, hourly rate, and hours worked). This is the most common payroll fraud. A more complex version of a payroll scheme includes the manipulation of variable compensation arrangements. A common variable compensation arrangement provides an employee with the opportunity to earn additional compensation based upon the achievement of certain performance metrics. For example, an employee could earn a commission based upon certain factors (e.g., sales multiplied by a fixed commission rate). In order to perpetrate this fraud, the employee would need to change the factors that influence the employee's incentive compensation.

The third payroll scheme—one that involves ghost employees—although not the most common of schemes, is typically the most costly since the perpetrator can potentially misappropriate large amounts over a short period of time. A ghost employee can be a former employee who has not yet been removed from the payroll system, a nonexistent person entered into the company's system using false documentation, or a real individual who has never worked for the organization.

This particular scheme was perpetrated by a country club controller and manager working in collusion to misappropriate $1.3 million using all three forms of ghost employees. The two created fictitious employees, kept former employees on the payroll, and added individuals to the payroll who had provided personal services to the two fraudsters. Electronic payments would then be made to the fraudsters' personal bank accounts based on the payroll information.[10]

Payroll fraud will inevitably increase an organization's payroll expenses. In applying detective measures, organizations can analyze duplications of payee addresses, bank accounts, social security numbers, and other forms of identifying information. Verifying overtime authorization by supervisors, comparing commission expenses for accuracy and increases, and reviewing withholding and tax deductions may assist in identifying a potential payroll fraud. Similarly as for other fraud schemes, organizations must ensure that there are sound internal controls over the functional areas where the schemes can manifest themselves.

Expense Reimbursement. Expense reimbursement schemes are another form of fraudulent disbursements. These schemes can include fabricated or overstated expenses as well as duplicate claims. Whether the purported expense was for a cab ride or a meal while traveling for business, the employee perpetrates the fraud by altering or fabricating receipts and other supporting documents in order to falsify expense reports. While these sums may seem immaterial on an individual level, they may represent large sums in the aggregate.

When employees know that their expenses are being closely scrutinized, a fraudulent expense reimbursement scheme is less likely to occur. The following specific examples can be implemented to combat or reduce fraudulent expense reimbursements:

- Review expense claims for appropriateness and flag any unusual purchases or expense categories (e.g., entertainment, alcohol).
- Analyze deviations from historical expense trends or actual versus budgeted expenses.
- Inquire if employees have observed any lifestyle changes or ostentatious lifestyles in excess of what is expected based on their pay.
- Communicate and train all employees on the company's expense reimbursement policies, the consequences of misrepresentation, and the way to report cases of suspected fraud.

Check Fraud. Check fraud is big business, resulting in an average of $15 billion in losses annually.[11] In the typical fraudulent disbursement scheme, the perpetrator prepares supporting documents (e.g., invoices, expense reports, time cards) to request payment from the organization. Check fraud schemes can become more complex as the fraudster takes control over the check in order to provide disbursement. Two common types of check fraud affecting organizations include:

- *Forgery.* One of the simplest and more prevalent check-tampering schemes, forgery is committed when a perpetrator forges the payee, endorser, or signature. An example of this check fraud scheme involves a former accountant who forged the signature of his organization's owner on checks totaling more than $1 million over a four-year period. The scheme was concealed by moving the organization's funds between bank accounts and altering bank statements. It was finally uncovered when the bank investigated a suspicious check.[12]
- *Alteration.* A perpetrator may alter a check to erase the information included on the check. The process of check washing erases the details of the check using a chemical solution. In a simple example of check alteration, a project accountant at a construction company prepared checks payable to a fictitious portable toilet vendor named "Mr. John." He then added his own last name to select checks. This scheme netted more than $2.8 million and was only discovered when an auditor was unable to verify the vendor.[13]

Check fraud schemes are typically perpetrated by employees whose duties lack segregation (e.g., check preparation, collection, and processing) and who have easy access to the organization's checkbook, bank statements, and, in some instances, signature stamps. To avoid being caught, the perpetrators may conceal their actions through improper journal entries and forced bank reconciliations to disguise the imbalances while creating false supporting documentation, such as fictitious invoices. As such, check fraud schemes usually exhibit red flags such as missing or voided checks, checks payable to employees or questionable payees, altered or dual endorsements, and even customer complaints regarding accounts they believed to be settled. Organizations can attempt to prevent check tampering by segregating the duties of their employees, requiring mandatory vacation time, instituting physical and technology controls over sensitive information, and establishing maximum dollar amounts on checks with the organization's banks or setting up an electronic payment processing system.

Wire Fraud. While technology continues to change the face of business, it too is contributing to the evolution of fraud schemes. Today's digital and online environment creates a platform for fraudulent wire transfers. Whereas in the past a fraudster had to undertake a series of steps to execute a scheme, now funds can be stolen with just a few keystrokes. Often, all the fraudster needs is knowledge of the organization's bank access codes and the ability to electronically transfer funds.

In one example, an accountant at a law firm made 114 fraudulent wire transfers totaling over $1 million to a personal bank account over a period of two years to pay off gambling debts. The fraudulent transfers were uncovered when the organization was audited due to an arson caused by the accountant when he was terminated from the firm.[14]

In another example, a former employee at a state treasurer's office was indicted by a grand jury for transferring $750,000 to a personal account. Once the employee transferred the funds, the fraudster attempted to cover up the shortfall in accounts by applying a payment that the office had received in error from another entity. The fraudulent transfer was uncovered when the organization that made the erroneous payment requested a return payment.[15]

To help prevent fraudulent wire transfers, organizations should implement authorization controls. This includes not only proper supporting documentation, but also different layers of authorization depending on the size of the transfer. In addition, businesses that conduct a high volume of wire transfers, such as financial institutions, should require that managers call customers to verify wire transactions that exceed a specified dollar threshold.

Noncash Fraud

The proximate goal of most asset misappropriation schemes is cash in pocket, hence the ubiquity of the cash fraud schemes discussed earlier in this chapter. One step removed from cash in pocket is theft of assets that are convertible into cash. Noncash fraud is any deed that results in the theft or misuse of noncash assets, including inventory, equipment, supplies, proprietary information, and trade secrets. Such schemes will be the focus of this section.

Inventory Theft

According to the ACFE's *2008 Report to the Nation on Occupational Fraud and Abuse*, frauds targeting noncash assets, including inventory, were noted as relatively common and were 16.3 percent of all asset misappropriation cases examined.[16] Every year, companies write down losses from inventory misappropriation from their retail locations, warehouses, or offices. This misappropriation of physical, noncash assets includes inventory (stock), equipment, supplies, and products. In this section, we will explore three common areas of inventory fraud—fictitious sales, asset requisition and transfer schemes, and purchasing and receiving.

Fictitious Sales. First, let us consider how fictitious sales would apply in the retail industry. A retail employee who is selling books may ring up a sale for a new bestseller that the employee has been waiting to read and then subsequently void the transaction in the register as damaged goods. In this scenario, the employee would be creating a fictitious sale for the purposes of misappropriating the book.

Another fictitious sales scheme can be perpetrated if the employee is not intending to be the end user of the particular bestseller. In this case, the employee would ring up a fictitious sale in a manner similar to the above scenario, but rather than take the book home to read, the employee resells the book online. This type of scheme allows employees to convert the organization's assets to cash when they do not intend to use the product or service themselves.

Asset Requisition and Transfer. A record scheme that perpetrators have used to steal inventory is asset requisition and transfer. This scheme can be perpetrated by placing internal orders for inventory that exceed the amount actually needed to complete a project. Creative fraudsters may even actually invent a project in order to requisition goods. In the latter, they would also need to create false paperwork that would allow them to remove and divert the inventory from a warehouse or storage facility. As an illustrative example, think back to our country club fraudsters. They may have had an opportunity to order additional equipment, which the club provides to its members. The fraudsters could then have taken the equipment and either personally used it or resold it to a third party. Another example would be if the club was undergoing a renovation and the fraudsters decided to renovate their own homes at the same time so they could take advantage of the supplies being ordered for the project.

Purchasing and Receiving. The third inventory theft scheme is purchasing and receiving. Any organization that is heavily involved in shipping and receiving products, including online retailers and manufacturers, as well as any other type of organization that receives products at their loading docks, is susceptible to this type of fraud. In this scheme, the fraudster is typically an employee who is in a position to falsify incoming or outgoing inventory records and has physical access to the inventory itself. The employee may alter one copy of a receiving report used for the inventory record to deduct the inventory stolen, which prevents the organization from detecting the missing inventory. However, to ensure that the vendor or supplier receives payment, the employee will not alter the original invoice submitted to the accounts payable department. In a variation of this scheme, an employee notifies the vendor that its inventory is being returned due to quality issues. The employee then ships the products back and misappropriates the replacement lot sent by the vendor.

Similar tactics can be employed with outgoing shipments of inventory. To pilfer outgoing inventory, an employee typically creates false shipping and sales documents to make it appear that the stolen inventory was sold. The employee may also forge packing slips to suggest that the inventory was released for delivery. This fabricated documentation allows an accounts receivable entry to be recorded in the organization's financial records. In order to cover their tracks, employees will take steps to make it appear as though there are more assets present than there actually are in inventory, a practice known as physical padding. In order to create the illusion of extra inventory, employees may stack empty boxes or empty canisters on shelves or move boxes from an unaudited warehouse to one that is subject to audit.

While much of the focus has been on employee-perpetrated fraud, external parties can also take advantage of purchasing and receiving schemes. Outside fraudsters must have knowledge of an organization's routines, procedures, and controls, or lack thereof. For example, a delivery driver can learn over time that the organization does not weigh or count its inventory upon receipt. Using this knowledge, the driver may withhold inventory yet charge the organization for delivery of the full inventory. Unscrupulous vendors or suppliers can apply the scheme by charging a company for a full order but only shipping a partial order.

Organizations should be aware of potential red flags relating to inventory theft. These may include locations where the inventory turnover is not consistent with corporate averages or declining margins. From a receiving perspective, the organization should also remain aware of any deliveries that are made or received at unusual times during the day or any vendor complaints. Finally, any unusual or unexpected findings resulting from either external or internal audits should be examined to understand the nature of variances. Each one of these red flags does not necessarily indicate inventory theft but, collectively, may be indicative of a more systemic problem.

Internal controls that may mitigate the risk of inventory fraud include the following:

- Require proper documentation of requisitions, receiving reports, perpetual records, raw material requisitions, shipping documents, and job cost sheets.
- Segregate employee duties with respect to the requisition of inventory, receipt of inventory, disbursement of inventory, conversion of inventory to scrap, and receipt of proceeds from disposal of scrap.
- Implement independent checks of purchasing or warehouse functions on an unannounced basis with a physical observation of inventory.
- Utilize analytic reviews (e.g., cost of goods sold increasing disproportionately to revenue).
- Institute physical safeguards of all merchandise and limit access to certain identified individuals.
- Integrate new technologies to gather information and observe employees on loading docks.

Asset Misuse

Misuse occurs when an employee engages in the unauthorized use of company assets. Although often tolerated, companies face significant unquantifiable losses every year from excess wear, tear, maintenance costs, and lost revenue. The many degrees of such personal use of company assets can lead to differing perceptions about what is and is not acceptable use. For example, is an office employee committing fraud by using a company telephone to make a personal call? What if the call was long-distance and incurred significant expense? How would this compare with someone in the company's maintenance department using company machinery to carry out construction at home?

Misuse of company assets can also occur when an employee uses a company discount to purchase a product or service and then resells it for a profit. For example, many retail employees receive discounts on their employer's products. Employees may buy merchandise at the discounted price, resell the products, and pocket the difference in price. An employee may also use company equipment to operate a side business (e.g., service company employees using the company's trucks and inventory to run their own side business). When an employee is misusing company assets to operate a side business, the cost to the company is not just the wear and tear on the inventory and equipment, but also a loss of employee productivity and other opportunity costs.

Companies should consider potential misuse of assets by executive-level employees. Examples of CFO or CEO misuse of company inventory or equipment abound, since executives often have access to higher-dollar items (e.g., corporate jet, entertainment, tickets, and laptops). According to the ACFE's *2008 Report to the Nation on Occupational Fraud and Abuse*, approximately 22 percent of noncash theft occurs at the executive level of employees.[17]

The most effective way for organizations to combat the potential misuse of assets is through instituting a zero tolerance policy. This policy should be clear so that employees understand what acceptable behavior includes, and should be disseminated to all employees. Additionally, all leaders within the organization should set the tone for employees regarding ethics and integrity and should promote a work environment that does not justify misuse of company assets.

Intellectual Property

Even intellectual property, which includes original creative thought such as patents, copyright material, trademarks, trade secrets, manufacturing processes, licensing rights, computer source code, research and development data, and chemical formulas, provides another opportunity for the misappropriation of assets. The true value of these intangibles is often unknown until they are lost to the organization by fraudulent means.

An episode at a Chicago airport offers a glimpse of the potential financial impact on an organization when it loses control of intellectual property. Just prior to a departing flight to China, a U.S. Customs and Border Protection agent stopped a passenger who had just resigned from her job at a telecommunications company to work for an overseas competitor. Upon inspection of the passenger's bags, approximately 1,000 paper and digital documents marked "Confidential" and containing technical plans for products that belonged to the passenger's former employer were found. The telecommunications company noted that it would have lost $600 million in the ensuing three years had the documents been copied by a competitor and used to create new telecommunication products.[18]

Lost sales, however, do not tell the whole story. For example, stolen design information can be used to make counterfeit products. These counterfeit products are often made with inferior components or ingredients that not only threaten the value of the core brand but can also pose severe health and safety risks to those who buy the product.

Similar to other types of asset misappropriation, intellectual property theft can be committed by those inside or outside the entity. Thefts can involve business partners, information brokers, consultants, foreign agents, suppliers, temporary employees, or vendors. However, former employees, competitors, on-site contractors, and corporate spies pose a significant risk. Employees may leak information to the public or act as moles planted within the organization by an unscrupulous competitor in order to steal proprietary information. Other ploys include market research scams used to obtain confidential operational and financial data.

To protect against this type of theft, organizations should be alert to employees who report lost security badges, access cards, or passwords; attempt to access sensitive computer files; or log hours in areas not related to their work function. Organizations must also be cognizant of missing files or computer disks, as well as reports of trespassing. To protect against external threats, companies should take care to control access to certain facilities and information and verify vendor and third-party credentials through due diligence. Hiring a corporate information officer or a security management consultant to develop a program to safeguard intellectual property may also be beneficial to those organizations with significant intellectual property.

Ponzi Schemes

For most of 2009, daily media accounts were filled with news of Ponzi schemes, making Ponzi schemes the *fraud du jour* for that year. The downturn in the economy that began at the end of 2008 and ran throughout 2009 led to the uncovering of nearly four times as many of these investment schemes in 2009 than in 2008. The two largest of such schemes, perpetrated by Madoff and Stanford, accounted for an estimated $58 billion in misappropriations.[19] While not the cause of the recent financial meltdown, Ponzi schemes have become one of the more visible symbols of a decade of excesses.

According to the Associated Press, an analysis of criminal cases at all U.S. Attorneys' Offices and the FBI, as well as criminal and civil actions taken by state prosecutors and regulators at both the federal and state levels, revealed that "tens of thousands of investors, some of them losing their life's savings, watched more than $16.5 billion disappear like smoke in 2009. While the dollar figure [in 2009] was lower than in 2008, that is only because Mr. Madoff, who pleaded guilty earlier [in 2009] and is serving a 150-year prison sentence, was arrested in December 2008 and did not count toward this year's [2009] total . . . In all," the Associated Press reported, "more than 150 Ponzi schemes collapsed in 2009, compared to about 40 in 2008."[20]

The reason for this upsurge in uncovering Ponzi schemes was clear, according to Lanny Breuer, assistant attorney general for the U.S. Department of Justice's criminal division. "The financial meltdown," Breuer stated, "has resulted in the exposure of numerous fraudulent schemes that otherwise might have gone undetected for a longer period of time."[21]

Ponzi schemes are fraudulent business ventures where investors are paid from other investors' funds rather than from operations. A Ponzi promoter typically spends money in order to raise more capital from investors, who are then utilized to return earlier investors' funds. The Ponzi eventually collapses when the creator is unable to provide enough cash flow to pay back early investors. These schemes can be simple or very complex; however, all of them are designed to deceive investors, and all share similar elements.

Ponzi operators are typically not engaged in genuine business transactions. Instead, Ponzi operators engage in transactions that are in the form of investments that have the color of legitimate transactions but, upon further review, lack economic substance. For example, Charles Ponzi himself was only in the business of collecting and distributing investor funds—mostly to himself. This is important since legitimate businesses are intended to create new wealth so as to be able to pay dividends to investors. This is not the case with Ponzi schemes, as these frauds are involved in little more than cycling and diverting an investor's hard-earned money.

Since there is no wealth created, the source of funds to pay investors can only come from later investors and not from operations. By providing returns to early investors, other investors are often enticed by the opportunity. Keep in mind that the majority of funds will be taken and pushed directly into the schemer's pocket, whose affluent lifestyle also serves as an advertisement for potential investors. The house of cards typically comes falling down when business or economic circumstances can no longer sustain the scheme or when investors seek to cash out and the promoter is unable to find enough new investors to pay back early investors.

The Better Business Bureau identified these Ponzis as "the biggest single fraud threat confronting American investors."[22] Why do people keep falling for this age-old scheme? First, people seem to be unable to stop chasing pipe dreams. Ponzi promoters may offer extraordinarily high returns; as an example, Charles Ponzi offered 50 percent returns in the 1920s. The promoters may also offer good returns regardless of whether in a bull or bear market, which was the case of Madoff, who reported extremely consistent returns of 10 to 12 percent each year.

Second, people are often attracted to the apparent success or exclusivity of the promoter. The promoters of Ponzis often have the same type of personality: charming, charismatic, trustworthy, and charitable. For example, Stanford had the trust of all his investors, especially considering that he was knighted in Antigua, where much of his illegal business dealings took place.[23]

Finally, and arguably, most problematic is that people will turn their money directly over to someone without a true understanding of who that person is.

Conclusion

It is extremely important to do proper due diligence on investment managers. This also includes understanding the methodology behind the investments. Many times, scam artists will provide a hard-to-understand strategy so that clients will not question them. Interestingly enough in 2001, *Barron's* reported that experts were beginning to question Madoff's methodology, and that when interviewed, Madoff said, "It's a proprietary strategy. I can't go into it in great detail."[24] These red flags, which often serve as warnings of a risk investment, are not always noticed by investors who are enamored and comforted by the high returns or other inducements. An important red flag: if it seems too good to be true, it probably is.

Currently, several government agencies are applying their resources to Ponzi scheme investigations. This is evidenced by the SEC issuing 82 percent more restraining orders and increasing investigations by 6 percent in 2009—both relating to Ponzi schemes and other securities frauds. Additionally, the FBI has increased the number of securities fraud investigations by 20 percent and increased agents assigned to high-yield investment fraud cases by over 50 percent for that same period. Further, the Commodity Futures Trading Commission has filed 31 civil actions in 2009 relating to Ponzis, which is double that of its 2008 actions. As these statistics highlight, the current economic environment and the media attention on Ponzis have bolstered enforcement measures in an effort to prevent additional fraud cases.[25]

Chapter 2

Financial Reporting Fraud

Timothy P. Hedley

Financial reporting fraud involves intentional or reckless conduct that results in the misrepresentation of financial information required both for internal managerial decision making and for external reporting purposes. Reporting manipulations can be as simple as the double counting of inventory or as complex as the fabrication of entire transactions, customers, or business operations. Its manifestations are constrained largely by the imagination and motivations of those engaged in manipulating financial records.

Almost 90 percent of financial reporting frauds involve the chief executive officer (CEO), the chief operating officer (COO), the chief financial officer (CFO), the chief accounting officer (CAO), and/or the controller.[1] This is evidenced by the involvement of Kenneth Lay, Jeffrey Skilling, and Andrew Fastow at Enron and Bernard Ebbers and Scott Sullivan at WorldCom. While these large, publicized frauds involved senior management, the Securities and Exchange Commission also brings enforcement actions against lower-level management and employees, and even against third parties for aiding and abetting the frauds perpetrated by others. For instance, the SEC filed a complaint against the former CFO of a third party, Terex Corporation, for aiding and abetting the securities law violations of United Rentals, Inc., for a fraudulent accounting scheme involving sale-leaseback transactions that were structured to improve United Rentals' 2000 and 2001 financial results by allowing for premature revenue recognition to improperly inflate profit.[2]

Additional contributors are Cassandra C. Cohen, Douglas E. Farrow, Marc L. Miller, and Charles H. Reid.

While it is estimated that only slightly more than 10 percent of frauds involve financial reporting, financial reporting fraud is by far the most costly.[3] The damage experienced by an organization may come in the form of significant fines and penalties imposed by governmental and regulatory agencies, deterioration of stock price, increased cost of capital, and significant loss of public trust due to the negative publicity. Consider, for example, Enron, whose market capital plummeted 26 percent to $8.9 billion in just 9 days after the SEC announced it was looking into certain Enron transactions.[4] An even larger loss was suffered by WorldCom, which had sustained a market cap loss of $186 billion by the time it filed for bankruptcy in 2002.[5]

In order to fully understand the nature of financial reporting fraud, it is important to recognize that it typically begins with manipulating the timing of transactions. U.S. generally accepted accounting principles (U.S. GAAP), as applied to commercial enterprises, require companies to recognize revenue when it is earned, regardless of when cash is exchanged, and to recognize expenses when obligations are incurred. Known as accrual accounting, this provides, in principle, a good picture of the results of operation for a period by matching revenues earned with the expenses incurred to generate those revenues. By intentionally manipulating the recorded timing of transactions, a company misrepresents its financial position or its results of operations.

Extending this general discussion, the following is an overview of the common financial reporting fraud schemes with particular focus on income statement manipulation, balance sheet manipulation, management estimates, and improper disclosures.

Income Statement Manipulation

An income statement can generally be manipulated by managing earnings or manipulating revenue or expenses.

Earnings Management

It is important to understand that a generally accepted definition of earnings management does not exist. Earnings management can represent perfectly ethical decision making on the part of management to achieve certain results. For instance, delaying necessary machine maintenance to a later period to improve the current period's bottom line would be a perfectly proper management of earnings.

For discussion here, the focus is upon abusive earnings management, which represents the intentional, material misrepresentation of bottom-line results. Such active earnings manipulations are undertaken for many purposes, including boosting current-year income to meet bonus targets, to meet consensus earnings estimates, or to smooth reported earnings over time. The desire to smooth earnings is generally a reaction of management to avoid the negative market reaction to volatility in year-over-year reported operating results. In other words, the market rewards predictability and consistency. However, the measure of true quality is in the consistent application of accounting principles and policies and in the consistency with which management makes estimates and uses judgment.

Revenue Manipulations

Revenue is the most commonly relied-upon metric in evaluating a company's performance and, not surprisingly, tends to be the most vulnerable to manipulation. In fact, one often-quoted study found that more than 50 percent of financial reporting frauds involved overstating revenue.[6] Since revenue is such an important metric, the pressure to manipulate is particularly acute near or soon after period-end when financial reports are due and analyst or other stakeholder expectations must be met.

Common revenue schemes include:

- Fictitious sales
- Channel stuffing
- Bill-and-hold transactions
- Round-tripping
- Manipulation of vendor rebates and allowances
- Manipulation of consignment sales
- Delayed revenue recognition

Each of these schemes will be covered in greater detail in the pages that follow; however, it is important to note that while many of these schemes involve manipulation of timing, as discussed in the introduction, many also involve completely fictitious transactions.

Fictitious Sales. Fictitious sales are typically straightforward and involve recording illegitimate or bogus sales transactions. For example, the fraudster could create a ghost customer or use a legitimate customer and falsify invoices without actually processing such invoices for product or service delivery.

The SEC charged executives at a medical equipment provider with, among other things, using fictitious sales of infusion pumps and consulting services that were not performed in order to overstate net sales by 62 percent and operating income by 229 percent. The motivation behind this scheme was reportedly to protect stock price and conceal reduced revenue resulting from decreased demand for their product. Once the fraud was publically announced, the company's market capitalization declined 95 percent, or $202.5 million.[7]

Channel Stuffing. When a company stuffs its distribution channels, it pushes—often through its sales department—more products through its distribution channels than its clients have ordered or can sell during that period or in a reasonable time thereafter. This behavior typically hinges on the knowledge that the company believes it has about future customer needs; or more commonly, it hinges on having customers accept goods in exchange for some future undisclosed benefit. Often, this fraud is committed when a company feels pressure to achieve forecasted sales, and is prevalent in those industries that experience high gross margins, such as consumer goods and pharmaceuticals.

In some cases, there can be collusion between the company selling the goods and the company purchasing the goods. As discussed at the start of this chapter, Terex Corporation paid an $8 million fine in 2009 for aiding and abetting an equipment rental company by agreeing to sell equipment at the end of the lease periods while guaranteeing the company against any losses.[8]

In another example in 2004, the SEC filed a civil action against a major U.S. pharmaceutical company for an alleged revenue scheme committed in order to meet both internal executive targets and external expectations. The SEC charged that at the end of each quarter in question, the company stuffed its distribution channels with excess inventory in order to inflate revenue. This scheme resulted in the improper recognition of approximately $1.5 billion in revenue from sales.[9]

Bill-and-Hold Transactions. A transaction where a company negotiates the sale of inventory but holds it at the company's facility is known as a bill-and-hold. To be recognized as revenue, bill-and-hold transactions must meet certain conditions. These conditions include having the risk of ownership transferred to the buyer. Normally, the company has a customer who has made a fixed commitment to buy the goods. There is a fixed schedule for delivery. In those instances where the goods are not shipped as scheduled, the buyer requests that the shipment be delayed, and the buyer has a substantial business purpose for delaying delivery. One typically expects that the new delivery date would be reasonable and consistent with the purpose of delayed delivery and the seller has not retained any performance obligations. Other conditions that one would expect to find in a legitimate bill-and-hold transaction would be that the purchase order specified a certain type of goods, the goods were segregated in the seller's inventory, the manufacturing process was complete, and the goods were ready for shipment.[10]

Due to the nature of the conditions required for a legitimate bill-and-hold, such transactions are susceptible to abuse. To illustrate, consider the case of Sunbeam, which artificially inflated the company's revenue by inappropriately recording $1.5 million in revenue from the sale of barbeque grills to a wholesaler in the first quarter of 1997. The revenue did not meet the criteria of U.S. GAAP since the wholesaler could return any unsold product to Sunbeam, which would assume all costs related to shipments both to and from the wholesaler. The wholesaler did not record any expenses related to this transaction and returned all barbeque grills to Sunbeam in the third quarter of the same year.[11]

In another example, Candie's, a shoe retailer, inflated revenue by $4.4 million through a similar bill-and-hold scheme. The company prematurely recorded revenue from invoiced shoe purchases that would not be delivered until a future date. This practice was against the company's disclosed revenue recognition policy, which stated that revenue was to be recognized upon shipment of product. By employing this practice, Candie's was able to convert a fourth-quarter loss into a profit.[12]

Round-Tripping. Round-tripping transactions are similar to fraudulent bill-and-hold transactions. The SEC stated in its *Report Pursuant to Section 704 of the Sarbanes-Oxley Act of 2002*, round-tripping "transactions involve simultaneous prearranged sales transactions, often of the same product, in order to create a false impression of business activity and revenue."[13] In other words, the company sells goods to another company with an agreement (typically undisclosed) to buy back the goods at a future time. This provides the appearance of legitimate business activity.

The SEC alleged that Collins & Aikman Corporation (C&A) entered into numerous round-tripping transactions totaling $14.8 million with Elkin McCallum, a member of C&A's board of directors and a supplier for the company. In this case, C&A received $3 million from McCallum to increase its 2001 income with the understanding that the funds would be returned. The transaction should have been recognized as a loan agreement. The money was later repaid by transferring equipment worth approximately $3 million to McCallum.[14]

In another case, the SEC alleged that in 2003 and 2004, Krispy Kreme engaged in a series of round-tripping transactions in connection with the reacquisition of franchises. In each disputed transaction, Krispy Kreme paid money to a franchise with the understanding that the franchise would pay the money back to Krispy Kreme in a manner that would allow Krispy Kreme to improve pretax income. In one of these transactions, Krispy Kreme increased the price paid for a franchise reacquisition by $800,000 in exchange for the franchise purchasing equipment for $800,000.[15] In essence, the transaction was without economic substance.

Manipulation of Vendor Rebates and Allowances. Vendor rebates or allowances are fees paid by vendors in exchange for marketing, promotions, and volume. Per U.S. GAAP, vendor rebates are treated as income of the receiving company and are recorded as earned when the final products are sold. Unfortunately, rebates and allowances are prone to manipulation.

In 2005, the SEC brought a complaint alleging Bristol-Myers Squibb (BMS) engaged in a series of improper transactions, including improperly accounting for rebates, in which "investors lost millions of dollars as a result." The complaint stated that BMS induced its two largest wholesalers to take excess inventory by covering their carrying costs and guaranteeing them a specified return on excess inventory. Because of this channel stuffing, the wholesalers purchased BMS's products in excess of demand, helping BMS meet its internal earnings targets and the consensus earnings estimates. When BMS's performance continued to fall short of expectations, the company then, among other things, understated the rebate amounts owed to Medicaid and prime vendors for rebates associated with the channel stuffing.[16] (See the previous discussion on channel stuffing.)

Manipulation of Consignment Sales. A consignment sale is a transaction contingent upon a third party having a right to return the purchased merchandise. Under U.S. GAAP, if a company sells a product and provides the buyer with the right to return the product, the ability to recognize revenue is only possible if certain conditions are met. These conditions require that the seller's price to the buyer be substantially fixed or determinable at the date of sale. In addition, it is essential that the buyer has paid the seller, the buyer is obligated to pay the seller, and the obligation is not contingent on resale of the product. Furthermore, the buyer's obligation to the seller would not be changed in the event of theft, physical destruction, or damage of the product. Finally, the buyer acquiring the product for resale has economic substance apart from that provided by the seller, and the seller does not have significant obligations for future performance to directly bring about the resale of the product by the buyer.[17]

For example, a manufacturer may sell a product to a retailer who can return the product if it is unable to sell it. Revenue for the manufacturer would only be recognized if the item is actually sold by the retailer. These types of selling arrangements are legitimate, but are ripe for abuse since such arrangements are susceptible to undisclosed sales conditions. In the preceding example, the manufacturer and retailer could negotiate the consignment sales with a side agreement that goes undocumented so that all deliveries to the retailer could be considered sales, but because of the side agreement, the retailer can return any unsold items. This would disallow the manufacturer from recognizing revenue.

A similar arrangement was abused by PowerLinx, Inc., a manufacturer of security products and underwater cameras. PowerLinx entered into arrangements whereby a third party would display the company's products without actually purchasing them. Under this arrangement, the company would ship the cameras to the dealers without releasing title and providing for no financial obligation unless the cameras were sold within 90 days. If the cameras were not sold, the third parties would return the cameras. Nonetheless, as soon as one of these agreements was entered into, PowerLinx recognized revenue even before cameras were manufactured, shipped, or sold.[18]

Delayed Revenue Recognition. The revenue schemes previously discussed relate to inflating revenue to make current earnings appear stronger. As mentioned earlier, there are occasions when a company may find it beneficial to delay the recognition of revenue, such as when earnings expectations and bonus targets have already been met. In such cases, a company may close the books early or not record current-period sales until the next period to make it easier to meet future targets, to protect against negative future earnings, or even to provide the illusion of consistent, positive, revenue streams ("income smoothing").

In a classic income smoothing case, Tyco International, from fiscal year ended June 30, 1997, through fiscal quarter ended June 30, 2002, used excess reserves to make period-end adjustments to enhance and smooth its reported results. The scheme was fairly simple: various Tyco business units moved earnings to reserve accounts in reporting periods in which it appeared that the units would not need the earnings to meet performance targets. If a business unit's earnings fell short of its performance target in a subsequent period, the unit would make up the shortfall by reversing reserves. In total, Tyco reversed at least $47.1 million from reserves to its income statement.[19]

While each of the revenue recognition schemes has its own nuances, they all share a common outcome—manipulating the top line to achieve a desired bottom line. Red flags that signal revenue recognition schemes include:

- Quarterly or annual revenue inconsistent with industry averages
- Consistently lower activity at the beginning of the period that does not have a reasonable explanation
- Alteration of sales, shipping, or invoice documents
- Unsubstantiated confirmations of receivables from customers
- Unusual spikes in sales, absent a similar increase in cash or receivables for the same period
- Discrepancies between the dates on shipping documents and other supporting accounting records, such as invoices or journal entries
- Unusual or unsubstantiated journal entries
- Unusual or complex sales arrangements
- Evidence of side agreements

- Unusually high number of credit memos issued after quarter- or year-end
- Evidence of significant nonrecurring gains
- Significant sales to unknown or new customers
- High volumes of product returned after quarter- or year-end

Further, one might find quarter-to-quarter revenue figures that do not appear to be consistent with economic events or industry averages. Abnormal patterns may be an indication that improperly timed transactions have been recorded. In addition, on the transactional level, a sample testing of transactions to confirm that the dates on all documents (e.g., sales, shipping, and invoicing) match the period in which the revenue is recorded may reveal an intentional manipulation of earnings. Last, improper revenue recognition schemes might be uncovered by making inquiries of sales and accounting personnel regarding period-close procedures. Such inquiries may provide an opportunity to gather information from the individuals performing the work, which may not otherwise be accessible through regular, observable reporting channels. A more comprehensive discussion on risk assessment techniques can be found in Chapter 7, "Prevention: Risk Assessment." Next, we turn our attention to expenses, another common area for income statement manipulation.

Expense Manipulation

To understand expense manipulation, it is important to understand that "expenses" and "costs" are not synonymous terms. Costs represent the cash or cash equivalent that an organization forgoes in exchange for something. For example, when an organization makes a purchase, the item purchased will represent an unexpired cost on the balance sheet. The unexpired cost is commonly known as an asset. Under U.S. GAAP, as assets are consumed or used, their costs flow to the income statement as expenses to properly match the costs incurred during the period with revenue earned during the same period. Therefore, deferring expenses will have the same effect upon the bottom line as overstating revenue.

The simplest way to use expenses to manipulate the bottom line is by understating or omitting expenses during a period. For instance, a company could simply store invoices in a file cabinet as the company receives them, or even put them in the trash, knowing that when the invoice goes unpaid, another invoice will be sent. The example is illustrative, but as we will see, expense schemes are as varied and nuanced as revenue schemes.

Capitalization of Expenses. As previously noted, assets are held on the balance sheet until consumed, at which time they are moved to the income statement as expenses. When assets or costs are held on the balance sheet, they are known as capitalized costs. When an expense is not moved to the income statement but is held on the balance sheet, it gives the appearance of a stronger bottom line.

In a notable case, WorldCom took certain operating costs that should have been recorded as current-period expenses and held them in capital accounts on the balance sheet. This manipulation allowed WorldCom to defer recognition of current-period expenses to future periods. This resulted in the company paying a $500 million penalty to the SEC—and WorldCom's CEO and CFO serving significant prison terms.[20, 21]

In a similar case, Bally Total Fitness Holding Corporation understated current-period advertising expense by improperly capitalizing advertisement production costs. In combination with other fraudulent acts, the company booked $513 million in net income when it should have booked a loss of $1.3 billion.[22]

Depreciation and Amortization. U.S. GAAP requires that depreciation and amortization be allocated by systematic and rational procedures to the period that the assets are expected to provide benefits.[23] For many assets, management judgment is required for determining the appropriate period of depreciation. By extending depreciation time frames, inflating salvage values, or aggressively capitalizing current-period expenses, management can increase current-period earnings.

This was the case at Waste Management, Inc. (WM), in the late 1980s and early 1990s when the company had approximately $6 billion on its balance sheet for trucks, containers, and equipment. In order to defer depreciation expenses for those assets, WM inappropriately extended the useful lives and salvage values of garbage trucks, which resulted in one of the largest financial statement restatements up to that time.[24]

Changes in accounting treatment of expenses, whether large or small, must be examined closely to understand the economic substance of the change. Some indicators that a company has concealed or deferred expenses may include:

- Recurring negative cash flows from operations or an inability to generate cash flows from operations while reporting earnings
- Significant pressure to meet quarterly earnings targets
- A large number of unusual or complex expense journal entries at the beginning or end of an accounting period
- Credits to expense accounts either in the week preceding a quarter or after the close period
- A lack of supporting documentation for journal entries
- Management frequently revising the quantum of depreciation charges during the close period
- Capitalization policies that are outside of industry norms

- Capitalized costs that are increasing more quickly than revenue
- A significant increase in capitalization of assets during the period
- Journal entries made by individuals who typically do not make entries

Balance Sheet Manipulation

For stakeholders trying to understand a company's financial position and earnings potential, it is imperative that the company's assets and liabilities be reported fairly on the balance sheet. Balance sheet items are particularly vulnerable to manipulation; these manipulations may include:

- Overstating inventory
- Failure to record asset impairment
- Misstating accounts receivable
- Restructurings and Big Baths

Overstating Inventory

Inventory represents goods and materials on hand, including merchandise for sale, and is one of the more commonly misreported items on the balance sheet.[25] By fraudulently overstating inventory, companies overstate assets, which will understate expenses. The simplest way to overstate inventory balances is to overstate the physical counts of inventory on hand. For example, management may double-count inventory on hand or include scrap, obsolete, damaged, or even sold goods that are not yet shipped.

For instance, a distributor of health and beauty products had a line of credit that allowed the distributor to borrow, in part, up to 60 percent of the value of its inventory. Executives created fictitious documentation for hundreds of millions of dollars in phony sales and nonexistent inventory in order to improve the company's borrowing ability. This scheme, along with other fraudulent activity, resulted in losses to investors, creditors, and other victims of an estimated $160 million, and it contributed to the company's ultimate bankruptcy.[26]

In one of the oldest and most famous fraud cases from 1939, McKesson & Robbins overstated its revenue by $10 million in an inventory scheme. In this case, the company's external auditors did not independently verify the company's inventory balances, but relied upon management's written representations. The auditor believed that the company's management was best qualified to measure inventory balances. This case became a major driver in establishing modern audit procedures that require independent audit evidence.[27]

Aside from conducting proper independent physical inventory counts, there are several ways to detect inventory overstatements. For example, a trending of gross margins and inventory days as compared with historic company trends and with competitors' margins may help detect instances of inventory overstatement. Are margins consistent or within company or industry norms? Are days in inventory trending unexpectedly upward? Is the relative mix of raw material, work in process, and finished goods consistent with reported operations, historic trends, and competitors?

Failure to Record Asset Impairment

U.S. GAAP requires companies to test their long-lived assets, investments, or asset group for impairment and recognize an impairment loss when the financial statement carrying value of those assets or asset groups exceeds its fair value and is not recoverable.[28] Asset impairments can be especially problematic in weakening market conditions when asset impairments are particularly challenging.

CenterPulse Ltd., a manufacturer of medical devices, offers an interesting example of the implications of not recognizing asset impairments. According to the SEC, in an effort to secure a large credit facility, CenterPulse inappropriately decided to not write off costs for certain impaired assets associated with a software system. This decision was not in conformity with U.S. GAAP and resulted in an 18 percent overstatement of Centerpulse's third-quarter 2002 pretax income.[29]

Misstating Accounts Receivable

Accounts receivable represents money owed to a company by customers for products and services provided on credit. Fictitious revenue schemes may include instances where fraudsters book bogus accounts receivable because the fictitious sales do not generate real cash or real receivables.

To illustrate, consider Platinum Software Corporation (PSC), which, according to an SEC action, recorded revenue from license agreements that were accompanied by side letters allowing the customer to cancel the agreement within a designated period. Revenue from these contracts was recorded with corresponding accounts receivable entries. Since the agreements would be canceled, the receivables were not paid. Analysts and investors began to take interest in PSC's receivables and noticed that days to collect receivables were higher than expected. Management then began to overstate cash receipts with understatements of receivables to allay concerns of analysts and investors about the soundness and collectibility of PSC's receivables.[30]

U.S. GAAP requires companies to record accounts receivable on the balance sheet at net realizable value, which is the value of accounts receivable less an allowance for uncollectible amounts. This means that when a company has determined that a particular account is uncollectible, it must write that amount off against the established allowance. Companies can manipulate earnings by understating this allowance for doubtful accounts or by not writing off against the receivables allowance those accounts known to be uncollectible.

Restructurings and Big Baths

Restructuring charges are typically incurred in connection with a business combination or a change in a company's strategic plan or in response to declines in demand, increasing costs, or other factors.[31] This is especially common when a company has suffered a period of significant losses. Unfortunately, when times are very bad or a company has little or no chance of meeting current-period stakeholder expectations, management may be tempted to clean up additional items on the balance sheet. This temptation may include writing off many items as part of restructuring charges. This reduces future expenses and improves reported future earnings and is known as a "Big Bath."

There are several motivations for taking Big Baths. For instance, an incoming CEO may want to start with a clean slate so that the first full year of the CEO's tenure is exceptional. For example, Al "Chainsaw" Dunlap, CEO at Sunbeam in 1996, cleaned up the balance sheet by taking a restructuring charge of $337.6 million that included $35 million in improper reserves, excessive write-downs, and premature expense recognition. More specifically, when the company decided to eliminate part of its household product line and sell its products to liquidators, the company included products from other product lines. This resulted in both an understated balance sheet value for household inventory that would be used in continuing operations and an overstatement of losses of $2.1 million so that when the products were sold in the following year, inflated margins were represented.[32]

For a company that is not doing well, and whose management believes its share price will suffer, there may be motivation to take a Big Bath, especially if the company is already taking a loss. Why not take as large a hit as possible? After all, memories are often short, and the Big Bath may help ensure that future results appear much better.

Management Estimates

Accounting estimates are approximations of a financial statement element, item, or account. Estimates are included in financial reports when particular amounts are uncertain—they are dependent upon the outcome of a future event or upon information related to events that have not yet occurred or cannot be gathered. Common examples include reserves for uncollectible accounts, reserves for loan losses, obsolete inventory, useful lives and scrap values, warranty claims, pension costs, percent of completion, contingent litigation losses, and fair values in nonmonetary exchanges.[33]

Good faith estimates are critical to stakeholders, because these estimates are the primary method for communicating forward-looking information. For example, a well-reasoned estimate of uncollectible accounts signals to investors an expectation of future cash flows from accounts receivable.

By their nature, accounting estimates are vulnerable to manipulation—first, because uncertainties exist in the underlying assumptions, and second, because there exists an inherent information asymmetry between the preparers of estimates and stakeholders. This is a powerful combination, because management, who may be intent upon deception, could take advantage of the uncertainties to mislead investors.

Take, for example, American Home Mortgage Investment Corp., where an internal company analysis showed that American Home's losses on delinquent second liens were escalating and that the company would lose at least 72 percent of the value of these loans after foreclosure. Management knowingly failed to reserve adequately for the losses expected from delinquent loans. In 2009, the SEC filed a civil action against certain senior officers of the company, alleging they understated "loan loss reserves by tens of millions of dollars, converting the company's losses into a fictional profit."[34]

Fair value, or mark-to-market accounting, further highlights the difficulties surrounding management estimates. Accounting standards require that certain financial instruments be recorded at fair value; however, determining fair value can be difficult, particularly during periods of economic stress when there is little or no market for some financial assets.[35] When there is no market for the financial assets, management uses its own pricing models to measure fair value, which may include management assumptions and estimates that are subjective and vulnerable to manipulation. Whenever accounting involves a management decision, "the distinction between what is legitimate and not legitimate is not always clear."[36]

Some red flags of manipulated estimates may include:

- Accounting principles that deviate from the industry standards or averages
- Accounting methods that seem to favor form over substance
- A change in accounting estimate over the prior year that is not substantiated
- An increase in reserve accounts with decreasing accounts receivable
- Journal entries made to accounts that contain significant estimates without proper support

Improper Disclosures

Financial statement disclosures are secondary information regarding items included or excluded from the body of the financial statements. They help to ensure that a reader is informed of the facts required to make sound decisions concerning the entity. The types of information in disclosures may include details of accounting principles and methods employed, transactions with related parties, executive compensation, significant risks, pension accounting, income taxes, legal proceedings, and contingencies.

According to the SEC, disclosure is mandatory where there is a known trend or uncertainty that is reasonably likely to have a material effect on the issuer's financial condition or results of operations. A good example is the requirement that preparers of financial statements disclose any changes in accounting principles. These changes should be justified on the premise that the new accounting principles properly match revenue with expense. Examples of changes in accounting principle may include a change in methods of depreciation, a change in valuing inventory, or a change in methods for accounting for long-term contracts.

Improper disclosures can take various forms, including misrepresentations; intentional inaccuracies; or deliberate omissions of information concerning changes in estimates, accounting policy changes, and related-party transactions. For example, in the American Home example discussed previously, the SEC also alleged that American Home made misleading disclosures regarding the riskiness of the mortgages the company originated and held and its liquidity, among other things. Further, the SEC complaint stated that the company failed to disclose entirely that American Home sold the majority of its multibillion-dollar mortgage portfolio to meet liquidity demands.

Conclusion

An undisclosed related party can be a powerful device in a fraudster's hand. According to the American Institute of Certified Public Accountants, "Related parties, such as controlled entities, principal stockholders or management can execute transactions that improperly inflate earnings by masking their economic substance or distort reported results through lack of disclosure, or can even defraud the company by transferring funds to conduit related parties and ultimately to the perpetrators."[37]

Consider the use of undisclosed related parties conducting business with the Escala Group, Inc. According to an SEC complaint, Escala engaged in a series of fraudulent undisclosed related-party transactions that led to a "secret and dramatic" manipulation of collectible stamp values. The SEC found that the misleading disclosures and omissions contributed over $80 million to Escala's revenue and drove its stock price from $1.47 per share to $32 per share in a few years. If the true nature of the undisclosed related-party transactions were known, investors would have realized that Escala had actually been partially manipulating the collectible stamps market through a series of transactions with its own parent company and other related parties.[38]

In another fraud case, the SEC found that between 1997 and 2001, Raytheon Company and certain members of its senior management made false and misleading disclosures and used improper accounting practices that masked the declining results of a subsidiary, Raytheon Aircraft Company (RAC). In particular, Raytheon failed to disclose fully and accurately "known risks, trends, uncertainties, and other information concerning the deteriorating" state of RAC's business and the negative effect the decline was having on asset values. As a result, Raytheon failed to recognize between $67 million and $240 million in losses.[39]

At Cardinal Heath, Inc., the SEC alleged that three former senior accounting and finance officers engaged in an earnings and revenue management fraud scheme that offered a false picture of Cardinal's operational results. This enabled Cardinal to claim it met "its publicly proclaimed financial targets between its fiscal years (FY) 2001 and 2004."[40] The fraud included the undisclosed inflation of Cardinal's reported operating revenue through improperly reclassifying more than $5 billion of bulk revenue as operating revenue, selectively accelerating, without disclosure, Cardinal's payment of vendor invoices too prematurely, and improperly classifying $22 million in anticipated litigation settlement proceeds. As a result, Cardinal materially misrepresented its trends in reported operating revenue and earnings.

Part II

Understanding Other Forms of Misconduct and Illegal Activity

Richard H. Girgenti

In Part I, we discussed various types of fraud and some of the strategies that companies should build in order to combat fraud. Given the global nature of business today, executives are also required to navigate a complex web of laws and regulations. Part II looks at forms of illegal conduct other than fraud that can undermine a company's earnings and, perhaps most importantly, its brand and reputation. While the myriad potential illegal acts that an organization may encounter are too numerous to cover here, we will examine some of the more common forms of illegal conduct that are receiving enforcement attention, including bribery and corruption (Chapter 3), money laundering and trade sanctions (Chapter 4), and the falsification of government claims and insider trading (Chapter 5). Our discussion of each begins by assessing the legal and regulatory framework and looking at what constitutes the various forms of illegality; our discussion concludes by highlighting compliance measures that can be adopted by businesses to prevent and detect this misconduct.

Chapter 3

Bribery and Corruption

Richard H. Girgenti
Michael B. Schwartz

Few enforcement topics have received more attention over the last few years than the issue of the bribing of foreign government officials by corporate entities. Yet this has not always been the case. Indeed despite an auspicious beginning in the mid-1970s, anti-bribery enforcement received little or no attention for over 20 years.

In the mid-1970s, in the wake of the Watergate scandal and as a result of investigations by the SEC, over 400 U.S. companies admitted to making questionable payments to foreign government officials, politicians, and political parties amounting to US$300 million. One of the organizations involved in such bribery was a major aerospace company. Executives at this company bribed foreign officials to favor their products not only in developing countries, but also in industrialized nations including Italy, the Netherlands, and Japan.[1] Scandals like these tested the public's confidence in the integrity of American businesses. In 1977, the Foreign Corrupt Practices Act (FCPA) was signed into law to restore this confidence. This act was amended by the International Anti-Bribery and Fair Competition Act of 1998, which was designed to implement the anti-bribery conventions of the Organisation for Economic Co-operation and Development (OECD). This amendment expanded the jurisdiction of the United States to prosecute foreign companies and nationals for corrupt payments within the United States.

Mr. Schwartz is a principal in KPMG LLP's Forensic practice in Houston, TX. He leads KPMG's national and global Anti-Bribery and Corruption services.
Additional contributors are Andrew J. Curtin, Kate Lyden, Brent McDaniel, Nimna Varghese, and Brian Wilson.

The FCPA also amended Section 30A of the Securities Exchange Act of 1934. It now contains a general rule prohibiting U.S. persons, entities, and issuers from giving or offering to give anything of value to any "foreign official" in order to obtain or retain business, to influence the official, or to induce the official to act in violation of his lawful duties. The prohibition against providing or offering "anything of value" to government officials includes not only cash, but also gifts, trips, and entertainment. Something seemingly innocuous, such as paying for a government official's dinner, may raise anti-bribery questions if the payment is intended or perceived as an attempt to influence the official to award business or take action favorable to the payor. Companies have paid substantial fines to settle proceedings brought for providing items of monetary value, including jewelry, gift certificates, perfume, first-class airfare, and the use of golf club memberships and condominium time shares. Political and charitable contributions have also come under close scrutiny. Other illegal payments have appeared in the form of bogus consulting payments, false items added to legitimate invoices, and even commissions or rebates that lack economic substance—all intended to disguise a bribe.

The term "foreign official" is defined in the FCPA as an officer or employee of any foreign government or any department, agency, or instrumentality of such government; any political party, official or candidate; any public international organization; or "any person acting in an official capacity for or on behalf of any such government or department, agency, or instrumentality, or . . . public international organization." This has been broadly interpreted by the DOJ and SEC to include employees of state-owned entities.[2]

The sole exception included in the FCPA to the prohibition of giving or offering anything of value to foreign officials applies to routine governmental action and appears in Section 30A(b) of the Securities Exchange Act. It provides that Section 30A(a) shall not apply to "any facilitating or expediting payment" to a foreign official "to expedite or to secure the performance of a routine governmental action." Routine governmental action is defined as that which is ordinarily and commonly performed by a government official, such as obtaining permits, licenses, or other official documents; processing governmental papers, such as visas and work orders; providing police protection or mail pickup and delivery; providing phone service or power and water supply; loading and unloading cargo or protecting perishable products; scheduling inspections associated with contract performance or transit of goods across country; and "actions of a similar nature."[3] While the last category is not well defined, it's generally viewed that the governmental action must be clearly ministerial in nature and the facilitating payment exception specifically does not include any decision to award new business, to continue existing business, or "to obtain any improper advantage."[4] Accordingly, a key question to be answered in determining if the facilitating payment exception applies is whether the foreign individual to whom the payment is made has discretionary authority over the matter at hand.

The statute provides two affirmative defenses to an alleged FCPA violation. To avoid liability for an otherwise actionable payment under the FCPA, a U.S. person, entity, or issuer must show that (1) the payment was lawful under the laws of the foreign official's country or (2) the payment was a reasonable expenditure for promotional activities. For the payment to be lawful under the laws of a foreign country, there must be a written statute or regulation to support the legality of the action. This is not the same thing as "traditional" or "customary" or "not enforced"—even if confirmed by local counsel. There must be a written law authorizing or supporting the payment. For promotional expenses to pass muster, the expenses must be reasonable, bona fide, and clearly connected to the business of the company.

The accounting provisions of the FCPA provide guidance for the maintenance of books, records, and internal controls. Section 13(b)(2)(A) of the Securities Exchange Act requires issuers* to maintain books, records, and accounts that, in reasonable detail, accurately reflect the transactions and dispositions of the issuer. Section 13(b)(2)(B) requires issuers to devise and maintain a system of internal accounting controls sufficient to provide reasonable assurances that transactions are authorized by management and are recorded as necessary to account for assets and to permit preparation of financial statements in conformity with U.S. GAAP. When read in conjunction with Section 30A, this, not surprisingly, means that payments to foreign officials must be accurately recorded in the books and records.

For 20 years following the enactment of the FCPA in 1977, the United States was the only country with a formal law that provided for the prosecution of domestic companies for paying bribes abroad to foreign government officials. During this period, bribery payments were not only legal but also tax deductible in many other countries.[5] This began to change in December 1997 when 33 other countries joined the United States (38 as of 2010) in signing the OECD Convention on Combating Bribery of Foreign Public Officials in International Business Transactions (the OECD Convention).[6]

The Corruption Perceptions Index (CPI) determined by Transparency International indicates the perceived level of public-sector corruption in 180 countries and territories.[7] According to the 2010 index, a selection of which is shown in Table 3.1, the majority of the 178 countries scored below 5 on a scale

---

* The FCPA's accounting provisions apply to publicly held U.S. companies considered "issuers" under the Securities Exchange Act. To qualify as an issuer under the FCPA, an entity either must be required to file reports with the SEC under §r15(d) of the Exchange Act or must have securities registered with the SEC under §12 of the Exchange Act. The definition of "issuers" is sufficiently broad to cover corporations with bonds or American depository receipts traded on U.S. markets or stock exchanges. Unlike the anti-bribery provisions, the accounting provisions do not apply to "domestic concerns" that are not issuers.

Table 3.1.

Rank	Country/ Territory	CPI 2010 Score	Surveys Used	90% Confidence Interval
Sampling from Top Third				
1	New Zealand	9.3	6	9.2–9.5
6	Canada	8.9	6	8.7–9.0
8	Switzerland	8.7	6	8.3–9.1
10	Norway	8.6	6	8.1–9.0
15	Germany	7.9	6	7.5–8.3
20	United Kingdom	7.6	6	7.3–7.9
22	United States	7.1	8	6.5–7.7
28	United Arab Emirates	6.3	5	5.4–7.3
30	Israel	6.1	6	5.7–6.6
30	Spain	6.1	6	5.7–6.5
54	South Africa	4.5	8	4.1–4.8
Sampling from Middle Third				
62	Ghana	4.1	7	3.4–4.7
67	Italy	3.9	6	3.5–4.4
69	Brazil	3.7	7	3.2–4.3
78	Greece	3.5	6	3.1–3.9
78	China	3.5	9	3.0–4.0
78	Thailand	3.5	9	3.2–3.9
87	India	3.3	10	3.0–3.5
98	Mexico	3.1	7	2.9–3.3
98	Egypt	3.1	6	2.9–3.4
101	Dominican Republic	3.0	5	2.7–3.2
Sampling from Bottom Third				
127	Syria	2.5	5	2.1–2.8
127	Belarus	2.5	3	2.1–3.1
134	Nigeria	2.4	7	2.2–2.7
134	Philippines	2.4	9	2.1–2.7
134	Ukraine	2.4	8	2.1–2.6
154	Russia	2.1	8	1.9–2.3
154	Cambodia	2.1	9	1.9–2.2
164	Venezuela	2.0	7	1.8–2.1
168	Angola	1.9	6	1.8–2.0
172	Turkmenistan	1.6	3	1.4–1.8

Source: Transparency International, "Corruptions Perceptions Index 2010," Transparency International Surveys and Indices, www.transparency.org/policy_research/surveys_indices/cpi/2010/results.

from 0 (perceived to be highly corrupt) to 10 (perceived to be very clean). Of the 178 countries, the Scandinavian countries were perceived to be some of the least corrupt countries, ranging from the high score of 9.3 for Denmark to 8.6 for Norway. On the other hand, the emerging BRIC (Brazil, Russia, India, and China) countries ranked in the bottom two-thirds of the index, with Brazil scoring at 3.7, China at 3.5, India at 3.3, and Russia at 2.1.

Article 1 of the OECD Convention states that each signatory should make it a criminal offense "to offer, promise or give any undue pecuniary or other advantage . . . to a foreign public official in order to obtain or retain business or other improper advantage." This includes obtaining permits or preferential treatment in relation to taxation, customs, and judicial or legislative proceedings. As currently written, the OECD Convention focuses on the conduct of public officials, but a wider scope may be addressed in future revisions.[8]

Each signatory to the OECD Convention agreed to work to impose "effective, proportionate and dissuasive non-criminal sanctions"[9] on offenders and to impose sanctions "when the offence is committed in whole or in part in its territory."[10] (The phrase "in part" typically refers to cases in which the direction to pay the bribe has been made from the home country.) In addition to criminalizing the payment of bribes to public officials, the OECD Convention also contains an agreement or a books-and-records provision that prohibits "the establishment of off-the-book accounts, the making of off-the-books or inadequately identified transactions, the recording of non-existent expenditures . . . as well as the use of false documents . . . for the purpose of bribing foreign public officials or of hiding such bribery."[11] The agreement also provides for mutual legal assistance between signatories, including extradition for bribery offenses.

In March 2010, the OECD Working Group on Bribery issued Good Practice Guidance on Internal Controls, Ethics, and Compliance, which offers business organizations a number of practices to consider in their efforts to effectively combat bribery and corruption. These "good practices" include adopting a "clearly articulated and visible corporate policy for prohibiting foreign bribery" that receives "strong, explicit and visible support and commitment from senior management"; instilling a sense of responsibility for monitoring and ensuring compliance at "all levels of the company" and providing select senior officers with an "adequate level of autonomy from management" to "report matters directly to independent monitoring bodies" at the company; ensuring "periodic communication and documented training"; and implementing specific measures to prevent and detect bribery by third-party business partners such as risk-based due diligence, as well as disciplinary procedures to address violations.[12]

These agreements and international efforts have also influenced other countries to draft their own legislation and enforcement actions. In the United Kingdom, the Bribery Act 2010 was enacted in April 2010 (now effective April

2011) with the following components: (1) a more effective legal framework to combat bribery in both the public and the private sectors; (2) two general offenses covering the offering, promising, or giving of an advantage, and the requesting, agreeing to receive, or accepting of an advantage; (3) a discrete offense of bribery of a foreign public official; and (4) a new offense of failure by a commercial organization to prevent a bribe being paid for or on its behalf, but it will be a defense if the organization has "adequate procedures" in place to prevent bribery.[13] This Bribery Act has many similar elements to the FCPA and is a comprehensive anti-bribery regulation. However, probably the largest difference between the two is that the Bribery Act allows for fewer affirmative defenses than the FCPA does, as the FCPA allows for "facilitating payments" and has language that allows for more open interpretation.

The challenge for many companies subject to laws criminalizing bribery and corruption is that they may be operating in geographies or with organizations where the concept of giving something before asking for something is part of the culture. Some companies complain that refraining from participating in culturally expected bribery norms puts them at a disadvantage when bidding alongside competitors with fewer ethical qualms or who are subject to fewer regulations because of the location of their headquarters.

This is particularly important in developing countries that may have weaker regulatory, legal, and enforcement regimes. The result, according to Ben Heineman, senior fellow on corporate governance at Harvard Law School and the Kennedy School of Government, as well as former senior vice president for law and public affairs at General Electric, is that bribery and corruption have a negative effect on societies and economies, especially in developing nations. According to Mr. Heineman, corruption "distorts markets and competition, breeds cynicism among citizens, stymies the rule of law, damages government legitimacy and corrodes the integrity of the private sector. It is a significant obstacle to development and poverty reduction. It also helps perpetuate failed and failing states, which are incubators of terrorism, the narcotics trade, money laundering, human trafficking and other types of global crime."[14] Despite these seemingly obvious negative effects, the bribing of government officials was long viewed in many parts of the world as culturally acceptable, a competitive necessity, and therefore an acceptable business practice.

In some places, laws can be vague and subject to interpretation and change, frequently without much notice to the general public. China, for example, writes or revises thousands of laws each year, some of which are left to interpretation by provincial or local judges who often have little or no legal background or experience.[15] Regardless, illicit payments and other forms of corruption result in significant business risks, ones likely to increase in light of increasing domestic and international regulatory scrutiny and law enforcement. Bribery risks can arise in a variety of circumstances. In addition to direct dealings with government officials, in-country third parties such as sales or marketing agents, consultants, joint venture partners, or distributors present substantial risks to organizations. These risks arise either when third parties make improper payments to government officials or when a prospective business entity may be owned by or affiliated with a government official or close relative.

Similarly, merging with or acquiring a majority stake or operational control in another entity could make an acquirer liable for past and future anti-bribery violations. Enforcement authorities expect acquirers, among other things, to conduct anti-bribery due diligence, to halt any ongoing activity involving bribery, and to obtain contractual provisions and representations confirming an acquired company's compliance with applicable anti-bribery laws.

For most of the 30-plus years of its existence, the FCPA was the only legislation enacted in response to widespread corruption scandals, and prosecutions under this act were rare. However, in the last few years, prosecutions under the FCPA have increased significantly.

Figures 3.1, 3.2, and 3.3 illustrate the increase in regulatory actions against corporations and individuals related to FCPA matters. The simultaneous prosecution of individuals and their employers who are believed to have violated the FCPA is not always the case; the DOJ and SEC seem to vary their approach based on the unique circumstances of each case.

Between 2005 and October 2009, the Criminal Division of the DOJ filed 57 cases—more than the number of prosecutions filed in the almost 30 years between the enactment of the FCPA in 1977 and 2005. According to the

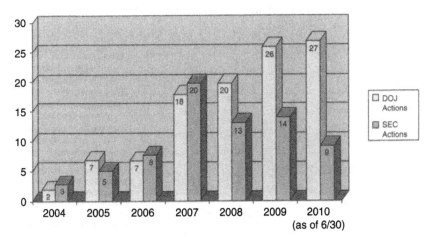

Figure 3.1. FCPA enforcement actions brought by DOJ and SEC, 2004–2010 (as of 6/30)
Source: 2010 Mid-Year FCPA Update, New York: Gibson, Dunn & Crutcher LLP, July 8, 2010.

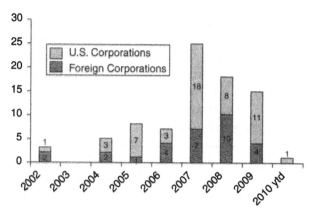

Figure 3.2. Total corporate matters initiated, 2002–2010
Source: Philip Urofsky and Danforth Newcomb, *Recent Trends and Patterns in FCPA Enforcement,*
New York: Shearman & Sterling LLP, March 4, 2010.

OECD's report on U.S. anti-bribery efforts released on October 15, 2010, the United States has more than 150 criminal and 80 civil ongoing FCPA investigations, many of which are parallel matters.[16] Some of the factors that have triggered this increase include:

- Penetration of U.S. companies into countries like oil-rich Nigeria, where energy concessions have an enormous value and there are other dynamics that resulted in a history of bribes being frequently solicited or paid
- The USA PATRIOT Act of 2001, which connected bribing foreign officials to the advancement of terrorist activity

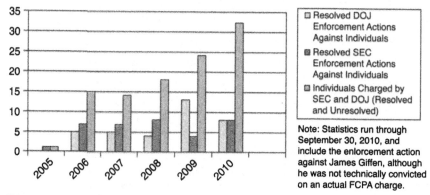

Figure 3.3. DOJ and SEC enforcement activity against individuals, 2005–2010 (through September 30, 2010)
Source: FCPA Autumn Review 2010, Washington, DC: Miller & Chevalier, October 8, 2010.

- The Sarbanes-Oxley Act of 2002, which made senior executives of public companies accountable for the accuracy of public disclosures related to a company
- A heightened sensitivity to potential FCPA violations in the targets of mergers and acquisitions
- A significant increase in voluntary disclosures

A brief look back over the last few years best illustrates the increasing breadth and severity of DOJ FCPA enforcement.

In February 2007, three subsidiaries of Vetco International Ltd. pleaded guilty to violating the anti-bribery provisions of the FCPA and agreed to pay $26 million in criminal fines. "This case represents the largest criminal penalty the Department of Justice has ever sought in a Foreign Corrupt Practices case," then-Deputy Attorney General Paul McNulty was quoted as saying at the time. It was an attention-grabbing sum, but such was the price tag for the criminal conduct described in the charging documents: making at least 378 corrupt payments totaling $2.1 million to induce Nigerian Customs Service officials to give the subsidiaries preferential treatment during the customs clearance process.[17]

Just two months later in April of that year, following its admission that it paid about $4 million in bribes to secure a contract for developing and operating an oil field in Kazakhstan, a subsidiary of Baker Hughes, Inc., agreed to pay $11 million in criminal fines, $10 million in civil penalties, and more than $24 million in profit disgorgement.[18]

In 2008, Siemens AG and three of its subsidiaries pleaded guilty to long-standing and systemic violations of the FCPA involving more than $1.4 billion in bribes paid to government officials across Asia, Africa, Europe, the Middle East, and the Americas. At the conclusion of this unprecedented investigation, the DOJ, the SEC, and the Munich Public Prosecutor's office collectively imposed on Siemens more than $1.6 billion in fines, penalties, and disgorgement of profits. Of that, $800 million was charged by U.S. authorities ($450 million going toward criminal fines), making the combined U.S. penalties the largest monetary sanction ever imposed in an FCPA case in U.S. history.

The globalization of anti-bribery and anti-corruption laws, regulations, and enforcement has led to parallel investigations in different jurisdictions by different agencies as was seen in the case of the Siemens AG investigation. Jeffrey Taylor, the U.S. Attorney for the District of Columbia at the time, said that the Siemens case "set the standard for multinational cooperation in the fight against corrupt business practices," while then-SEC Division of Enforcement Director Linda Chatham Thomsen characterized the end result as "a testament to the close, coordinated working relationship among the SEC, the U.S. Department of Justice, and other U.S. and international law enforcement."[19]

In 2009, Kellogg Brown & Root (now known as KBR, Inc.) paid $402 million in criminal FCPA penalties for its participation in a decade-long scheme to bribe Nigerian government officials to obtain government contracts.[20]

The focus on business combinations has resulted in more investigations and harsher penalties for corporations, for both acquirers and acquisition targets. According to the *2008 Anti-bribery and Anti-corruption Survey* conducted by KPMG LLP, only 36 percent of the respondents said they felt their organization's level of FCPA due diligence in a merger, acquisition, or other transaction in the past five years was "adequate." Twenty-seven percent described their organizations' FCPA due diligence as "minimal."[21]

In addition to other more frequently considered negative effects (e.g., revenue degradation, loss of public trust, and criminal prosecution), bribery and corruption violations may also impact the target's valuation. If an acquirer discovers during its due diligence that the target obtains business through the use of bribes, the acquirer will need to assess the impact that discovery may have on the quality of earnings resulting from the cessation of those suspect business practices. Such considerations may cause the acquirer to lower its bid, walk away from the transaction, or request guidance from federal regulators.

In June 2007, eLandia International Inc. acquired Latin Node Inc., a company that provided telecommunications services over the Internet. In April 2009, Latin Node Inc. pleaded guilty to violating the FCPA in connection with improper payments in Honduras and Yemen, agreeing to pay a $2 million fine. As a result of its postacquisition due diligence, investigatory efforts, and subsequent self-reporting to the DOJ, eLandia closed its just-acquired Honduras operations, terminated senior management in that country, and wrote off almost its entire $20-plus million investment due to the corrupt payments eLandia had not uncovered during its preacquisition due diligence.[22]

Bribery and corruption due diligence, which is discussed in more depth in Chapter 9, is, of course, most relevant in transactions that share certain types of high-risk characteristics. These high-risk characteristics include the degree of interaction with government and government officials, the geographic location of the target, the target's culture and governmental structure, the industry within which the target operates, the local accounting standards and laws regarding payment of bribes, the lack of an existing bribery and corruption compliance program and related internal controls at the target, and a customer base that includes governmental entities and agencies.

An analysis in "The Effectiveness of Laws against Bribery Abroad," by Alvaro Cuervo-Cazurra, assistant professor at the Moore School of Business, University of South Carolina, reveals that investors from countries that have implemented laws against bribery abroad have become more sensitive to host-country corruption, shown through reductions in foreign direct investment in those countries perceived as corrupt after their home countries had implemented these anti-bribery laws. The implications of the findings of the study suggest that laws against bribery abroad appear to be effective, but only when the legislation in place is coordinated in multiple countries.[23]

However, there may also be unintended business consequences of anti-corruption regulation and the difficulties involved in navigating a global patchwork of regulation. According to a December 2009 survey published by Dow Jones,[24] over two-thirds of companies (70 percent) were delaying or abandoning business initiatives abroad as they collected information they needed to confidentially assess corruption risk. Sixty-five percent of those companies surveyed delayed or abandoned plans for new partnerships or entry into new markets due to legal questions arising from unclear anti-corruption regulations. Forty percent decided against entering emerging markets for fear of running afoul of anti-corruption regulations. Despite these concerns over potential negative consequences, companies doing, or intending to do, business overseas can implement programs and controls that can mitigate their concerns and safely navigate these challenges while taking advantage of cross-border commercial opportunities.

On July 21, 2010, the Dodd-Frank Wall Street Reform and Consumer Protection Act (Dodd-Frank Act) was signed into law in the United States. This act was created in response to a number of economic developments from 2008 to 2010 and is supposed to promote further financial stability and accountability. The Dodd-Frank Act provides the SEC with new powers of enforcement by including a "whistleblower bounty program." Under this bounty program, if the information provided by a person or persons leads to a successful SEC enforcement, the person or persons could receive 10 to 30 percent of the monetary sanctions in excess of $1 million. The Dodd-Frank Act will most likely increase the number of cases brought by the SEC against individuals and corporations and could provide a strong deterrent for other individuals and companies considering paying bribes.

Other deterrents for paying bribes are in the works now, as more bills are being introduced calling for greater accountability and greater repercussions for violations of anti-bribery acts. The Overseas Contractor Reform Act, if passed, would mandate the debarment of those found to be violators of the FCPA from additional or future federal government contracts. While the language of this bill is currently limited, the Overseas Contractor Reform Act could turn into a significant and effective piece of legislation in the prevention of bribery.

An FCPA Compliance Program

Policy and court filings by the Department of Justice clearly indicate that in making charging and disposition decisions, the government places considerable weight on whether and to what extent a company had a preexisting and effective compliance program. In Part IV, we will discuss the elements of an effective compliance program. However, to the extent that a company is multinational or seeks to operate globally, the government also expects that an organization's compliance program will be effectively designed and implemented to reduce the prospect of violations of bribery laws. The DOJ's Opinion Procedure Release 04-02[25] lays out a basic framework for FCPA compliance programs and procedures. Its principles have been followed in numerous deferred and nonprosecution agreements involving FCPA-related issues as well as in the OECD's Good Practice Guidance mentioned earlier in this chapter. While many of these compliance program elements are common to all compliance programs, others are specific to the risk of an FCPA violation.

- The effectiveness of an FCPA compliance program is, more often than not, initially viewed through the lens of the code of ethics that drives it, more specifically, the FCPA-specific policies and procedures enshrined in such a code. The many components in a code of ethics usually include a preamble, broad policy statements, specific policy statements (which may include FCPA compliance requirements), and reporting mechanisms for employees. Ideally, any company with a myriad of global operations and businesses should include FCPA-specific policies and procedures in its code of ethics.
- The applicability of the FCPA-specific policies and procedures should be expanded to include all directors, officers, employees, and business partners—including, but not limited to, agents, consultants, representatives, joint venture partners, and teaming partners—involved in business transactions, representation, business development, or retention in a foreign jurisdiction (respectively, agents and business partners) that are reasonably capable of reducing the prospect that the FCPA or any applicable foreign anti-corruption law will be violated.
- Establishing accountability standards plays a key role in the execution and monitoring of an FCPA compliance program. Independent senior employees reporting directly to a compliance committee of the audit committee of the board of directors should be given the responsibility for the implementation and oversight of the program and should be accountable in case there is a lapse in its functioning. The rising number of prosecutions of business executives, i.e., individual employees in FCPA-related violations, highlights the importance of establishing and maintaining standards of accountability.
- The relevance of training cannot be understated in making an FCPA compliance program effective. According to the *2008 Anti-bribery and Anti-corruption Survey* conducted by KPMG, only one-quarter of organizations with communication and training programs said training is mandatory for

all employees. The remaining 75 percent said they used a risk-based approach.[26] Training and communications should be formal and specialized and should be a coordinated effort by multiple departments within a company—including legal, compliance, human resources, and internal audit. It should extend to agents and business partners of a company in the various jurisdictions where the company operates.

- A reporting mechanism such as a hotline, managed independently, should be set up. The effectiveness of internal reporting mechanisms such as hotlines is especially critical in light of recent enhancements and protections afforded corporate whistleblowers under the Dodd-Frank Act. All employees, agents, and business partners should be aware of the existence of the hotline and be encouraged to use it to report suspected violations of the code of ethics or suspected illegal conduct. The appropriate department within the company should investigate the merit of any alert received through the hotline. The *2008 Anti-bribery and Anti-corruption Survey* conducted by KPMG revealed that only slightly more than one-quarter (27 percent) of companies with a hotline extended the hotline to parties outside their organizations with whom they have a business relationship, including agents and business partners.[27]

- Companies must investigate actual or alleged incidents related to bribery and corruption. External counsel or FCPA consultants may be engaged to investigate on behalf of the company, especially if the company does not have adequate resources to investigate such a complaint in a certain part of the world.

- After investigating the claims, if the suspected violation of the ethics code is proved, appropriate disciplinary procedures should be initiated.

- In addition to setting up internal control processes, companies should design stringent processes for dealing with agents and business partners. Preretention due diligence requirements and postretention oversight pertaining to all agents and business partners should be done. Further, complete records pertaining to such due diligence should be maintained. The Department of Justice's Opinion Procedure Release 08-01 elaborates on elements of an effective due diligence on a joint venture partner and describes maintenance of evidence of this due diligence centrally.[28] A committee consisting of senior officials within the business should review and document the appointment of agents and business partners and all contracts and payments related to such appointment. In all agreements, contracts, and renewals thereof with all agents, business partners, and other third parties, the following provisions should be included in contracts:
  - Representations and undertakings to not engage in corrupt activities
  - Compliance with foreign anti-corruption laws and other relevant laws

- ○ Allowance for internal and independent audits of the books and records of the agent, business partner, or other third party to ensure compliance with the foregoing
- ○ A provision for termination of the agent, business partner, or other third party as a result of any breach of applicable anti-corruption laws and regulations or representations and undertakings related thereto

- Among the different types of payments that present an FCPA compliance risk are promotional expenses, facilitating payments, charitable contributions, lobbying, and travel and entertainment expenses. Of these, facilitating payments are probably the most difficult to discern as being legitimate or otherwise. Facilitating payments should only be made if certain criteria are met, including modesty of the amount, infrequency of the payment, payment to a low-level government official performing ministerial and nondiscretionary duties, legality under local law, necessity to secure or expedite a routine government action, and appropriate recording of the payment in the books and records of the company. The DOJ has not looked favorably on facilitating payments in recent years, and it should be noted the April 2010 U.K. Bribery Act and March 2010 OECD Good Practice Guidance contain no similar exception. In each instance, the company should obtain legal advice before making such payments. As a result of these interpretive and compliance challenges and subsequent events, including the U.K. Bribery Act and OECD Good Practice Guidance mentioned previously, it was not surprising that KPMG's *2008 Anti-bribery and Anti-corruption Survey* found that only approximately 25 percent of the companies surveyed allowed facilitating payments to be made, while approximately 75 percent did not.[29]
- As a part of the aforementioned due diligence procedures, due care should be applied to help avoid delegating discretionary authority to individuals whom the company knows, or should know through the exercise of due diligence, to have a propensity to engage in illegal or improper activities. Due care is achieved through thorough background checks locally and in other geographies where the individuals operate. Background checks should also shed light on whether agents, business partners, or other third parties have government affiliations or relationships that may create heightened risk for an organization.
- A system of internal accounting controls to keep accurate books, records, and accounts should be implemented.
- Independent and objective audits by outside counsel or forensic accountants performed three years apart, at most, should be part of the FCPA compliance program to help assess whether the code of ethics, including its FCPA-specific provisions, is implemented in an effective manner.

Conclusion

An effective FCPA compliance program in today's environment requires managing risk arising from laws and regulations in many global jurisdictions. Of course, the precursor to designing and implementing an effective anti-bribery and anti-corruption compliance program is to assess and understand the risk of bribery and corruption occurring throughout the organization. Coordination across all business units and among various geographic locations of the company will help produce a comprehensive risk assessment and facilitate the development of a highly effective and manageable compliance program.

Chapter 4

Money Laundering and Trade Sanctions

Teresa A. Pesce

I t is difficult to estimate the amount of money laundered, but reliable studies[1] cite global figures in excess of $3 trillion annually.[*] If convicted of money laundering, an individual or institution can face a criminal fine of up to $500,000 per charge or twice the value of the property involved in the offense and, for an individual, an additional 20 years of imprisonment. In addition, civil forfeiture actions brought by the government may result in the seizure of funds connected to the offense.

While money laundering is often associated with the acts of individuals, financial institutions can also be implicated. In fact, law enforcement appears to be intensifying its focus on the banking sector in an effort to quell questionable transactions. Over the last few years, the Department of Justice has prosecuted, deferred prosecution on, or brought civil penalty actions against many financial institutions on money laundering charges.[2,†] Because of their central role in all forms of monetary transfers, financial institutions of every type—be they commercial banks, broker-dealers, money service businesses (MSBs),

Ms. Pesce is a principal in KPMG LLP's Forensic practice in New York, NY. She leads KPMG's Anti–Money Laundering services for the Americas region.

Additional contributors are Laurence Birnbaum-Sarcy, Marikay A. Corcoran, Jim Dowling, Stephen D. Marshall, and Alan Williamson.

[*] Note, however, that Reuter and Truman regard this as an upper limit and that the actual amount is difficult or impossible to define.

[†] According to the U.S. Department of Justice, between 1994 and 2001, over 18,000 federal defendants were charged with money laundering.

insurance companies, alternative-value transfer businesses, unregulated financial businesses, or even nonfinancial companies—must have robust anti–money laundering (AML) programs and processes in place.

Recent enforcement actions in the United States demonstrate the importance of having strong AML systems and controls. In July 2008, the Securities and Exchange Commission fined online stockbroker E*Trade $1 million for failing to follow its own procedures to identify and verify its customers, a fundamental element of any prevention program. The regulator made note of the fact that the deficiencies that led to the action were brought to the attention of E*Trade management by employees and auditors, but management failed to respond properly. In January 2009, E*Trade was again fined $1 million, this time by the Financial Industry Regulatory Authority (FINRA), for failing to have a program to detect suspicious activity that suited the particular risks of its business model.[3]

If two financial institutions are used as conduits for criminal conduct, law enforcement will be less likely to press criminal charges against the one with a strong AML program that was unwittingly used.[4,*] This is true even for unregulated financial companies. The criminal and civil penalties found in the U.S. Criminal Code (Title 18) apply to all persons and institutions subject to U.S. criminal laws, whether or not they are covered by AML regulations. According to the Financial Action Task Force (FATF), in order for countries to effectively implement FATF's recommendations, they must "require financial institutions and other businesses and professions to implement effective measures to detect and prevent money laundering and terrorist financing."[5]

Background and Regulatory Framework

The meaning of the term "money laundering" has changed over time. The historical conception of money laundering involved narcotics trafficking, reporting of large currency transactions, and forfeiture of narcotics proceeds. It appears that the earliest judicial use of the phrase occurred in 1982 in a published opinion denying the petition of a Colombian citizen to lift a freeze order involving $4 million. The money was seized for forfeiture to the U.S. government after an investigation involving large quantities of cash delivered to a small Florida bank in bags and cardboard boxes.[6]

This classic definition of money laundering consists of three stages: placement (placing cash from illegal sources into the legitimate financial system), layering (concealing fund ownership or origin, usually through nontransparent structures

---

* The 2009 Federal Sentencing Guidelines Manual, §8B2.1, "Effective Compliance and Ethics Programs," states, "Diligence of an organization in seeking to prevent and detect criminal conduct has a direct bearing on the appropriate penalties."

and multiple transactions), and integration (reintroducing laundered funds into the legitimate economy through the purchase of goods or services).

The AML provisions of the Bank Secrecy Act (BSA), originally aimed at the reporting of cash transactions over $10,000, have evolved through legislation, regulation, and enforcement actions. AML laws now require not only aggregation, detection, and reporting of cash transactions, but also the implementation of related sophisticated controls aimed at understanding customers and their transactions in order to detect, investigate, and report suspicious activity.

Money laundering was independently criminalized in 1986 with the passage of the Money Laundering Control Act, which also directed banks to establish and maintain procedures to ensure and monitor compliance with the BSA. Other laws followed,* but the most significant—after the BSA itself—is probably the USA PATRIOT Act of 2001, passed in the wake of the September 11 attacks. The USA PATRIOT Act and its subsequent implementing regulations strengthened the government's ability to fight money laundering and added specific provisions requiring counterterrorist financing (CTF) measures. The USA PATRIOT Act formally defined the elements of an AML program, extended the reach of AML program requirements to many nonbank financial institutions (e.g., broker-dealers, insurance companies, mutual funds, money service businesses, jewelry dealers, casinos), and created specific requirements for information sharing,[7,†] customer identification,[‡] and enhanced customer due diligence.[§]

Under the USA PATRIOT Act,** a financial institution is required to have an AML program with four distinct elements:

- Internal policies, procedures, and controls
- An independent audit function to test the program
- A designated AML compliance officer
- An ongoing employee training program

These elements are discussed more fully in the pages that follow.[8]

The BSA and the USA PATRIOT Act require financial institutions to file suspicious activity reports (SARs) to an agency of the U.S. Treasury Department,

---

* Other laws include the Anti-Drug Abuse Act of 1988, the Annunzio-Wylie Anti–Money Laundering Act (1992), the Money Laundering Suppression Act (1994), and the Money Laundering and Financial Crimes Strategy Act (1998).

† Sections 314(a) and 314(b) of the USA PATRIOT Act define methods for financial institutions to share information with law enforcement and other financial institutions, respectively.

‡ Section 326 of the USA PATRIOT Act requires a customer identification program (CIP).

§ Section 312 of the USA PATRIOT Act requires enhanced due diligence for certain correspondent accounts and private banking relationships.

** Section 352 of the USA PATRIOT Act requires financial institutions to have anti–money laundering programs.

the Financial Crimes Enforcement Network (FinCEN). The definition of "suspicious activity" under the USA PATRIOT Act, however, is broad and is used to cover crimes and misconduct ranging from identity theft to computer intrusion and securities fraud.[*] This has resulted in a gradual broadening of the definition of money laundering beyond the original "classical" understanding.[†]

International standards also demand that financial institutions maintain AML and counterterrorist financing programs to prevent, detect, and report illicit transactions. Organizations such as the FATF and the Basel Committee on Banking Supervision have developed core principles that financial institutions operating in the international marketplace are expected to follow. FATF, an intergovernmental body, independently assesses and measures the AML/CTF regimes of nations and maintains a list of noncooperative countries and territories (NCCTs) to designate those countries of highest money laundering concern. The original list, published in 2000, identified 15 countries as noncooperative. In 2001, the FATF added another 8 countries. Over time, these countries worked to institute the FATF recommendations; and at present, no countries remain on this list, although recently FATF has identified other countries presenting varying levels of money laundering concern.[‡] Moreover, international industry groups, such as the Wolfsberg Group (made up of representatives from 11 global financial institutions),[§] have also developed guidance to combat money laundering.

In addition to AML measures, financial institutions must also implement programs to comply with trade sanctions. In the United States, the sanctions

---

[*] Suspicious activity includes "criminal violations . . . and transactions conducted or attempted by, at, or through . . . [the institution] if [the institution] knows, suspects, or has reason to suspect that the transaction: may involve potential money laundering or other illegal activity (e.g., terrorism financing), is designed to evade the BSA or its implementing regulations . . . [or] has no business or apparent lawful purpose or is not the type of transaction that the particular customer would normally be expected to engage in, and the bank knows of no reasonable explanation for the transaction after examining the available facts, including the background and possible purpose of the transaction." See 12 CFR 208.62, 211.5(k), 211.24(f), and 225.4(f) (Board of Governors of the Federal Reserve System); 12 CFR 353 (Federal Deposit Insurance Corporation); 12 CFR 748 (National Credit Union Administration); 12 CFR 21.11 (Office of the Comptroller of the Currency); 12 CFR 563.180 (Office of Thrift Supervision) (does not apply to Savings and Loan Holding Companies); and 31 CFR 103.18 (FinCEN).

[†] For example, FINRA recently notified its broker-dealer members that failure to detect and prevent an unregistered stock offering could be a failure of their AML program; see "FINRA Reminds Firms of Their Obligations to Determine Whether Securities Are Eligible for Public Sale," Regulatory Notice 09-05, January 13, 2009.

[‡] In February 2010, and then updated in June 2010, FATF published two lists commonly referred to as the "blacklist" and the "graylist." On the blacklist (www.fatf-gafi.org/dataoecd/17/5/45540828.pdf) "FATF identified jurisdictions that have strategic deficiencies and, along with the FATF-style regional bodies (FSRBs), works with them to address those deficiencies that pose a risk to the international financial system." The graylist (www.fatf-gafi.org/dataoecd/17/4/45540819.pdf) cites "jurisdictions that have strategic AML/CFT deficiencies for which they have developed an action plan with the FATF."

[§] The Wolfsberg Group consists of representatives from Banco Santander, Bank of Tokyo-Mitsubishi UFJ, Barclays, Citigroup, Credit Suisse, Deutsche Bank, Goldman Sachs, HSBC, J.P. Morgan Chase, Société Genéralé, and UBS.

program is administered by the Office of Foreign Assets Control (OFAC), an office of the U.S. Treasury Department. OFAC administers and enforces economic and trade sanctions, based on U.S. foreign policy and national security goals, against designated foreign countries, terrorists, international narcotics traffickers, and activities related to the proliferation of weapons of mass destruction. OFAC acts under presidential wartime and national emergency powers, as well as authority granted by specific legislation, to limit transactions and freeze foreign assets under U.S. jurisdiction. Many of the sanctions are based on United Nations and other international mandates, are multilateral in scope, and involve close cooperation with allied foreign governments.[9] OFAC does not examine institutions for compliance with sanctions, so it has entered into memoranda of understanding with U.S. regulatory agencies such as the Federal Reserve, the Office of the Comptroller of the Currency, the SEC, and even state regulators such as the New York State Banking Department. Financial industry regulators now generally include OFAC compliance in their AML compliance examinations.

In light of the intense scrutiny that regulatory agencies apply to AML and sanctions compliance, as well as the legal, financial, and reputational risks associated with program failures, institutions are well advised to maintain robust AML/CTF and sanctions controls. Thus, to the best of their ability, firms should have in place programs to prevent money laundering and terrorist financing, to detect and investigate suspicious activity if it occurs, and to report such events when detected. When firms maintain sound, thoughtful, and up-to-date programs commensurate with the risks presented by their business and client base, they not only help reduce their exposure to money laundering, but are more likely to engender goodwill with regulators and law enforcement authorities. The latter are then less likely to impose harsh sanctions or penalties in the event of a money laundering event.

Fundamental Principles of Anti–Money Laundering Programs: Prevention, Detection, and Response

AML laws and regulations are better understood through their evolving legal and historical context, but their application requires straightforward principles:

- Prevention of money laundering at an institution
- Detection and reporting when it does occur
- Response to issues, problems, and the ever-changing threat posed by resourceful criminals and terrorists

This section explores these principles in more detail.

Prevention

Although the absolute prevention of money laundering is impossible, financial institutions must do their best to deter this type of activity. The law recognizes that no institution, no matter how sophisticated its program, can prevent all questionable transactions. But it does require that firms detect and report any suspicious activity they do find.

A good prevention program is tailored to the needs of the institution. This means understanding the nature of the business conducted, assessing the risks inherent, and building a program that addresses those risks adequately. Although the legal and regulatory structure in the United States is largely rules-based, the growing consensus among regulators and practitioners is that a risk-based program, using the rules as a foundation, is a better course of action. As James Freis, director of FinCEN, said in a speech in October 2008, "Under the risk-based approach to BSA compliance, FinCEN does not expect that banks will develop anti–money laundering programs meeting an unnecessary and arbitrarily high standard, or will detect and report every single unusual and suspicious transaction."[10]

Rationale behind a Risk-Based Approach. A *rules-based* AML program is often thought of as a "check-the-box" approach, one based strictly on the requirements of AML laws and regulations. In designing such a program, the organization applies rules to set standards for relevant processes and to identify, report, and resolve any anomalies that surface. Because it applies the same rules uniformly across business lines and products, a rules-based approach offers consistency. What it lacks, however, is flexibility. In addition, different processes have different risk profiles. By applying the same rules to all accounts and transactions, limited resources may be spent on low-risk areas, while high-risk issues may be missed. The program can become a mechanical exercise, based on routine and not the judgment of compliance professionals.

A *risk-based* approach, on the other hand, requires that organizations analyze and identify the money laundering risks that exist in their operations and establish appropriate controls to mitigate them. A tailored program allows an organization to focus its activities on higher-risk areas and apply more appropriate controls to lower-risk ones. This makes for better use of financial, operational, and compliance resources.

The Risk-Based Program. Although every reputable company should agree that it should prevent and detect money laundering, two factors make perfect compliance impossible. First, money laundering and sanctions risk change over time, as a result of either business changes or regulatory changes. The guilty plea by

Chiquita Banana in March 2007 to violations of OFAC sanctions offers one example. Historically, Chiquita did business in Latin America by paying a local terrorist organization not to interfere with Chiquita employees or facilities. Times changed, and the bandits changed, becoming members of a sanctioned revolutionary group, but Chiquita did not realize that this meant that its risk had also changed. Chiquita continued to pay what was now considered a foreign terrorist organization. As a consequence, Chiquita paid $25 million to settle with the DOJ. Second, a company may realize its risks but fail to address them adequately. In the E*Trade matter discussed earlier, the broker had a monitoring program to detect suspicious activity, but relied on manual monitoring and review for securities trading activity. Although that might be adequate in some circumstances, FINRA found that it was not adequate for a firm doing millions of online trades annually.

Understanding the Business Model. A number of factors go into designing a risk-based AML compliance program. Each organization is unique and should be assessed based on its individual profile. The first step in creating a risk-based program is understanding the organization itself. This begins with studying the industry in which the entity operates, particularly since legal and regulatory requirements may vary by industry. For instance, although there are common principles such as "knowing your customer" and monitoring transactions, elements of the program specific to an institution will differ depending on whether the institution is a bank, an investment bank, an insurance company, an MSB, or other type of financial institution.

The size of the institution is also important. A large institution with numerous branches and subsidiaries, a large number of employees, and high volumes of diverse transactional activity requires a sophisticated AML compliance program. Such a program should be designed with extensive resources such as a large group of experienced compliance professionals and advanced technology solutions. A medium-sized or small institution can achieve a similar level of compliance by establishing a less extensive program. For instance, automated monitoring solutions may not be called for in a small institution or one with a limited number of transactions. In such cases, manual or semiautomated monitoring may make more sense, as long as such monitoring remains effective and alerts can be reviewed and resolved. Similarly, there are no set rules for the number of compliance personnel needed to develop, implement, and maintain a strong program. The size of AML compliance teams can range from a single BSA officer to a BSA officer supported by dozens or even hundreds of AML compliance professionals and investigators—again, this is dependent on the size, number, and type of transactions and the risk profile of the institution in question.

Global Implications. A global institution with a parent or holding company in one country and subsidiaries, affiliates, and representative offices throughout the world will need an AML compliance program tailored to its organizational structure.[11,*] Often, global minimal standards will be set for the entire organization and managed centrally by the head office. Local divergence will usually be approved if local requirements are more stringent than the global standard chosen for the organization. On the other end of the spectrum, an institution operating exclusively in one country will likely be subject to a more straightforward and uniform set of requirements.

The fundamental issue that institutions should address is determining in whose hands compliance responsibility lies. While compliance risk is ultimately owned by the business, responsibility for getting it right is shared by the business and the AML compliance professionals who support it. As such, institutions should decide whether they wish to adopt a centralized or decentralized AML program. But this too can mean different things to different organizations. Where the AML compliance function is centralized, day-to-day AML duties tend to rest largely with a corporate compliance department. A centralized compliance function arguably makes a program simpler and easier to explain to home regulators, but it places a heavy burden on the central function and may give the firm a competitive disadvantage in some markets. When the function is decentralized, AML roles and responsibilities generally shift more broadly to the business lines, with supervision by the compliance department. Decentralized programs are typically less expensive for the home office to maintain and more adaptable to local markets, but it is often more difficult for the department to ensure that standards are applied consistently, leading to the possibility that local regulators will find the program wanting with difficult consequences for the company even in its home jurisdiction. More effective programs leverage the knowledge of the customer and the business model that front-end personnel have to offer and the corporate compliance department's understanding of AML requirements.

Assessing the Risks. In assessing risk, a firm should consider the products and services it offers its customers, the type of customers it has, the volume of transactions, the geographic reach of its business, the different risk profiles of different countries, and the channels through which its products are delivered. Frontline business personnel should be involved in this analysis. The assessment can come from informal meetings among business, operations, and compliance

---

* According to KPMG International's *Global Anti–Money Laundering Survey 2007*, "nearly 85 percent of internationally active banks reported that they had a global AML policy in place" in 2007.

personnel, or it can adopt a more formal methodology such as that recommended by the Committee of Sponsoring Organizations. In any case, the assessment must be documented and acceptable to both business and compliance. Once the institution has assessed the risks associated with its products, customers, volumes, geography, and channels—that is, the inherent risk in its businesses—it should evaluate existing AML controls to determine what risks are well or easily managed and where risk may still exist even after controls are applied. The institution should review its policies and procedures, evaluate their relevance to its business operations, and determine whether they meet legal and regulatory requirements.

In the United States, banking regulators are mandated to assess the risk profile of each organization they examine and to evaluate the adequacy of the organization's AML risk assessment process. They expect financial institutions to perform an enterprisewide money laundering risk assessment as part of an integrated AML program. In the event the organization does not have an enterprisewide risk assessment, examiners will conduct their own at the outset of their examination. In such a case, the resulting risk assessment may be at odds with the organization's view of its own business risk, and the organization may find itself in fundamental conflict with examiners during the course of the exam. Thus, an institution that understands its business best is well advised to be proactive in assessing its risk and tailoring its program accordingly.

U.S. bank examiners are explicitly told by the Federal Financial Institutions Examination Council (FFIEC),* "There are many effective methods and formats used in completing a BSA/AML risk assessment; therefore, examiners should not advocate a particular method or format. Bank management should decide the appropriate method and format, based on the bank's particular risk profile."[12] This means that organizations are free to identify their risk assessment method and format, although they may occasionally encounter criticisms by their examiners for failing to fully develop the assessment process. On the other hand, examiners are less likely to challenge the process if the assessment methodology is well reasoned and, above all, well documented.

While the exact methodology and format of the risk assessment may vary from institution to institution—indeed, it may vary based on the business assessed—a number of factors generally should be considered.

Products and Services Offered by the Institution. A key question that should be answered when designing a risk assessment is whether the institution offers products and services to its customers that present a high risk of

---

* The FFIEC is a formal interagency body empowered to prescribe uniform principles, standards, and report forms for the federal examination of financial institutions by U.S. banking regulators.

money laundering. Products and services often considered as higher risk include:

- Private banking (i.e., the provision of banking services exclusively to high-net-worth individuals through a dedicated resource)
- Correspondent banking (i.e., money transfers for customers of other banks whereby the correspondent bank does not know the "customer's customer" or the ultimate source of funds)
- Payable through accounts (i.e., accounts offered by a bank that effectively give check-signing authority to customers of another bank)
- U.S. dollar drafts (i.e., checks drawn on a bank that can be assigned to a third party and are effectively negotiable instruments)
- Electronic banking (i.e., banking transactions where bank personnel never meet the customer face-to-face)
- Trade finance (i.e., provision of credit in trade transactions for customers of other banks)
- Lending activities (e.g., loans secured by cash collateral and marketable securities)
- Any product or service offered where the ultimate underlying beneficial owner of the funds is not known to the institution

Retail banking can also be high risk depending on the client base, branch locations and activity, and extent of cash business.

Types of Customers. The firm should determine whether it is doing business with what are generally considered to be high-risk types of customers. Additionally, it should determine if it is dealing with another entity—that actually knows or should know the ultimate beneficial owner of the funds—that is in fact dealing with high-risk customers. High-risk customers include, for example:

- Politically exposed persons (PEPs), also known as "senior foreign political figures," because of the increased risk of becoming involved in public corruption or graft[13],[*]
- Cash-intensive businesses (e.g., convenience stores, restaurants, retail stores, liquor stores, cigarette distributors, privately owned ATMs, vending machine operators, and parking garages)

---

[*] KPMG International's *Global Anti–Money Laundering Survey 2007* found that 81 percent of responding banks considered PEP status as a key risk factor, and 71 percent had specific procedures for identifying and monitoring PEPs on an ongoing basis.

- Foreign financial institutions, particularly those based in high-risk jurisdictions
- Nonbank financial institutions (NBFIs) (e.g., casinos and card clubs; broker-dealers in securities; and dealers in precious metals, stones, or jewels). NBFIs also include MSBs, i.e., businesses engaged in selling money orders or traveler's checks, money transmission, check cashing, currency exchange, currency dealing, and stored value.[*]

A financial institution should also be wary of doing business with informal financial organizations such as hawalas (commonly used in Middle Eastern countries for transferring value between trusted but unregulated intermediaries outside the banking system). These entities present a variety of risks, not least of which is the possibility that they may be associated with crime or terrorism.[14,†]

Volume and Size. The amount of activity in each line of business should be considered. This includes the frequency of transactions, as well as their average size. If a corporate operation transfers funds or some valuable commodity very frequently in relation to its overall size (commonly referred to as "high velocity"), it presents a higher risk of money laundering than an operation that transfers funds infrequently relative to its size ("low velocity"). Thus, a small customer that is an active trader presents a higher possibility of money laundering risk than a large customer that is not active. Transaction size cannot be discounted, however, since, arguably, a company would be more likely to have resources to expend on understanding a few large transactions, and the reputational or headline risk of a large transaction is usually higher.

Geographic Risk. The risks associated with the geographic location of the entity and its operations, customers, and business activities are key to any money laundering risk assessment. For instance, the institution must consider whether it operates in jurisdictions with lax or no AML laws, regulations, or government supervision or whether it operates in a jurisdiction that has a highly regulated regime. Similarly, management should assess its customer base and establish the nationality, country of origin, and country of residence of each customer, as well as the AML legal and regulatory environment in those countries. Risks associated with a customer's customers may also need to be evaluated. Also critical is

---

[*] The institution may itself be an NBFI and likely considered inherently high risk by regulators.

[†] FinCEN's 2002 report to Congress on informal value transfer systems (IVTS) states, "While it appears that the majority of IVTS activity is legitimate in purpose, these systems have been used to facilitate the financing of terrorism and in furtherance of criminal activities. For this reason, many governments have begun to look at this issue in terms of the need for regulatory and legal controls and in terms of their ability to conduct successful financial investigations in cases where IVTS has been used."

an evaluation of the jurisdictions where, or through which, customers are trans-acting business. For instance, a number of countries or regions have been iden-tified as high risk by governmental agencies and international organizations. FinCEN, the State Department, and the Drug Enforcement Administration have rated the AML risk of countries and regions. Within the United States, high-intensity drug trafficking areas (HIDTAs)* and high-intensity financial crime areas (HIFCAs)† are considered high risk. Internationally, FATF maintains a list of noncooperative countries or territories.‡ Transparency International, another well-recognized, nongovernmental organization, provides a corruption index that lists countries with a high degree of public corruption. In addition, certain countries, organizations, and individuals, including state sponsors of terrorism, are sanctioned by governments and supragovernmental organizations such as the United Nations. In the United States, doing business with countries and persons on the OFAC sanctions list is prohibited.§

Channels. The institution should consider the channels through which it does business. For example, business conducted over the Internet or by phone, where there is no personal interaction with the customer, presents an inherently higher risk since it is more difficult to discern by whom, or for whom, the business is being conducted. Another example that may present increased risk is a business process that relies on a customer or outside third party to identify and assess the risk associated with the ultimate beneficial owner of the funds.

Sanctions. When developing its AML compliance program, an institution should also develop a sanctions compliance program to ensure that customers

---

* Approximately 14 percent of U.S. counties in 45 states are designated as HIDTAs. There are 33 HIDTA headquarters throughout the United States. Information on specific counties is available through the HIDTA Web site, www.whitehousedrugpolicy.gov/hidta.

† HIFCAs are in New York–New Jersey, Los Angeles, Chicago, San Juan, San Francisco, and the Southwest border states. Information on specific areas can be obtained on the FinCEN Web site at www.fincen.gov/law_enforcement/hifca.

‡ At the time of this writing, there are no countries on the NCCT list; however, from time to time, the FATF expresses concern about the AML/CTF regimes in particular countries, e.g., Iran, Uzbekistan, Turkmenistan, Pakistan, Sao Tome, Principe, and the northern part of Cyprus. As noted in a previous footnote, FATF published the "blacklist" (www.fatf-gafi.org/dataoecd/17/5/45540828.pdf)—consisting of "jurisdictions that have strategic deficiencies" with whom they work, "along with the FATF-style regional bodies (FSRBs), to address those deficiencies that pose a risk to the international financial system"—and the "graylist" (www.fatf-gafi.org/dataoecd/17/4/45540819.pdf)—comprising "jurisdic-tions that have strategic AML/CFT deficiencies for which they have developed an action plan with the FATF."

§ The modern U.S. sanctions regime began during the Korean War, when President Truman blocked all Chinese and North Korean assets. Currently, 13 countries are on the OFAC list, but in some cases, the sanctions apply only to certain individuals or activities in the country. The sanctions programs are complex, and each case should be considered individually. See www.treas.gov/offices/enforcement/ofac/programs.

and transactions are appropriately screened against the OFAC's sanctions lists, including those issued pursuant to country-specific sanctions programs, the Specially Designated Nationals (SDN)* List, and other sanction lists as appropriate for the location of the business, customer, or beneficial owner of the funds. As with the AML compliance program, a sanctions compliance program requires sufficient, well-trained resources to maintain the program; review potential matches; communicate with OFAC or, in the case of global institutions, other non-U.S. regulatory authorities with enforcement authority for non-U.S. sanction programs; and, when required, block accounts, reject payments, or take other appropriate action concerning the property of specified countries, entities, and individuals.

Compliance with OFAC's requirements is mandatory for persons and entities subject to U.S. jurisdiction, regardless of industry. Liability is strict, and the potential fines for violations can be steep.

Recent OFAC enforcement actions have resulted in multimillion-dollar penalties. While these have been enormous, they could have been larger. In accordance with the recent OFAC enforcement guidelines, OFAC mitigated the penalties, since the parties substantially cooperated and implemented prompt and thorough remedial responses.

Additionally, for global institutions, an understanding of OFAC requirements and liability is essential, but it is also important to fully understand the risks, requirements, and penalties associated with other non-U.S. sanction programs.

Resources. Finally, the assessment should address whether sufficient resources have been allocated to focus on the risk inherent in the business, whether they are appropriately deployed, whether they have sufficient seniority and expertise given their assigned responsibility, and whether they receive adequate and frequent training. The institution should also assess any technology solutions it has deployed, for instance, confirming that it is using transaction monitoring systems that allow for the effective identification of potential suspicious activity commensurate with the level of risk posed by the business. For example, in the E*Trade sanction previously discussed, FINRA stated that "while E*Trade provides its customers with online, self-directed electronic access to the securities markets, its AML program lacked automated electronic systems specifically designed to detect potentially manipulative trading activity in customer accounts."[15] The specific type of activity that E*Trade failed to detect was matched or "wash" trades, which could be indicative of market manipulation or other types of securities fraud.

---

* "Specially designated nationals" are individuals with whom U.S. nationals and residents are prohibited from doing business.

Design. After an organization conducts a detailed assessment, it should have a better understanding of its money laundering and terrorist financing risks, the degree to which it is controlling those risks, and any gaps or weaknesses that exist in its AML compliance program. With this information, the firm may enhance its AML compliance program commensurate with its type of business, size, and risk profile. The design should be aligned with a strategy clearly established by senior management and documented in detailed policies and procedures. As noted earlier in the chapter, Section 352 of the USA PATRIOT Act requires an effective program to have four core elements:

- The establishment of internal controls to ensure ongoing compliance
- Independent testing of AML compliance
- Designation of responsibilities for managing BSA compliance
- Training

The Establishment of Internal Controls to Ensure Ongoing Compliance. Internal controls should help identify operations vulnerable to abuse by money launderers and criminals, provide for periodic updates to the entity's risk profile, and reflect an AML compliance program tailored to manage risk. Internal controls should also meet all regulatory record-keeping and reporting requirements and provide for timely updates in response to changes in regulations. In addition, internal controls should help identify reportable transactions so that required reports, such as SARs and currency transaction reports, are filed on a timely basis.

The deferred prosecution of the money transfer agent Sigue Corporation provides a good example of a risk that was ignored. Sigue operated through a network of authorized delegates, primarily mom-and-pop stores, located in neighborhoods with large Mexican populations. Its primary business was sending remittances to Mexico and Latin America. The U.S. government's investigation found that a significant number of Sigue's authorized delegates allowed customers to structure their transactions to evade reporting requirements, and this activity was detected by Sigue's transaction monitoring systems. Yet Sigue did not follow through and investigate the transactions or realize the broader issues revealed by the persistent violations.[16]

A major control element—and perhaps the best defense against money laundering is for a firm to follow the principle of "know your customer" (KYC). Understanding the nature of customers, their expected or anticipated normal activities, and the risks associated with the customers and their businesses is critical to a firm's management of money laundering risks. In the first instance, a firm may choose not to do business with certain clients or client types that present a risk deemed unacceptable to the company's business model. By understanding its customers and their anticipated activities, firms can more effectively monitor transactions for anomalies and red flags indicative of money laundering or terrorist financing. Thus, firms should implement risk-based customer due diligence policies, procedures, and processes and identify what is considered anticipated normal activity for the customer. Transactions that are not consistent with the anticipated normal activity would be flagged as unusual, potentially suspicious activity and be subject to review. Firms should also develop methods for conducting enhanced due diligence for high-risk customers. In addition, Section 326 of the USA PATRIOT Act requires financial institutions to implement a written customer identification program. The CIP enables the institution to form a reasonable belief that it knows the true identity of each customer. As part of a CIP, financial institutions must obtain and record information that identifies each person who opens an account.

Independent Testing of AML Compliance. Firms must test the overall integrity and effectiveness of their AML compliance program, including policies, procedures, and processes, and review their risk assessment for reasonableness given their risk profile. The test should include appropriate risk-based transaction testing to verify the institution's adherence to BSA record-keeping and reporting requirements and the effectiveness of the monitoring systems used for AML compliance. The review can be conducted by an internal or external audit function; however, the audit cannot be conducted by any individual involved in the implementation or oversight of the AML program itself. While the frequency of an audit is not specifically defined in any statute, a sound practice is for the institution to conduct independent testing every 12 to 18 months, commensurate with the AML risk profile of the institution. If compliance issues are identified in an independent review, it may be good practice to advance the date of the next review to help ensure that appropriate corrective actions have been taken. In addition, an institution should evaluate management's efforts to resolve violations and deficiencies noted in previous audits and regulatory examinations, including progress in addressing outstanding supervisory actions, if applicable. Significant audit findings should be reported directly to the audit committee or board of directors. It is ultimately management's responsibility to correct any deficiencies.

Designation of Responsibilities for Managing BSA Compliance. Although the requirement is for *an* individual, rarely can the entire AML function of a firm rest in the hands of one person. In general, the BSA officer is the most senior AML compliance officer in the organization. Depending on the size, structure, and risk of the firm, that officer may be supported by a team ranging from a modest-sized group of compliance officers to a large staff covering many functions. Irrespective of how the AML compliance function is structured, however, overall responsibility for implementation of the program rests with the BSA officer. Such individuals must be knowledgeable of BSA and AML requirements and coordinate and monitor day-to-day compliance. The BSA officer should regularly apprise the board of directors and senior management of ongoing compliance.

Training. The institution must ensure that appropriate personnel are trained on an ongoing basis in AML laws and principles. Such training is usually given annually. Training should include regulatory requirements and incorporate current developments such as changes to laws and related regulations or to the institution's internal AML policies, procedures, and processes. Training should also be tailored to an employee's specific responsibilities. Thus, ongoing training of the compliance staff—who should keep abreast of changes to not only laws and regulations, but also regulatory guidance, regulatory expectations, and leading industry practices—is critical.[17,*]

Although it is essential that the above elements be included in an AML compliance program, the design elements must also fit the business model of the institution. All stakeholders should have a role in the process. This also helps to foster greater buy-in when implementing the program.

Implementation. Once a firm designs an AML program commensurate with its risk, it must ensure that the program is fully implemented. This requires the commitment of senior management. Based on responses to KPMG International's *Global Anti–Money Laundering Survey 2007* from 224 banks in 55 countries, over 70 percent of respondents reported that their most senior levels of management took an active interest in AML compliance, while only 1 percent reported that senior management took little interest.[18]

Like the program itself, the implementation plan should be risk-based. It is common and sensible for the plan to focus first on weaknesses identified by regulators, audits, or compliance reviews. This approach mitigates regulatory risk and may take advantage of existing firm project structures. The implementation plan should be approved by senior management and agreed upon by stakeholders, and it should provide a reasonable timetable for enacting program elements and enhancements. A common practice is to form a steering committee, representing affected business, operational, and technology groups to which the program managers report on a regular basis.

The plan should set forth agreed priorities, milestones, and target dates for completion. Any changes to the plan should be agreed upon by appropriate

---

* According to KPMG International's *Global Anti–Money Laundering Survey 2007*, 93 percent of North American banks require AML training of over 80 percent of staff, while 38 percent of European banks do.

business leaders, and any slippage in completion dates should be explained. The plan should be a collaborative effort involving all stakeholders. AML programs generally affect more than one business unit, so close cooperation is necessary to help ensure that changes made in one area do not have an unintentional negative impact in another. Further, AML programs may require implementation of technology systems across business units, with the result that firms may find it necessary to coordinate fundamental issues such as client data formats and systems. This can be a benefit as well as a burden, since integration of client data may lead to better understanding of the business needs of clients, clearer lines of responsibility for clients, and increased sales opportunities.

Finally, it should not be forgotten that the plan serves many purposes. Besides the important function of coordinating and monitoring needed change, it also provides an explanation and indication of commitment to auditors and regulators. In sum, the plan is a blueprint for change, with objectives, metrics, budgets, and a desired end state that may also be reviewed by regulators.

Evaluation. An AML compliance program, once created, should not remain static. Programs require ongoing, independent evaluation, because the AML requirements and money laundering risks evolve continuously. It is incumbent upon those responsible for maintaining the program to ensure that it keeps pace with changes in legal and regulatory requirements, the regulatory and enforcement environment, business models, products, customers, and leading industry practices. An example of industry-formulating leading practices in changing markets is the response to the growing prepaid card market. Prepaid cards are similar to cash in their portability and anonymity, and they are an attractive alternative to credit cards when credit is restricted or unavailable. This has resulted in a coordinated industry effort to define leading practices and standards to appropriately mitigate the obvious risks.[19]

Risk assessments should be undertaken at least annually or as substantive changes occur. Customer risk rankings should be revisited using a risk-based plan; e.g., if frequent news accounts or regulatory actions seem to involve a particular country or industry, it is sensible to look at the risk rankings for customers in that country or industry first.

Transaction monitoring systems should be regularly tested and tuned to help ensure that they provide quality output without overburdening those responsible for reviewing alerts. The output of the system should be kept relevant and meaningful, providing viable productive leads without the endless noise of "false positives." Training must be kept relevant as well. Internal audit programs need to keep pace with all the above to ensure that the independent testing requirement serves its intended purpose—to help ensure the program is working as designed.

As discussed previously, independent testing, one of the four core elements of an AML compliance program pursuant to Section 352 of the USA PATRIOT Act, can be performed by the company's internal audit group, by an outside firm, or by an independent team from the company's compliance department.

Detection

Critical to any robust AML program is the ability to detect suspicious activity in the organization. No matter how strong the program may be, it is likely that unusual and reportable events will occur. Whether a questionable event occurs at account opening, during the life of a client relationship, or by insiders able to manipulate a firm's systems, firms must have controls in place reasonably designed to produce alerts so that events can be investigated and, if warranted, reported to authorities. An appropriately designed detection program provides multiple lines of defense—from frontline personnel, such as sales or branch personnel, to support functions, including account opening and funds transfer. Further, detection programs will usually have some method of monitoring transactions to detect unusual, potentially suspicious activity and also will likely have an ongoing quality assurance program to help confirm that the program is operating properly. It is important that the program leverage all sources of information throughout the institution.

Techniques to identify events may differ depending on the stage at which the event occurs, the size of the institution, the product being monitored for suspicious transactions, and the volume and type of transactions processed. As with all aspects of an AML program, the detection mechanism should be tailored to the size and shape of the risk being addressed.

Multiple Lines of Defense. As discussed, no AML program will likely ever be completely effective and able to prevent every instance of money laundering. Financial institutions, therefore, are obligated to report suspicious activities through SARs. Regulators interpret this by requiring firms to do more than wait for suspicious activity to come to their attention; they must monitor for suspicious activity with the aim of detecting and reporting possible money laundering. When attempting to identify potentially suspicious activity, a financial institution relies on a combination of both vigilant employees and risk-based transaction monitoring controls. Often, frontline personnel, transaction monitoring systems and mechanisms, and middle- and back-office staff all play an important role in the detection of money laundering or terrorist financing activity. While automated transaction monitoring systems are useful in that they allow financial institutions to monitor large volumes of transactions and more readily identify potential anomalies for further investigation, they are no substitute for vigilant personnel.

Frontline Personnel. As a result of the global reach of financial institutions and their correspondent relationships, acceptance into a financial institution provides an entry point into the financial system on both a local and an international scale. The frontline employees within financial institutions constitute the crucial first line of defense in detecting money laundering activity[20,*] since they are the ones who have initial contact with customers.

Frontline personnel are employees with client contact, handling accounts and transactions with customers in person or over the phone (e.g., bank tellers, customer service personnel, or account representatives). Although these frontline personnel are not part of the compliance staff, they must be trained to identify red flags related to transactions or account openings and to escalate their suspicions of potentially suspect activity to the appropriate internal departments. Institutions must have risk-based programs in place to collect both identifying information and due diligence—KYC information—on customers. Customer-facing staff members are typically in the best position to evaluate the information, or lack thereof, provided by the client at account opening, or otherwise to determine if the situation should be further analyzed and, if necessary, escalated to the appropriate internal department for consideration. The interpersonal interaction that frontline personnel are able to have with customers allows them to note details about a specific customer or transaction that may not be obtained by automated transaction monitoring systems or back-office personnel.

In addition to raising awareness through training initiatives, management should also develop written policies and procedures that provide clear guidance to employees on how to recognize specific money laundering risks, how to obtain adequate information to fully understand the risk, how to bring situations presenting risk or potentially suspicious activity to the appropriate person or group, and what types of information they should include when doing so. For example, individuals involved in account opening should be trained in identifying high-risk customers such as PEPs. Procedures should reinforce the training that employees receive with respect to the specific steps necessary to identify potentially suspicious activity and the avenues for escalation, if appropriate.

Automated Transaction Monitoring Systems. Transaction monitoring systems allow financial institutions to observe financial transactions and detect patterns of activity that may be indicative of money laundering activity, such as multiple transactions just below reporting thresholds, large or frequent transactions with countries or businesses that present high risk for money laundering, or transactions inconsistent

---

* According to KPMG International's *Global Anti–Money Laundering Survey 2007*, 97 percent of banks rely on staff vigilance and reporting of suspicious transactions, even though they may also review exception reports or have sophisticated monitoring systems.

with the known business of the customer. These systems help identify activity that may not necessarily appear suspicious to frontline personnel because they cannot view aggregate customer activity across businesses or identify patterns over time. For example, software may aggregate information to detect the structuring of transactions to avoid reporting requirements, flag transfers of large sums of money that are not commensurate with the stated purpose of the account, detect an unusual number of transactions in and out of an account with no apparent business purpose, or detect unusual deposits. These scenarios, and many others dependent on the business line and customer bases, could be indicators for money laundering. Transactions flagged by automated transaction monitoring systems can then be reviewed by frontline personnel who may be able to provide appropriate explanations to substantiate the legitimacy of the transaction.

While the various levels of personnel in a company are important to a comprehensive AML program, technology plays an ever-increasing role. AML software enables companies to monitor far more information than would be possible for an organization's staff to monitor manually. Such software generally processes the firm's transaction data using defined rules or scenarios to detect patterns of activity that can be reviewed by a group of professionals trained in AML principles and investigations. As noted in the E*Trade example discussed previously, the larger or more active the firm, the more important it is to have some method beyond manual examination of transaction records to detect suspicious activity. Further, as financial institutions are increasing their online presence, customer contact with frontline personnel is decreasing. Implementation of automated systems is an effort to bridge this gap. Transaction monitoring is typically a complex and expensive undertaking,[21] but generally involves defining the type of situations that are of interest, choosing a methodology that can help detect those situations, and making sure that the system is finding the right situations.

Detection Scenarios. Two main strategies are employed by automated monitoring systems to identify suspicious activity: rules-based strategies and behavioral strategies. Rules-based strategies monitor transactions and trigger red flags when a rule is broken. An example would be large-dollar-value transactions moving money out of the country. A firm may set a "rule" placing any transaction of this sort over a specified dollar threshold on a daily, weekly, or monthly exception report for closer review. These reports should then be scrutinized to determine whether the activity is in fact potentially suspicious. Setting the thresholds for rules is an important step in designing a transaction monitoring system and is explained in more detail in the "Tuning and Validation" section that follows. Conversely, behavioral strategies monitor transactions and identify suspicious patterns. For instance, a customer transferring a sum of $9,000 would not necessarily trigger a red flag. However, if that customer continually transfers sums of money just under $10,000, a behavioral strategy should identify this activity as suspicious as it could indicate a structuring tactic used to avoid transaction reporting requirements. Behavioral strategies tend to be much more complex, as they must define what a customer's typical activity is—i.e., the customer's profile—and identify whether the customer's activity is suspicious and falls outside historical transaction norms. Using behavioral strategies in conjunction with rules-based approaches enables a transaction monitoring system to detect many different types of suspicious behavior.

Tuning and Validation. To help maintain an effective system, it is important that firms regularly review the rules or parameters set in the systems. Monitoring systems should produce high-quality alerts without a high proportion of false positives that cause reviewers to waste time reviewing what is actually normal activity. Conversely, if a very large portion of alerts result in the filing of the SAR, chances are the system is not sensitive enough, and suspicious transactions may be slipping through the cracks. Periodically tuning the system helps ensure that threshold levels remain current and relevant and keeps the institution up-to-date with regulatory requirements. In addition, the system should adapt to a continually changing marketplace. Tuning a system to eliminate rules that produce almost exclusively false positives is vital, as is adding new rules to keep up with the new trends in money laundering and fraud.

One of the more challenging aspects of an automated system is defining which activity the system should identify as suspicious and which activity should be considered business as usual. While some of the system's risk scenarios may not require calibration, others, such as suspicious large-dollar transactions, require a certain level of tuning. The first step in tuning the system is determining the proper thresholds. Systems regularly identify high-dollar transfers as suspicious, but "high-dollar" is a subjective term. A neighborhood bank with mostly small personal accounts, for instance, will typically see transactions with much lower dollar amounts than a large bank with large corporate customers. A global financial institution, however, will likely also maintain small personal accounts and large corporate accounts as well. For an institution that primarily has large, institutional businesses as its customers, large-dollar transactions may be the norm and small-dollar transactions the exception. Therefore, setting the thresholds the system defines as suspicious will vary greatly from one institution to another. The thresholds may likely differ at the account level within an institution as well.

As transaction monitoring systems identify suspicious activity, they generate reports alerting an organization of potential issues. At this point, the matter should be transferred from the transaction system to a person to review the red flags and determine the appropriate next step.

Back- and Middle-Office Functions. In addition to customer-facing and front-office personnel, unusual and potentially suspicious activity can be detected by employees such as operations staff, who process actual transactions. Who touches or sees transactions, in what way, and where in the organization it takes place depends on the size of the institution, the type of business conducted, the volume of transactions processed, and the risks associated with the products and client types. It is often the case that operations staff members have a clearer view of details that are inconsistent with the stated purpose of a transaction and also have a less immediate financial incentive to "get the deal done."

Once frontline, back-office, or middle-office personnel identify and escalate instances of potentially suspicious activity, a person or persons experienced in fraud and AML should assess the referrals to determine whether such potentially suspicious activity is in fact indicative of money laundering and thus requires an SAR filing. This same compliance team should generally also review alerts elevated from automated transaction monitoring systems.

The compliance team, composed of middle- and back-office personnel, is largely responsible for creating, administering, and monitoring the financial institution's compliance with AML regulations, including compliance oversight, creation and maintenance of policies and procedures, risk ratings, advice and guidance regarding enhanced due diligence, and training initiatives. The team should strive to ensure consistency across the company's business units and entities.

Leveraging Other Processes and Data Points. Information gleaned from external sources, such as requests under the information-sharing provisions of USA PATRIOT Act Section 314(a) or 314(b) or subpoenas, can assist banks in identifying potentially suspicious activity and should be appropriately leveraged. For example, the receipt of criminally related subpoenas from law enforcement should cause an institution to heighten its scrutiny of named accounts or customers. Similarly, accounts of individuals identified through 314(a) requests should be scrutinized for potentially suspicious activity. In either case, documentation supporting such reviews should be maintained to support the conclusion reached and the rationale for it. The SAR should be filed if appropriate.

Quality Assurance. An AML program should include one or more appropriate quality assurance programs for testing and monitoring. The foundation for a successful program is based on the value assigned and resources provided by senior management. Effective testing and monitoring programs feature diligent follow-up procedures and continuing improvements of existing systems and controls.

A quality assurance program is a business process by which management is able to gain comfort that the program is operating as it is designed to do. For example, the group that initiates customer relationships and records customer information might include periodic sampling of new customer information by a manager to ensure that information is appropriately recorded and understood. For some higher-risk businesses or business units, it may be appropriate for the company to have a further level of review. A compliance function or some independent group may perform sampling on the quality assurance program to provide an additional layer of comfort.

A fortunate element of automated systems is that much of the information needed for their implementation is in existing systems. Businesses typically collect customer and transactional information for commercial, legal, and regulatory reasons. Thus, automated monitoring systems typically have software that takes data from systems that are already in place. Perhaps the most difficult and important part of a system configuration and installation is the data analysis, which may help ensure systems are compatible and able to share information without human interaction. The AML system clearly benefits by having data that do not have to be manually entered; however, the firm's existing databases benefit as well. A properly configured transaction monitoring system creates exceptions when required data are missing. This helps guarantee that customer records are entered in their entirety, and a rise in data quality generally follows.

Response

An AML program is dynamic and must adjust with changes in the firm's risk profile, in response both to external events, as a result of audit or regulatory criticism, and to issues revealed by suspicious activity or, in the worst case, actual money laundering within the institution.

Responding to Internal Detection of Suspicious Activity. There will likely be occasions in which a business suspects or knows that money laundering has occurred at the institution. Such situations will help test the program's effectiveness and demonstrate to internal and external stakeholders the institution's commitment to AML compliance.

Evaluating the Depth and Scope. The first step an institution must take upon learning of suspicious activity is to report it appropriately. Usually, this will involve a period of fact gathering so that accurate and useful reports can be made. As the facts are developed, the firm should also evaluate the depth and scope of the problem. Is the problem "deep," and does it indicate a major flaw in the AML program? Second, is the problem of large "scope," meaning is it widespread throughout the organization? If the problem is either deep or widespread, it is likely that the firm will be required to have extensive dealings with law enforcement and regulators. In such a case, the company is well advised to engage experienced assistance from outside the organization to help in managing the law enforcement and regulatory relationships.

Dealing with Law Enforcement and the Regulators. Federal law enforcement agencies maintain robust SAR review and data analysis programs in order to initiate and support investigations of possible money laundering. There are 80 SAR review teams operating across the United States, analyzing reported data to identify evidence of financial crimes.[*] Although it is the duty of financial institutions to report suspicious activity, law enforcement is tasked with investigating and determining if a crime has been committed. Recent increased communication among regulatory and law enforcement organizations, interagency collaboration, and information sharing among organizations are indicative of collaborative efforts in the fight against money laundering. In fact, FinCEN Director James Freis stated, "In exercising our statutory authority, FinCEN works closely with a wide variety of federal and state regulatory and law enforcement agencies."[22]

It is important to remember that notifying law enforcement does not fulfill the requirement to file a timely SAR. If law enforcement has been notified prior to the SAR filing, this information should be reflected in the SAR itself.

Monitoring versus Closing Accounts. Merely filing the SAR on a customer is not, in itself, reason for closing a customer's account. Instead, a determination on whether to close a customer's account should be made with knowledge of the facts and circumstances surrounding the SAR filing and the customer's activities. The closure of an account as a result of suspicious activity is an organizational decision and should be made with the input of senior management, legal counsel, and other appropriate personnel. However, if the organization decides not to terminate the relationship after filing the SAR, it should consider whether to execute enhanced due diligence or monitoring on the customer. The decision and its rationale should be documented.

In some cases, law enforcement may want accounts or relationships to remain open despite potentially suspicious or illicit activity. While institutions are not required to maintain relationships in such cases, such requests may enhance law enforcement efforts to combat money laundering, terrorist financing, or other crimes. On the other hand, regulators may not agree that the reputational or financial risks of maintaining an account in which suspicious activity has occurred are justified. So if a law enforcement agency asks an institution to maintain a particular account, the institution should ask for the request in writing. This writing

---

[*] The Money Laundering and Financial Crimes Strategy Act of 1998 requires a periodic national money laundering threat assessment and a responsive national money laundering strategy. The most recent threat assessment was released in 2005, and the most recent strategy was released in 2007.

should document that the requesting law enforcement agency has asked the institution to maintain the account and the purpose of this request. After the expiration of this request, the ultimate decision to maintain or close an account or relationship should be made based on the institution's own criteria and rules.

Responding to Inquiries by Law Enforcement about Suspicious Activity. One of the more common and significant sources of information about suspicious activity at an institution is communications from law enforcement as it follows leads from other investigations. The nature of such communications depends on the firm, its relations with law enforcement, and its legally required response to certain types of requests. The communications can come in as informal phone calls, 314(a) requests, national security letters, subpoenas, or court orders.

Triage the Problem. An inquiry from law enforcement should prompt additional due diligence on the relevant customer, that customer's transactions, and others known to be related to the subject customer (e.g., affiliates, relatives, counterparties, frequent business partners). The institution should assess all available information, including the law enforcement inquiry, in accordance with its risk-based AML compliance program. The assessment should include whether the customer has caused any alerts to be generated in the firm's monitoring system, whether any employee has expressed concern or lack of comfort with the customer, whether the firm has received a subpoena or other legal process concerning the customer, and whether there have been recent relevant negative news stories about the customer. In some cases, suspicious activity may require immediate attention. In such instances, in addition to filing a timely SAR, an institution should immediately notify by telephone an appropriate law enforcement authority and the firm's primary regulator.[23] Delays in the suspicious activity reporting process can significantly diminish the usefulness of any information to law enforcement.

If the suspicious activity has a high degree of reputational risk, senior management and appropriate regulators should be informed immediately. If the activity indicates a deep problem of significant scope, the same calls should be made, but it may be appropriate to investigate the facts more fully so that the problem is better understood and a more complete account can be given to the regulator. On no account, however, should filing the SAR be delayed beyond the appropriate deadline.*

---

* A financial institution is required to file a suspicious activity report no later than 30 calendar days after the date of initial detection of facts that may constitute a basis for filing a suspicious activity report. If no suspect was identified on the date of detection of the incident requiring the filing, a financial institution may delay filing a suspicious activity report for an additional 30 calendar days to identify a suspect. In no case shall reporting be delayed more than 60 calendar days after the date of initial detection of a reportable transaction (www.fincen.gov/forms/files/f9022-47_sar-di.pdf).

Defendant versus Witness. Money laundering is a criminal offense, and law enforcement officers will, at some point, consider whether the company itself has criminal liability. If law enforcement agents or prosecutors refer to the firm as a "target" or a "subject" of the investigation, or if law enforcement is silent about the firm's involvement, it is likely that the firm will become a defendant in the case. In such a circumstance, the firm should engage competent experienced criminal counsel at once.

In most cases, the firm will simply be a witness in the action. Usually, this means producing documents, meeting with law enforcement to explain the documents and underlying processes, and, in some instances, producing a witness to testify to their authenticity. Even if the firm is a witness, however, it should review its business to determine if it is exposed to similar or related activity elsewhere in the firm.

Responding to Observations about the Effectiveness of the Compliance Program. All programs are subject to review, either by an independent auditor, internal or external, or by a regulator. It is likely that, over time, there will be findings regarding the strength of the program. It is critical that comments received by auditors and examiners be examined closely and reacted to with all due haste to ensure no program lapses.

Internally Generated Observations (Internal Audits or Compliance Self-Assessments). Analyzing findings from internal assessments can guide the allocation of resources and help shape enterprisewide risk assessments. Furthermore, periodic self-assessments allow continual enhancements of an institution's AML program. Finally, prompt detection and remediation of program weaknesses are likely to be viewed favorably by regulators, while failure to address a known issue may give the impression that the company did not take its responsibilities seriously.

To help ensure the completeness of a response, the review or audit should thoroughly document its scope and any findings or recommendations. Once completed, deficiencies should be tracked, and corrective action should be documented. The company should also consider whether the findings have broader application outside the immediate context of the review.

The results of reviews and audits are regularly requested by regulators, and so all documentation should be prepared with this audience in mind. In addition, it is good practice for the company to confirm, after the review or audit, but before a regulatory review, that changes implemented as a result of a review or audit are having the intended effect.

Externally Generated Observations (Regulators or External Examiners)—Dealing with Regulators during an Examination. Dealings with regulators should be candid, proactive, and prompt. All requested materials should be available in a neat and organized presentation prior to the beginning of the examination, but if they cannot be ready, that information should be given to the regulator as soon as possible, along with a deadline that the company is confident it can meet. If the company is aware of material issues before the examination begins, it should consider disclosing those issues prior to the formal initiation of the examination. Self-disclosure can foster a good working relationship with examiners, who may feel more confident that the institution is candid about issues; and in addition, self-disclosure may also serve to focus the examiner's attention on issues already being addressed.

Generally, an examination will begin with a kickoff meeting attended by the regulators and the representatives of the business they will be examining. It is often advisable to use this meeting to discuss the business and any changes that took place after a prior exam.

During the examination, questions should be answered as promptly as possible. If a question involves a subject not within the immediate responsibility of the person being asked the question, the responding person should confirm an understanding of the question with the questioner, promptly investigate, and get back to the regulator as quickly as possible. If the regulator points out an issue or concern, an explanation or a plan to correct the issue should be formulated as quickly as possible and discussed with the regulator. This may make the difference between a formal finding against the company and a more informal recommendation.

At the conclusion of the examination, there may be an informal closing meeting with the persons who have had day-to-day contact with the regulators, as well as a formal closing with senior management. Careful notes should be made during these meetings in case the final report does not match the statements at the informal closing.

Responding to the Regulator's Report. Arguably, the best defense to regulatory sanctions is a proactive and comprehensive AML compliance program. However, when a weakness is discovered in an AML program, the institution may be cited for violation. A violation of one portion of an AML program may not necessarily lead to an overall program failure. But where there is significant noncompliance or recurring or fundamental failures, an AML program failure may be declared.

Regulators can deem an institution's AML compliance program to be fundamentally insufficient, feature systemic and recurring noncompliance, or have isolated and technical noncompliance with AML requirements. Any of these issues may cause the regulatory authority to initiate an enforcement action that may involve regulatory fines or sanctions.

When regulators determine a component of an institution's AML program is insufficient to effect the desired corrective action, a formal and public action in the form of a written agreement or cease and desist (C&D) order may be issued. C&D orders are issued to ensure that actual or apparent conflicts of interest or unsound practices do not continue at financial institutions.

In other cases, the regulatory authority may issue a memorandum of understanding (MOU). An MOU is not a formal enforcement procedure, but is an informal vehicle used to monitor an institution's compliance program. An institution's failure to comply with an MOU can result in formal sanctions or action against the institution.

Conclusion

Financial institutions should utilize their regulators on a consistent basis. If an institution is unclear about a regulatory requirement or an appropriate remediation of a program weakness, it should consider contacting its regulator. Regulatory bodies want institutions to be in compliance with regulatory requirements and often respond positively to such contacts. However, the responsibility for interpreting regulatory requirements remains with the regulatory experts within the company. Outside an established "no-action" program, a regulatory agency will not be bound by the advice of its employees.

Chapter 5

Falsifying Government Claims and Insider Trading

Richard H. Girgenti

Government Procurement and Contracting Fraud

The economic crisis that began in 2007–2008 has led to unprecedented amounts of federal spending, most notably the Troubled Asset Relief Program (TARP) and other economic stimulus programs enacted in late 2008 and 2009. It has also made scrutiny of potential government fraud, waste, and abuse a mantra of the federal regulatory and law enforcement community. Organizations now have more exposure to the risk of procurement fraud as governments at every level have increased investigations and prosecutions. Current efforts to expand health care appear to assume that potential additional costs can be funded, in part, from the prevention and detection of fraud and waste. The financial crisis has spawned new regulations and enhanced federal enforcement efforts in the American Recovery and Reinvestment Act (ARRA, or Recovery Act) and the Fraud Enforcement and Recovery Act of 2009 (FERA). The financial crisis, the authorization of hundreds of billions of dollars in new federal funding, and a desire to strengthen regulatory and oversight controls have put fraud, waste, and abuse on center stage. New standards for transparency and accountability provide powerful incentives for companies to improve governance practices and related compliance and anti-fraud programs and controls. Whether an entity is a direct recipient of federal funding or a federal contractor, few businesses are exempt from the expanding oversight.

Additional contributors are Graham J. Murphy, Amanda Rigby, and Nimna Varghese.

The False Claims Act (FCA) is among one of the government's main weapons of choice in the arsenal of laws in place to protect government against those who seek to defraud it. The FCA has been the primary mechanism for recoveries in fraud actions in a broad cross section of industries doing business with the government, including health care, pharmaceutical, medical device, defense (including contracts in the Afghanistan and Iraq conflicts), oil and gas, computer, import-export, and real estate and construction. Universities and other educational and research institutions that receive government money also fall within the purview of the FCA. FCA actions have been brought in the areas of disaster relief and assistance loans and agricultural subsidiaries. The recent rash of foreclosures will likely result in additional FCA prosecutions for falsified applications for HUD-assisted mortgages.

Enacted in 1863 to curb corruption in the procurement of Civil War material, the FCA provides for substantial civil penalties and treble damages from any person or organization that makes a false or fraudulent claim to the U.S. government for money or property. Under the statute, a person can be held liable for "knowingly" (1) presenting or causing the presentment of a false or fraudulent claim for payment or approval, (2) making a "false record or statement to get a false or fraudulent claim paid or approved by the Government," or (3) conspiring to defraud the government "by getting a false or fraudulent claim allowed or paid."[1] Point 2 is important, because it means that criminal liability need not involve the necessity to prove that a fraud was committed—it is sufficient, and often easier, for the government to prove that there was a falsification of material fact simply by pointing to, for instance, a false statement on an application for federal moneys.

Qui tam is another important provision of the FCA; it is short for a Latin phrase, "*qui tam pro domino rege quam pro se ipso in hac parte sequitur,*" which roughly means "He who brings an action for the king as well as for himself." The *qui tam* provisions of the FCA empower private individual whistleblowers (dubbed "relators") to file suit on behalf of the government and share in any recovery. For high-dollar frauds, the bounty can be lucrative: 15–25 percent of the total proceeds of a successful suit if the United States intervenes in the *qui tam* action and up to 30 percent if the United States declines and the relator pursues the action alone.

Although the FCA was enacted in 1863, new laws and regulations continue to expand its reach. The FCA became a significant enforcement tool after Congress enacted amendments in 1986, including the provision of stiffer penalties and damages and the expansion of the rights of private citizens to bring actions. In November 2008, a new rule was finalized that amended the Federal Acquisition Regulation to require mandatory disclosure by federal government contractors of (1) violations of any federal criminal law involving fraud, conflicts of interest, bribery, or illegal gratuities connected to any aspect of a federal government contract or subcontract; (2) violations of the civil False Claims Act; or (3) any "significant" overpayments on a contract. The mandatory disclosure must be made as a "timely" written disclosure, and contractors that violate these rules can face stiff penalties, including suspension or debarment from government contracting.[2]

As a result of the economic recession, states and municipalities facing similar financial pressures to those of the federal government have also passed false-claims laws. These state laws have been critical in many fraud investigations at the state level in health care and other industries. Effective January 2007, Section 6031 of the Deficit Reduction Act of 2005 offered a financial incentive—a 10 percent reduction in Medicaid payment owed to the federal government—to states enacting false-claims laws that are "at least as effective" as the federal FCA.

In May 2009, the FERA was signed into law, which modified the FCA in a way that increases the liability exposure of every company that does business with the federal government, as well as those that provide goods or services that are reimbursed by federal funds. FERA legislatively overruled a 2008 Supreme Court decision[3] that the FCA only applied to frauds directed against the federal government directly, and not to frauds indirectly committed by subcontractors against prime contractors working on projects funded by federal dollars. This means that FCA liability may now be triggered by any false claim made to any recipient of federal money so long as that money is used to "advance a Government program or interest."[4] The practical implication is that FERA enhances law enforcement capabilities across a staggering array of federal programs and assistance areas, including financial services, energy, housing, health care, disaster relief, agriculture, education, defense, and infrastructure.

Where does all this lead? In November 2009, the Department of Justice announced that it had secured $2.4 billion in settlements and judgments in cases involving fraud against the government during its 2009 fiscal year ending September 30, almost double the $1.34 billion in penalties collected just one year earlier.[5] According to DOJ statistics, a total of more than $21.6 billion was recovered under the civil FCA between 1986 and 2008. More than $14.3 billion[6] was recovered from the health-care industry (broadly defined to include pharmaceutical and medical device industries).

Two-thirds of the 2009 total came from health-care fraud recoveries, the biggest going to the Department of Health and Human Services (HHS) through its Medicare and Medicaid programs.[7] Earlier in 2009, HHS announced the creation of a new task force, the Health Care Fraud Prevention and Enforcement Team (HEAT), to raise the level of interagency coordination in criminal and civil enforcement of health-care fraud. The Civil Division of the Justice Department is pursuing allegations of a variety of schemes including engaging in "off-label" marketing, which is the illegal promotion of drugs or devices that are billed to Medicare and other federal health-care programs for uses that were neither found safe and effective by the Food and Drug Administration nor supported by the medical literature; paying kickbacks to physicians, wholesalers, and pharmacies to influence drug or device purchases; establishing inflated drug prices for federal reimbursement and then marketing the "spread" between federal reimbursement and the provider's lower cost; and failing to report accurately the "best price" for a drug in order to reduce rebates owed under the Medicaid program.[8] Because health care is such a significant proportion of all federal spending, a lightning rod for cost and funding debates, and a target-rich environment for abuse, safeguarding the integrity of government programs in this area is expected to remain a top law enforcement priority into the future.

Of course, there are other new laws that will likely influence FCA enforcement in the near term. Speaking about the American Recovery and Reinvestment Act of 2009 and the Troubled Asset Relief Program only a month after ARRA became law, Earl Devaney, chair of the Recovery Act Transparency and Accountability Board, observed, "I'm afraid that there may be a naive impression that given the amount of transparency and accountability called for by this act, no or little fraud will occur. My 38 years of federal enforcement experience tells me that some level of waste and fraud is unfortunately inevitable."[9] Following that view, the inspectors general of almost all federal agencies have increased their staffs with additional funds available through ARRA, and have been vocal about enhancing and implementing additional anti-fraud programs and controls to carry out their mandate.

At a 2009 conference cosponsored by KPMG LLP and Willkie Farr & Gallagher, Neil Barofsky, the special inspector general for TARP (SIGTARP), observed the challenge for his office as follows: "You can't push $3 trillion out as quickly as the government is without there being opportunities for them to corrupt the process. We want to make sure that those considering crossing the line know someone's watching."[10] Through September 30, 2009, SIGTARP has opened 61 investigations and has 54 ongoing criminal and civil investigations. These investigations cover complex issues concerning suspected TARP fraud, accounting fraud, securities fraud, insider trading, bank fraud, mortgage fraud, mortgage servicer misconduct, fraudulent advance-fee schemes, public corruption, false statements, obstruction of justice, money laundering, and tax-related investigations.[11]

In the case of organizations accepting government funding or working with the government, there should be a heightened sense of awareness of the possibility of procurement and contracting fraud. Some of the measures an organization may institute to prevent and detect such instances include the following:

- A written code of ethics that, in addition to establishing general standards of business conduct, also addresses permissible and prohibited employee interactions with government officials, including specific limitations on gifts, entertainment, and political contributions as well as what constitutes lobbying. Since prohibited interactions with government employees and government contracting requirements vary not only between the states and federal governments, but also from state to state, the code should also provide guidance applicable to employees in all locales in which an entity operates and, at the same time, be detailed enough to address issues specific to certain geographies.

- Nuances of the code should not be left to the interpretation of the employees, and the organization should provide adequate guidance to the employees to enable them to act judiciously. Since the requirements of government contracting can be challenging to understand, even among those experienced in such activities, many leading organizations have established government contracting units or positions within the general counsel's office to provide guidance to employees. Some have even gone further, requiring deal boards to approve all government proposals and contracts. To effectively navigate the various state and federal laws on pay-to-play activities, some organizations require preapproval for any gifts, entertainment expenses, or political contributions to ensure compliance with the myriad requirements.

- Periodic training should be held for the employees who deal with government officials to help them understand their responsibilities in interacting with those officials, including pay-to-play requirements, lobbying considerations, and requirements for government contracting.

- Interactions with government agents or government employees should be subject to monitoring and oversight by the compliance group within an organization.

- Hotlines or an ombudsman should be in place for employees, customers, suppliers, investors, and other key stakeholders to alert the organization regarding a potentially fraudulent matter. Such a mechanism should be accompanied with protection for the whistleblower from purported retaliation.

- The compliance group members within an organization should be provided with adequate resources so that they can help the organization meet expected ethical standards.

- In the case of an entity that deals with governmental or quasi-governmental agencies, when a fraudulent act is engaged in by an employee of the organization acting as the latter's agent, or the organization itself is a victim of fraud, the entity should inform the appropriate regulatory agency.

Many more measures and mechanisms may be instituted; however, ultimately, the organizations are the ones that choose one action or make one decision over another, which may result in negative consequences.

Insider Trading

In late 2009, the Department of Justice and the Securities and Exchange Commission announced an unprecedented insider trading scheme allegedly perpetuated by Raj Rajaratnam, the founder of the hedge fund Galleon Group. With each passing day, more details emerged that suggested far-reaching implications for the hedge fund industry, which is still reeling from the impact of the recent market crisis. The Galleon matter represented the first time that court-authorized wiretaps have been used to target significant insider trading on Wall Street.

In unveiling the case against Galleon and its founder, U.S. Attorney Preet Bharara said:

> Today, we take decisive action against fraud on Wall Street. This case should be a wake-up call for Wall Street. It should be a wake-up call for every hedge fund manager and every Wall Street trader and every corporate executive who is even thinking about engaging in insider trading. As the defendants in this case have now learned the hard way, they may have been privy to a lot of confidential corporate information, but there was one secret they did not know: we were listening. Today, tomorrow, next week, the week after, privileged Wall Street insiders who are considering breaking the law will have to ask themselves one important question: Is law enforcement listening?[12]

Illegal insider trading refers to buying or selling a security in breach of a fiduciary duty or other relationship of trust and confidence while in possession of material, nonpublic information about the security. The prima facie insider trading case is a simple exchange of cash for misappropriated, nonpublic material information. In the case of Galleon, the Justice Department and the SEC alleged that Mr. Rajaratnam went too far for a trading edge. They described a tangled web of hedge fund managers, analysts, C-level executives, and consultants who all traded tips with one another. The quid pro quo often involved money, sensitive information, or sometimes even the promise of future favors.

Examples of insider trading cases that have been brought by the SEC are cases against:

- Corporate officers, directors, and employees who traded the corporation's securities on the basis of material, nonpublic information
- Friends, business associates, family members, and other "tippees" of such officers, directors, and employees, who traded the securities after receiving such information
- Employees of law, banking, brokerage, and printing firms who were given such information to provide services to the corporation whose securities they traded
- Government employees who learned of such information because of their employment by the government
- Other persons who misappropriated and took advantage of confidential information from their employers

Source: U.S. Securities and Exchange Commission, "Insider Trading," 2001, www.sec.gov/answers/insider.htm.

There may be more such cases going forward, especially as the SEC expands its use of sophisticated data-mining systems to track suspicious trading patterns. Ironically, the activities at Galleon were discovered by traditional techniques that are most often used in organized crime, such as wiretaps and informants.

The rules governing the broad definition of illegal insider trading stem from Section 10(b) of the Securities and Exchange Act of 1934.

Rule 10b5-1, Trading "on the Basis of" Material Nonpublic Information in Insider Trading Cases, lays out the conditions when a transaction may be deemed to be "on the basis of" material nonpublic information. Subject to the affirmative defenses in Rule 10b5-1, a purchase or sale of a security of an issuer is "on the basis of" material nonpublic information about that security or issuer if the person making the purchase or sale was aware of the material nonpublic information when the person made the purchase or sale. The rule permits persons to trade in certain specified circumstances where it is clear that the information they are aware of is not a factor in the decision to trade, such as pursuant to a preexisting plan, contract, or instruction that was made in good faith.

Rule 10b5-2, Duties of Trust or Confidence in Misappropriation Insider Trading Cases, clarifies how the misappropriation theory applies to certain non-business relationships:

- "Whenever a person agrees to maintain information in confidence;
- "Whenever the person communicating the material nonpublic information and the person to whom it is communicated have a history, pattern, or practice of sharing confidences, such that the recipient of the information knows or reasonably should know that the person communicating the material nonpublic information expects that the recipient will maintain its confidentiality; or
- "Whenever a person receives or obtains material nonpublic information from his or her spouse, parent, child, or sibling, provided, however, that the person receiving or obtaining the information may demonstrate that no duty of trust or confidence existed with respect to the information, by establishing that he or she neither knew nor reasonably should have known that the person who was the source of the information expected that the person would keep the information confidential, because of the parties' history, pattern, or practice of sharing and maintaining confidences, and because there was no agreement or understanding to maintain the confidentiality of the information."[13]

Subsequent legislations in 1984 and 1988 codified in Section 21A of the Securities Exchange Act include civil penalties for insider trading violations of up to three times the sum of profit gained or loss avoided by any person purchasing or selling a security while in possession of material nonpublic information; in the case of controlling persons, the monetary penalty shall not exceed the greater of $1 million, or three times the amount of the profit gained or loss avoided as a result of such controlled person's violation.

As information has become increasingly commoditized, hedge funds have relied on everyone from doctors and meteorologists to corporate executives to give them an informational edge. This has created more ambiguity as to when engaging in legitimate, shoe leather research and trading rumors ends and when illegally paying for market-moving information begins. With more sophisticated tools at its disposal, the SEC has increased its scrutiny of potential insider trading violations. Figure 5.1 shows the SEC's year-by-year enforcement of insider trading. The SEC brought 61 enforcement actions in 2008 versus 42 actions in 2004.

In 2009, the SEC's Enforcement Division announced that it was launching national specialized units, three of which will focus on derivatives and securitized products, broad-based insider trading and market manipulations, and fraud

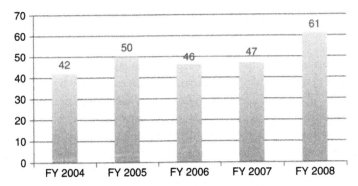

Figure 5.1. Insider trading enforcement actions
Source: U.S. Securities and Exchange Commission, "SEC's Year-by-Year Enforcement of Insider Trading," *Spotlight on Insider Trading*, www.sec.gov/spotlight/insidertrading.shtml.

among hedge funds and investment advisors. Some recent actions by the SEC highlight the pervasiveness of insider trading across industries and geographies and the increased scrutiny by regulatory agencies on insider trading and other market abuses.

- The vice chair of International Securities Exchange Holdings Inc. (ISE), along with two of his associates at a financial consulting firm, Marshall Tucker & Associates LLC, traded on material nonpublic information regarding the merger of ISE and Eurex Franfurt AG that resulted in illegal profits of over $1 million. The SEC action was contemporaneous with a criminal complaint against the three men in the U.S. District Court for the Southern District of New York.[14]
- An Italian resident, Cristian De Colli, used insider information on a potential merger between DRS Technologies, Inc., an American company, and Finmeccanica S.p.A, an Italian aerospace company, to reap illegal profits of $2.1 million on an initial investment of approximately $422,000. This action by the SEC highlights the fact that enforcement action against insider trading has assumed greater priority.[15]
- The SEC charged seven individuals and two companies involved in an insider trading ring, alleging that Matthew Devlin, a former registered representative at Lehman Brothers Inc., traded on and tipped his clients and friends with confidential, nonpublic information about 13 impending corporate transactions. Some of the individual's clients and friends, three of whom worked in the securities or legal professions, tipped others who also traded in the securities of the companies involved in the transactions. In this instance the illegally made profits amounted to $4.8 million.[16]

In a speech on November 5, 2009, Robert Khuzami, director of the SEC Division of Enforcement, said:

> There is a basic principle that governs our capital markets, and that is that there is one set of rules, and everyone is expected to play by that one set of rules. That principle gives investors confidence that the markets are fair. Insider trading is a corruption of that basic principle . . . Those who commit insider trading, who think that there are two sets of rules, run the risk of detection by law enforcement. And that is a trade with only one rule—and that rule is, if we prove our case, your misconduct will be known to all, you will be penalized, and you may well go to jail.[17]

Preventing Insider Trading

Some of the measures that can be initiated by management to prevent illegal trading include the following:

- As with every compliance program, a strong code of ethics explains what constitutes insider trading and encourages personnel to refrain from insider trading. For instance, investment advisors subject to the Investment Advisers Act of 1940 Rule 275.204A-1 are required to establish, maintain, and enforce a written code of ethics that, at a minimum, establishes standards of business conduct and reflects fiduciary duties. The code should set out ideals for ethical conduct premised on fundamental principles of openness, integrity, honesty, and trust. In the wake of scandals like the Galleon case, companies in industries other than financial services may need to rethink whether and how their codes of ethics approach illegal insider trading.
- Most importantly, the code of ethics should be accessible to every employee with ease. Further, there should be appropriate means to resolve any doubts or queries employees may have on certain requirements in the code, for example, a dedicated legal and compliance team for personnel issues, a summary of frequently asked questions, and such other means.
- Management should set up ethical wall barriers within the organization to prevent the appearance of or the actual sharing of information between groups with conflicting business interests. Material nonpublic information should be limited to individuals on a "need-to-know" basis. The ethical barriers should be a combination of physical and technological segregations.
- All employees should be given periodic training that educates them both about the legal framework within which the company operates and about the different types of activities that are or appear to be insider trading.

The training should also highlight to the employees that not only may insider trading be dependent on one's actions, but that providing information to another may also be construed as such in the eyes of the regulators, thereby explaining the relevance of being vigilant. Some companies instruct employees to end conversations with third parties the moment these conversations begin to give the employee more information than the employee needs to know. Following periodic training, employees should be asked to certify their understanding of what is being required of them. Such certifications should be retained by the company.

- The company should have stringent rules around personal trading by employees. In the case of global organizations, the rules should be region-specific and adhere to the company's code of ethics. Employees may be required to obtain prior approval (i.e., preclear) before directly or indirectly acquiring beneficial ownership in any security in an initial public offering or in a limited offering. The purpose is to help ensure that employees do not misappropriate investment opportunities that should first be offered to eligible clients or that employees do not receive a personal benefit for directing client business or brokerage. Employees should be required to report their personal holdings and transactions on a periodic basis.

- Mechanisms should be set up to report any violations of the code of ethics promptly to the chief compliance officer or to any other person designated in the code of ethics. An environment that protects persons who report violations and encourages them to speak freely, such as preventing retaliation or permitting anonymous reporting, should be created by management.

Conclusion

There is an increased need for companies to create awareness internally around the issue of insider trading, examine the ways in which one can run afoul of prohibitions on insider trading, and institute measures to help prevent illegal insider trading.

Part III

A Framework for an Effective Compliance Program

Chapter 6

Building an Integrated and Comprehensive Compliance Program for Sustainable Value

Richard H. Girgenti
Ori Ben-Chorin

E ffective fraud and misconduct risk management should begin with a well-designed and properly executed ethics and compliance program that seeks to prevent, detect, and respond to fraud and misconduct. However, to be truly effective and sustainable, the program should be thoroughly integrated into the organization's overall governance and risk management framework as well as its business strategy and operations, and not be an isolated set of activities within an organization. And yet traditional thinking on the management and oversight of ethics and compliance programs has too often tended to focus on the individual roles of key players or controls and less on how these roles and controls should operate in concert with one another and within the larger context of an organization's governance, risk, and compliance architecture.

At a minimum, the compliance program should have well-designed controls and processes. Leadership should provide strong visible support for the program.

Mr. Ben-Chorin is a director in KPMG LLP's Forensic practice in Washington, DC. He provides Fraud Risk Management services to corporate clients.
Additional contributors are Scott Avelino and Nimna Varghese.

Directors should provide attentive oversight. The compliance function should be independent and properly resourced. However, the success and ultimate maturity of the program will rest on the organization's ability to embed a culture of ethics and integrity.

This chapter begins with a discussion of the basic elements of compliance program management and oversight, as outlined in the Federal Sentencing Guidelines, §8B2.1. It then examines the role of the compliance program within the organization's larger governance, risk, and compliance architecture. Next the chapter takes an in-depth look at the duties of the compliance function, as well as other related functions. Finally, the chapter focuses on the role of the board of directors. Along the way, the discussion touches on prevailing guidance for each role and elaborates on practical ways each of the players within the organization can promote and drive integrity internally.

Authoritative Guidance

The principal guidance for what constitutes an effective compliance and ethics program can be found in the Sentencing Guidelines, which establish minimum requirements for organizations in structuring their compliance function and thereby allow for mitigated penalties in the event of corporate crimes.

Originally adopted in 1991 and amended on November 1, 2004, and April 7, 2010, the Sentencing Guidelines provided federal judges with guidance to be used in sentencing organizations convicted of criminal conduct. Organizations that can demonstrate good corporate citizenship actions, including voluntary disclosure of misconduct to the government, full cooperation with governmental authorities, and an effective compliance and ethics program to prevent, detect, and respond to fraud and misconduct, can mitigate potential criminal sanctions.

The principles behind the Sentencing Guidelines are important, not only because they created a judicially recognized framework that rewards responsible, well-governed organizations, but because they also provided a sound model that organizations could follow to manage business conduct and a standard that influences government enforcement policies, actions, and director and officer liability in civil litigation.

As originally adopted, the Sentencing Guidelines stated that in order for an organization's compliance program to be creditworthy, the program must have, "at a minimum," seven categories of compliance activities. Later revisions to the Sentencing Guidelines in 2004 expanded upon the original seven requirements, making it more explicit that organizations were expected to promote a culture of ethical conduct, tailor each program element based on compliance risk, and periodically evaluate program effectiveness. Specifically, the amended Sentencing Guidelines called on organizations to:

- Promote a culture that encourages ethical conduct and a commitment to compliance with the law
- Establish standards and procedures to prevent and detect criminal conduct
- Ensure that the board of directors and senior executives are knowledgeable and exercise reasonable oversight of the ethics and compliance program
- Assign a high-level individual within the organization to ensure that the organization has an effective program, and delegate day-to-day operational responsibility to individuals with adequate resources, authority, and direct access to the board
- Use reasonable efforts and exercise due diligence to exclude individuals from positions of substantial authority who have engaged in illegal activities or other conduct inconsistent with an effective program
- Conduct effective training programs for directors, officers, employees, and other agents and provide such individuals with periodic information appropriate to their respective roles and responsibilities relative to the ethics and compliance program
- Ensure that the program is followed, including monitoring and auditing to detect criminal conduct
- Publicize a system, which may include mechanisms for anonymity and confidentiality, whereby employees and agents may report or seek guidance regarding potential or actual misconduct without fear of retaliation
- Evaluate periodically the effectiveness of the ethics and compliance program
- Promote and enforce the program consistently through incentives and disciplinary measures
- Take reasonable steps to respond appropriately to misconduct, including making necessary modifications to the program

Finally, the Sentencing Guidelines require that in implementing these requirements, the organization must periodically assess the risk of criminal conduct and then take appropriate steps to design, implement, or modify elements of the compliance program to reduce the risk of criminal conduct from taking place.[1]

Additional amendments to the Sentencing Guidelines in 2010 enhanced the reporting obligations of the individual who has operational responsibility for the program (i.e., the chief compliance officer) to the organization's highest governing authority (the board or an appropriate subgroup such as the audit committee).[2] The amendment makes it clear that an organization may benefit from a significant reduction in fines where (1) the individuals with operational responsibility for the program have a "direct reporting obligation" to the governing authority (express authority to communicate personally on the implementation and effectiveness of the program or any matter involving existing or potential criminal conduct); (2) the program detected the misconduct before it was discovered outside the organization or before detection was reasonably likely; (3) the organization reported the offense to the government in a prompt manner; and (4) individuals with operational responsibilities for the program did not participate in, did not condone, or were willfully ignorant of the misconduct.

The amended Sentencing Guidelines also clarified steps that the organization must take to properly respond to criminal conduct. The Sentencing Commission commented that the organization must self-report the misconduct, cooperate with authorities, and take reasonable steps, as warranted, to provide restitution to victims of the criminal conduct. To prevent further similar misconduct, the organization also must act appropriately, including assessing the program and making modifications to ensure that it is effective.

While the Sentencing Guidelines provide some measure of how the government may evaluate whether a compliance program is effective, they do not provide systematic guidance that management can use to specifically develop or measure the effectiveness of compliance program elements. Rather, the Sentencing Guidelines give organizations leeway to create individualized programs and controls within the context of the Sentencing Guidelines' requirements. It is also important to note that the Sentencing Guidelines' overarching requirement that the organization exercise "due diligence" to ensure that the program is "generally effective" necessitates that management incorporate into the program those practices that peer organizations with mature compliance programs have generally found to correlate with effective compliance management.[3]

Linkage with Governance, Risk, and Compliance Frameworks

Governance, risk, and compliance (GRC) is generally intended to define an integrated framework for thinking about those structures, policies, and procedures that focus on generating long-term value. The goal should be to implement ethical and effective oversight and operations of a business by the board of directors and management (governance) with an organization's systematic approach to assessing and managing risks (risk management), as well as to ensure that the organization and its employees adhere to laws, regulations, and company standards of conduct (compliance). More than just a technology tool, GRC is a strategic and holistic approach to rationalizing risk management, controls, assurance structures, and processes with data management structures, supported by a strong corporate culture to deliver both high performance and compliance with relevant laws and regulations.

As risks become inherently more complex, compliance environments become more rigorous; and in turn, regulators typically enhance their scrutiny of both board oversight and corporate actions. Under such circumstances, the challenges for GRC functions can increase exponentially. In responding to such challenges, many organizations too often employ siloed or patchwork approaches, which lead to duplication of functions, spiraling costs, and multilayered GRC processes. However, the more mature organizations understand that effective GRC activities require an enterprise model that will bring together complex and disparate risk and compliance activities and will direct these efforts more efficiently and in alignment with corporate strategy.

Such a model helps leaders gain intelligence and insight into what they need to know. It also instills agility into critical governance efforts, pointing the way to merging risks and helping to clarify an organization's strengths and weaknesses so that leaders can take advantage of such knowledge as they plan strategic initiatives. An effective GRC framework should:

- Protect and enhance business value by fostering a risk-aware culture, support informed decision making, and address multiple compliance and assurance layers
- Enhance operational efficiency by rationalizing risk management, controls, and assurance structures and processes, as well as intelligent use of IT and data management structures
- Provide a proactive and dynamic approach by enabling the organization to more quickly, consistently, and efficiently respond to challenges arising from evolving risk profiles and rapidly changing regulatory requirements
- Support a linkage to strategy by enabling the organization to meet compliance objectives while improving performance through the use of an integrated framework in support of strategic objectives

By employing a holistic GRC framework that serves as a lens to view specific risks and facilitate a flow of consistent and timely information, a resilient and informed organization can optimize risk, strengthen culture and behavior, and enhance its governance, organization, and infrastructure.

Management and Oversight

To be effective, a comprehensive compliance program must have not only a strong support structure and oversight within an organization's legal, audit, and compliance functions, but also strong leadership from top executives as well as key managers throughout the organization who have substantial authority.

Executive Leadership

Effective fraud and misconduct risk management starts with executive leadership. When an organization's leadership demonstrates clear and unequivocal support for ethical behavior and compliance with the law, the effect can be transformative. An example of this occurred in the early 1990s as the financial securities firm Salomon Brothers became embroiled in a major corporate scandal. The issues at Salomon Brothers involved irregularities in the firm's bids in three U.S. Treasury security auctions, which enabled it to sidestep rules limiting its own share of the total securities issued. It later emerged that Salomon's top executives had been aware of, and failed to report, these irregularities. The firm's share price tumbled, the CEO resigned, and the prospect of criminal indictment loomed. The firm was suffering badly from a loss of public trust, investor confidence, and the prospect of serious government regulatory action.

But Salomon's fortunes turned when billionaire investor Warren Buffett took over as interim chair. He made his intentions clear by stating, "My job is to clean up the sins of the past and capitalize on the enormous attributes that this firm has."[4] It was immediately evident that as chair, Buffett also saw his role as that of a chief compliance officer (CCO). Buffett's words and actions sent a clear signal that unethical behavior would not be tolerated when he remarked, "If you lose money for the firm by bad decisions, I will be very understanding. If you lose reputation for the firm, I will be ruthless."[5] Buffett responded to the unfolding scandal by investigating those at the heart of the misconduct. Those implicated in misconduct were let go, including several senior-level executives.

Recognizing the need to create a safe communication channel for reports of misconduct, Buffett offered himself as a direct point of contact, providing his private telephone number and demanding that each person "report, instantaneously and directly . . . any legal violation or moral failure on behalf of any employee."[6] In all, it appears that Buffett took clear ownership of ethics and compliance issues, acted decisively against known wrongdoers, and made available both formal and informal channels for raising ethical concerns. What he in fact was doing was beginning the work of clearing the way for a cultural change so that a culture of ethics and integrity could take hold within the organization.

Buffett's actions helped stave off intrusive government scrutiny; business picked up, and the company's share price eventually rebounded. While Salomon's recovery was certainly aided by the talent and hard work of its employees, regulator restraint and investor confidence were influenced in great part by the ethical culture Buffett helped to instill.

In much the same way as Warren Buffett's leadership influenced the culture at Salomon Brothers, other C-level executives and senior managers have an opportunity to help shape the ethical culture of their own organizations. And they can do so by setting the "tone at the top" and a clear expectation for ethical conduct, as well as by creating incentive systems that motivate employees to act in ethical ways. The resulting culture of high ethics and integrity can then become the organization's first line of defense against fraud and misconduct. When tone at the top only manifests itself in an occasional speech or e-mail to employees, it can ring hollow and instead breed damaging cynicism. The challenge for leaders, then, is to move beyond mere messaging on issues related to ethics and compliance, and to engage directly in leading the design, implementation, and evaluation of programs and controls that prevent, detect, and respond to ethics and compliance risks.

Regulatory Guidance. The Sentencing Guidelines offer the prevailing framework for the role taken by an organization's senior-level executives in organizational ethics and compliance when they mandate that "high-level personnel" must ensure that the organization has an effective compliance and ethics program.[7] In the context of a compliance and ethics program, such personnel are defined as individuals who have substantial control over the organization or its policy making (e.g., director; executive officer; head of a major business unit or function such as sales, administration, and finance; or an individual with substantial ownership interest).[8] The Sentencing Guidelines thus require the organization to assign formal compliance responsibilities to organizational leaders who have ultimate responsibility for ensuring that the program is effective.

Moreover, the Sentencing Guidelines require both high-level personnel and "substantial authority personnel" to be knowledgeable about the content and operation of the compliance program, perform their compliance duties with "due diligence," and promote a culture that encourages ethical conduct.[9] In this context, substantial authority personnel can be defined as individuals who can exercise a substantial measure of discretion when acting on behalf of the organization. This would include individuals beyond the C-suite, such as those who can exercise substantial supervisory authority (e.g., a plant manager or a sales manager) or any other individuals who, while not part of management, nevertheless can exercise substantial discretion when acting within the scope of their authority (e.g., when negotiating or setting price levels or when approving significant contracts).[10] To be considered knowledgeable, these individuals must receive specialized training, as appropriate to their individualized roles and responsibilities, to enable them to report on the design and operational effectiveness of the program.

Senior Leadership Responsibilities. An organization's senior leaders are responsible for promoting a culture of high ethics and integrity, and doing so is integral to a compliance program's effectiveness. There are three areas, in particular, where leadership can play a pivotal role in driving an ethical culture.

The first is in setting performance goals for the organization and its employees. For example, when senior management sets unrealistic targets (e.g., earnings-per-share targets) that are divorced from internal or market realities or are based solely on Wall Street expectations, employees may feel pressure to act in illegal or unethical ways in order to "make their numbers." Instead, as Thomas Donaldson, the influential professor of business ethics at the Wharton School of the University of Pennsylvania, put it, "Goals must map with the company's underlying values,"[11] and recognizing the connection between goal setting and the pressures to commit misconduct is critical for leaders who seek to promote ethical conduct.

Second, through strategic decision making, leadership can steer employees toward, or away from, business environments where the pressures or opportunities for misconduct may be high. In choosing to go forward, for example, with a business deal that offers good opportunities for reward, but also poses inherent risks that are greater than can reasonably be controlled, leadership places the organization in a difficult position. Doing so communicates a willingness to tolerate results, regardless of how obtained. Of course, some measure of risk is inherent in the business decision-making process, and risky decisions may often lead to high rewards. However, management should weigh such strategic decisions carefully and communicate unambiguously to all employees that performance and results must be achieved in an appropriate and ethical manner.

Third, the manner in which managers and employees are rewarded is a clear indication of the standards of conduct valued by leadership. In this matter, rewards and incentives for performance (and equally, consequences or repercussions) can send perhaps the strongest message about leadership's commitment to integrity. For example, performance metrics that focus on business results alone may communicate the idea that the means by which success is achieved are secondary to achieving successful results. Such a message focuses on the "what" and not the "how" of performance, and it can create an environment in which employees may act in illegal or unethical ways to achieve performance metrics. To discourage unethical or illegal behavior, leadership should devise additional incentives or reward structures for employees who exemplify core values and promote high ethics and compliance practices. Rewarding ethical behavior in this manner can provide positive examples for employees to follow and demonstrate institutional support for ongoing compliance program initiatives.

Few actions can demonstrate leadership's high regard for acting with integrity more clearly than setting realistic business goals, avoiding high-risk business opportunities, and rewarding ethical behavior. Weaving such actions into an organization's operational fabric provides leadership with its best chance of promoting a culture that encourages ethical conduct.

Compliance, Legal, and Internal Audit Functions

Creating and maintaining a culture of ethics and integrity is not only the responsibility of an organization's senior leadership team or those who exercise substantial authority, but also that of a variety of other individuals serving in various support functions. For example, because a compliance program should reach all employees, many organizations find it necessary to design and implement a compliance function infrastructure that includes staffing at both the headquarters level and at various field locations. Likewise, the organization's legal function can help support the program by ensuring the availability of adequate legal advice and by assessing legal risks. Finally, the internal audit function can serve the compliance program's aims by evaluating and providing feedback with respect to the design and operational effectiveness of programmatic elements. In the next few pages, we will examine the drivers for such functions, as well as key attributes for their effectiveness.

The Compliance Function. The increasing prevalence of compliance functions is reflected in the number of dedicated compliance professionals and the industry associations that represent them. For example, when the Ethics & Compliance Officer Association (ECOA) was founded in 1991, it had only 12 members. Today, the organization has over 1,400 professional members.[*] Currently, the Society of Corporate Compliance and Ethics (SCCE),[†] founded in 2002, has over 1,000 members, and the Open Compliance and Ethics Group (OCEG) has over 13,000 members in over 46 countries.[‡] This trend is complemented by a number of organizations that support industry-specific compliance professionals, as well as by the number of publications and forums held on compliance-related subjects every year.[§]

---

[*] The ECOA (www.theecoa.org) is a professional network association to promote discussion among those individuals who hold positions of responsibility in their respective organizational ethics and compliance functions.

[†] The SCCE (www.corporatecompliance.org) facilitates annual symposia on ethics and compliance programs designed to be a forum for professionals involved in the compliance industry.

[‡] The OCEG (www.oceg.org) is a nonprofit organization founded in 2002 when a consortium of 17 different organizations came together to sponsor the development of an ethics and compliance framework. OCEG offers guidance, standards, and benchmarks for integrating governance, risk management, and internal controls.

[§] For example, the Health Care Compliance Association (www.hcca-info.org) was set up in 1996 to provide an ethical network and resources to the health-care profession. Today, it has over 5,300 members and 35 corporate members.

The basic design framework for compliance functions is provided by the Sentencing Guidelines, which require that:

- A specific individual or team of individuals within high-level personnel be assigned overall responsibility for the compliance program
- Specific individual(s) be delegated day-to-day operational responsibility for the compliance program with regular reporting to the board of directors, per 2010 amendments
- Those tasked with operational responsibility for the program be given adequate resources, appropriate authority, and direct access to the organization's governing authority[12]

These guidelines are played out in the practices and lessons exhibited by leading compliance functions. The following paragraphs illustrate the Sentencing Guidelines' tenets in action.

Key Attributes of an Effective Compliance Function. An effective compliance function draws its success from having the right levels of authority, responsibility, competency, objectivity, and resources. A compliance function that has these five key attributes will likely be better positioned to manage emerging ethics and compliance challenges and can proactively pursue compliance goals. It is important to note, however, that there is no one "right design" for a compliance function; each organization must consider a variety of factors, including size, geographic dispersion, industry, risks, compliance history, and enforcement priorities, to name a few, in the design of the compliance function and its responsibilities.[13]

Authority. Having in place the right level of authority for the ethics and compliance program necessitates designating a high-level individual within the organization to serve as a CCO, with overall responsibilities for ensuring employee compliance with laws, regulations, and company standards. Such a CCO is often assisted by a deputy and guided by subject matter experts (SMEs), who will often be part of a compliance committee and can advise the CCO on matters related to implementation of the program.

On occasion, organizations struggle to determine who would be an appropriate "high-level individual" to head up ethics and compliance efforts. To be sure, such an individual must be seen as a senior member and have unrestricted access to information necessary to pursue compliance goals (e.g., involvement in strategic planning that may include new acquisitions as well as internal audit or investigative findings). The CCO should also have the responsibility of coaching other executives on ethical matters—illustrating the ethical dimensions of business decisions and helping drive integrity into business processes.[14]

But more than all such attributes, an inquiry into whether the CCO is "high level" enough should include an assessment of the CCO's upward reporting relationships, as these can be crucial in determining whether the individual truly has the requisite authority to serve as head of a compliance function. Optimally, a CCO would report directly to the highest levels of management (e.g., to the chief executive) and, at the same time, would have unfettered access to, and a reporting relationship with, the board of directors, as set forth in the 2010 amendments to the Sentencing Guidelines. A CCO with such reporting relationships is typically considered to have an appropriate level of authority and independence to bring about required organizational change.

Responsibility. The responsibilities of the CCO differ significantly from those of other staff and SMEs within the compliance function. As illustrated in the examples in Table 6.1, the challenge is often for the CCO to drive the overall design and implementation of the compliance function's strategy, while

Table 6.1.

Chief Compliance Officer (CCO)	Risk-Specific Compliance Managers (SMEs)
Risk Assessment	
• Establishes criteria for conducting compliance risk assessments	• Execute compliance risk assessments within areas of expertise
• Compiles results of risk assessments performed by SMEs	• Share leading practices for compliance risk assessment
• Facilitates prioritization of aggregated risks and program needs	• Identify connectivity of compliance risks across locations and functions
Policies and Standards	
• Establishes criteria for companywide policies and standards	• Identify or respond to policy needs within their areas of expertise
• Compiles policies generated by SMEs	• Draft policies that conform to company criteria
• Works with applicable committee to approve new policies	• Identify redundant or ineffective policies
Due Diligence	
• Establishes criteria for employee and third-party due diligence	• Identify specific due diligence needs relative to particular risk areas
• Works with relevant functions to help ensure due diligence takes place	*(continued)*

Table 6.1. (*Continued*)

Chief Compliance Officer (CCO)	Risk-Specific Compliance Managers (SMEs)
Communication and Training	
• Establishes criteria for compliance communication and training	• Identify training needs within their risk areas
• Develops common templates and technology platforms for delivery	• Develop and deliver training content as needed
• Tracks delivery and effectiveness of training	• Coordinate timing and delivery of training across locations and functions
Auditing and Monitoring	
• Administers hotline and forwards issues to SMEs as appropriate	• Follow up on hotline calls related to their risk areas
• Establishes criteria for compliance auditing and monitoring	• Oversee compliance audits within their risk areas
• Compiles results of compliance audits	• Coordinate timing of compliance audits across locations and functions
• Presents audit results to applicable committee and the board	
Investigation	
• Establishes criteria for investigations	• Perform or advise on investigations involving their risk areas
• Oversees initial processing and close-out of investigations	• May perform ad hoc investigations on routine, insignificant matters
• Advises senior management and the board on significant matters	
Remediation and Corrective Action	
• Establishes criteria for discipline, accountability, and corrective action	• Provide input on disciplinary guidelines relative to their risk areas
• Works with legal and human resources to effect disciplinary action	• Modify program elements to prevent and detect future violations
• Works with legal and others on disclosures and remedies	

Chief Compliance Officer (CCO)	Risk-Specific Compliance Managers (SMEs)
Report Results	
• Establishes criteria for compliance metrics and score cards	• Populate score cards and metrics for their risk areas
• Compiles metrics generated by SMEs	• Identify continuous improvement plans
• Communicates results and plans to applicable committee and board	
• Coordinates process considering disclosures in sustainability report	

Source: KPMG LLP, 2010.

working in tandem with others who have subject matter expertise in specific compliance risk areas.

Competency. Designing, implementing, and evaluating ethics and compliance program initiatives require compliance professionals with strong qualified competencies. As such, the CCO and other compliance personnel should have adequate credentials, experience, and training to be successful in their roles. Even beyond experience and training, a CCO should possess "leadership credentials that allow him or her to be accepted as a high-ranking officer of the organization and a respected member of the senior executive team."[15]

The professional credentials for a CCO are not set in stone, but typically they are understood to include a certain level of education, experience, professional training, and certification in a relevant compliance area. This may include having a background in law, public accountancy, finance, law enforcement, or human resources, among others. As such, a CCO should bring to the task appropriate professional credentials and a level of experience that can enable the CCO to understand the vulnerabilities that give rise to fraud and misconduct and to "demonstrate knowledge of business operations enough to be able to speak the language of management" and "relate the standards of the organization in terms that will be meaningful to workers at all levels." Such skills can help the CCO forge strong alliances with other key organizational functions and engage other executives on strategic and operational issues in a way that draws their genuine consideration.[16]

Other compliance program staff should also possess strong credentials. For example, such personnel should possess a genuine personal commitment to acting with integrity and to "doing the right thing" in all circumstances, personally and professionally. Having the requisite experience, professional training, and certification is also helpful to compliance personnel; in addition, however, they should possess good people skills that can motivate the personal behavior of others, the political astuteness to navigate difficult interpersonal situations, discretion in handling confidential matters, and patience to endure the hurdles often found on the road to high organizational ethics and integrity.[17]

Objectivity. Since compliance personnel may also be influenced by the same organizational pressures that can drive misconduct generally, they may need additional support to maintain a level of objectivity and independence from others within the organization. Such independence is often accomplished by having compliance personnel report directly through the compliance function and up to the board. This avoids having their performance determined by those individuals the compliance staff is assigned to monitor. Steps to support independence can include, for instance, requiring that the board ratify the appointment, removal, and performance appraisal of the CCO and, perhaps, even other key compliance personnel.

Resources. Common sense, as well as relevant regulatory guidance, dictates that the compliance program should have sufficient resources to carry out its mandate.[18] While the definition of "sufficient resources" may vary from one organization to another, certainly the size of the organization and the nature of its risks are factors in determining the need for resources. For example, in geographically dispersed organizations, the compliance function may need to rely on a network of dedicated employees who have, as an added task, compliance responsibilities (e.g., in training or communicating to local employees), and such employees may also have a dotted-line relationship to the CCO.[19]

But what are "enough resources" for a compliance function? This perhaps vexing question was recently answered by the Ethics Resource Center in a leading study when it said, "Resources can be considered adequate when organizations have funding to comprehensively promote standards, educate the workforce, audit and monitor compliance, and receive/respond to incidents that are potential violations of those standards in a timely manner."[20]

The Legal Department. An organization's in-house attorneys, and especially the general counsel (GC), are indispensible participants in the process to prevent, detect, and respond to potential fraud and misconduct. In many organizations, such professionals are chiefly charged with ensuring the availability of adequate legal advice to management as well as assessing and responding to legal risks.

The GC's position is often so highly regarded that many organizations combine the positions of GC and CCO into one. But while assigning oversight of the compliance program to the GC may satisfy the Sentencing Guidelines' requirement for someone "within high-level personnel of the organization" to have oversight of the program, organizations should evaluate carefully the considerations raised by practitioners and government officials on the matter of assigning the job of CCO to the GC.

There is a point of view raised by some practitioners against assigning the job of CCO to the GC that bears consideration. The reasoning is that the GC serves a management function in giving legal advice to management on business decisions and, therefore, may not be as independent as a CCO should be. Those who would advise against the GC serving as CCO would also point out that having in-house counsel function as CCO creates the risk that the organization's need to maintain attorney-client privilege in certain matters can potentially be compromised because of this dual role.

Whether serving as CCO or supporting the compliance function, the GC can play a vital role in an organization's compliance program by:

- Conducting legal risk assessments
- Providing updates on relevant laws and regulations to appropriate compliance staff for communication to relevant employees and agents
- Ensuring appropriate legal content of compliance training and communications
- Overseeing and coordinating internal investigations related to violations of standards and laws
- Overseeing voluntary disclosure of violations to the government
- Assisting in conducting compliance audits as appropriate (e.g., review of contracts for standard and legally required language)
- Reporting results of compliance-related efforts to the CCO, CEO, board audit committee, and others, as appropriate
- Providing ongoing compliance-related advice to operations staff on an as-needed basis

The Internal Audit Department. Since the Sentencing Guidelines also require organizations to take reasonable steps to "ensure that the organization's compliance and ethics program is followed, including monitoring and auditing to detect criminal conduct,"[21] an organization's internal audit department has a critical role to play.

Historically, the internal audit function served as a conduit for an organization's management and board to evaluate the effectiveness of controls the organization has in place to record, process, summarize, and report financial data. In more recent times, these more traditional duties have grown to include operational and efficiency reviews, including audits of compliance with applicable laws and regulations, and evaluations of the effectiveness of an organization's ethics and compliance program.

The criticality of an internal audit to the compliance function is obvious. After all, both the compliance and internal audit functions operate with a degree of independence from management, which is designed to enable effective evaluation of operations. Both typically report to the governing authority of the organization, usually the board of directors; and specifically, it is common for both to report to an audit committee of the board. Additionally, both play a role in conducting and responding to risk assessments and helping the organization adapt to emerging risks. Moreover, it can also be said that many of the skills and competencies inherent within an internal audit are well suited for aspects of compliance administration, particularly in evaluative capacities. It then comes as no surprise that some organizations have integrated compliance functions into their internal audit departments.

The Role of the Board of Directors

Just as management and compliance professionals play an important role in effecting compliance within an organization, so too does an organization's governing authority, typically the board of directors. Effective fraud risk management requires a board that is committed to driving the values and standards that it expects all aspects of the company to embrace. The board should apply these values as a filter to drive all its decisions—from selecting the organization's chief executive, to shaping strategic goals, to evaluating management's performance and influencing organizational management of risk and compliance.

The board's oversight of compliance activities involves each of the functions and individuals who are charged with compliance responsibilities. It is through such functions and individuals that boards and other governing authorities have an opportunity to influence the compliance systems and ethical culture relied upon by an organization to prevent, detect, and respond to fraud and misconduct. The board's role is important for the following reasons:

- For the compliance program to succeed, it must be viewed as a high priority—involving the board helps secure institutional and practical support.
- Compliance efforts do, on occasion, uncover sensitive information regarding management wrongdoing, and the board is in the best position to lead the appropriate response.
- Enforcement authorities demand evidence of high-level support for the compliance program, and direct involvement by the board in launching and monitoring the compliance program fulfills this need.

Responsibilities

The responsibilities of an organization's board of directors are described in the Sentencing Guidelines, which require the governing authority to "be knowledgeable about the content and operation of the compliance and ethics program and . . . exercise reasonable oversight with respect to the implementation and effectiveness of the compliance and ethics program."[22]

The first requirement, to be knowledgeable about the content and operation of the program, is a duty that falls on every board member and cannot be delegated to a board committee. At a minimum, it requires every board member to understand the dimensions of the program and, generally, how it operates. Such detailed knowledge can be gained in a number of ways, including periodic reporting by members of the compliance function, briefings by external specialists on the design and operational effectiveness of the program, and trainings on relevant issues.

In addition to being knowledgeable about the content and operation of the compliance program, the board must exercise "reasonable oversight" over the program. Board members have a "duty of care" that, along with directors' "duty of loyalty," makes the board's oversight of the compliance program essential.

Exercising diligent oversight over the compliance program entails obtaining a clear understanding of how well the program is designed and implemented, as well as how effective it is in mitigating the risk of fraud and other misconduct. While this duty can conceivably be borne by the board as a whole, it is typically delegated to a board committee that specializes in organizational oversight, often the audit committee or a risk committee. To effectively exercise reasonable oversight, boards must directly monitor and respond to information presented to them. In other words, directors have a duty to react and to work proactively to ensure that the compliance program is effective.

As a practical matter, directors' diligent oversight over the compliance program may include:

- Regular attendance and participation in board meetings where compliance issues are discussed
- Initiation of board agenda items relating to compliance
- Continuing review of compliance reports generated by the CCO on the implementation and impact of the compliance program
- Initiation of inquiries when alerted by circumstances that warrant investigation and are not otherwise being addressed by management

Generally, in fulfilling its oversight role, the board should focus on ensuring that it has a reasonable basis for believing that adequate systems have been designed and implemented to prevent, detect, and respond to fraud and misconduct. In fact, due to the influential decision of the Delaware Chancery Court in the well-known Caremark case and its progeny, a director who is diligent in ensuring board oversight of the compliance program may be protected from personal liability when employees harm the organization by engaging in criminal conduct.[23] By contrast, a director who fails to ensure adequate oversight responsibility will likely receive no such protection.

Additional Opportunities for Boards to Further Ethics and Compliance

In addition to providing leadership, focus, and oversight, a board can further an organization's compliance program in a number of very specific ways. These include engaging the CEO, maintaining the independence of the CCO, and ensuring that the board is receiving timely and appropriate information.

Engaging the CEO. As discussed earlier, the chief executive and senior management team are critical drivers of an organization's ethical culture.[24] As such, board members should utilize their influence with the CEO and the senior management team to help ensure they are appropriately driving the organization's culture. The board's influence in such matters is especially critical because the board is typically involved in the process of selecting the CEO, evaluating and rewarding the CEO's performance, and overseeing the achievement of ethics and compliance program goals.

Boards can also create incentives for ethical performance and disincentives for failing to perform in accordance with the company's ethical standards. In this matter, so-called clawback provisions are becoming more common in executive compensation packages, requiring the repayment of incentive payments when illegal or unethical behavior occurs.[25] Combining the proper mix of incentives for high integrity with disincentives for misconduct can motivate executives to achieve results in a proper way.

Engaging and Safeguarding the Mandate of the CCO. While the board of directors is charged with oversight for the organization's compliance program, from a practical perspective, day-to-day management of the program is delegated to other individuals within the organization, and especially the CCO, who is typically held accountable for the effectiveness of the program. And yet the board is uniquely empowered to support the CCO's mission, safeguarding the latter's independence and imbuing the position with the necessary influence to perform a sometimes very difficult job. This can be achieved by giving the CCO unfettered access to the board, providing the individual with a dotted-line reporting relationship directly to the board, and requiring the board's assent to hire or fire the CCO.

Monitoring the Compliance Program. An effective board must receive timely and relevant information to be able to evaluate whether risks are being addressed properly and whether the program is operating effectively. The 2010 amendments to the Sentencing Guidelines reinforce the importance of regular reporting by the compliance group to the board. While the level of detail required may vary, generally the information required will encompass regular updates on the activities of the compliance function, including key performance indicators such as the number and type of allegations of misconduct received, the steps taken to investigate the allegations, the rate at which cases were closed, the number substantiated, and the type of disciplinary and remedial actions taken. Moreover, a properly informed board will be briefed regularly with respect to progress on major compliance initiatives, the results of compliance audits and risk assessments, and the outcome of efforts to evaluate the effectiveness of the organization's ethics and compliance program.

To illustrate, an effective board may seek to gather information that can answer the questions in Table 6.2.

Table 6.2.

Aligning Oversight
- Do stewards of the ethics and compliance program have the requisite levels of authority, responsibility, competencies, objectivity, and resources to do their jobs effectively?
- Does the compliance function have optimal participation from relevant corporate functions, e.g., legal and internal audit?
- Do the audit and compensation committees discuss how to address fraud and misconduct risks that may arise from executive compensation plans?
- Do management's actions (e.g., annual goal setting, strategic planning, budgeting, resource allocation, and incentive compensation) align with the goals of the organization's ethics and compliance program, or do they send mixed messages?
- How independent is the compliance function from management; e.g., does management filter compliance information presented to the board?

Assessing Risk
- What are the bases for organizational risk assessments (e.g., inputs and methodology)?
- Have internal controls been tailored based on an assessment of the types of fraud and misconduct risks that are likely to arise in the business today?
- Is the organization's program poised to anticipate and react to new ethics and compliance risks, or is it backward-looking and "fighting the last war"?

(continued)

Table 6.2. (*Continued*)

- What are the new risk areas that may be on the horizon, and how will current risk levels change?

Preventing Misconduct

- What controls are in place to prevent fraud and misconduct from occurring in the first place?
- Has training been tailored to the risks employees face, and is it effective in guiding their behavior?
- Is the organization performing the right level of due diligence on employees and third parties operating on its behalf internationally?
- Does the compliance program target the underlying pressures, rationalizations, and opportunities faced by managers and employees to engage in misconduct?
- Do performance evaluations include a balanced examination of business results and the means used to achieve them?
- What controls exist to guard against override of controls by management?

Detecting Misconduct

- What controls are in place to detect wrongdoing when it occurs?
- What are the sources for reports of misconduct (e.g., hotline, human resources, security, line management, regulators, etc.)? What sources could be included that are not currently included?
- Are concerns that get raised through nonhotline channels getting routed to the right place?
- How would a report implicating senior management in serious misconduct be handled and routed?
- Does the compliance program leverage feedback from alternative sources, such as customer complaints or employee exit interviews?
- Are fraud analytics embedded in computer-based auditing and monitoring systems to detect suspicious events or transactions?
- Have data analytic routines been expanded to address international risk areas, such as bribery and corruption?
- How can we build in early warning signals to identify indicators that suggest ethics and compliance risk?

Responding to Misconduct

- What controls are in place to respond appropriately to allegations or concerns when they arise?
- Has the organization equipped frontline supervisors with the knowledge and tools to address allegations and concerns in an appropriate manner?
- Is there a uniform understanding across the business of what allegations require investigation, by whom, when, and in what manner?

- What factors should guide whether managers are held accountable for the wrongdoing of subordinates?
- Who should be involved in a decision to voluntarily disclose potential compliance violations to the government?
- What is the average case-closure time for investigations?
- How are the root causes of misconduct and control weaknesses assessed once a violation is detected? Is corrective action routinely taken? What are examples?
- What steps are taken to administer discipline consistently for similar offenses?

Evaluating Effectiveness

- Have internal controls been evaluated recently to ensure they are operating effectively?
- Have compliance controls been designed in a manner consistent with minimum legal and regulatory criteria as well as industry practices that companies have generally found to be effective?
- What metrics and key performance indicators should be used to monitor the effectiveness of the program? Are employee perceptions and attitudes toward the program tracked formally?
- How does the organization demonstrate good governance and corporate social responsibility to external stakeholders?
- How does the organization define success for ethics and compliance programs? Is it purely from a risk-avoidance perspective, or has the organization identified ways the program can accrue benefits to the brand and the bottom line?

Source: KPMG LLP, 2009.

Conclusion

In summary, organizations are well served in preventing, detecting, and responding to issues of fraud and misconduct when they have the benefit of well-designed and comprehensive compliance programs. Leading organizations look beyond simply establishing compliance programs and seek to integrate them into the organizations' overall governance and risk management frameworks. This integration provides the opportunity not only to create truly effective compliance programs, but also to achieve sustainable business value.

Part IV

A Model for Managing Fraud and Misconduct— Prevention, Detection, and Response

Timothy P. Hedley

In Part III, we discussed how leading organizations recognize that they must adopt an integrated approach to governance, risk, and compliance. This requires organizations to coordinate numerous, interconnected activities, including internal audit, operational risk, legal, ethics and compliance, Sarbanes-Oxley, and enterprise risk management (ERM), among others.

In Part IV, we cover one of the more significant risk areas for organizations to address when managing governance, risk, and compliance—the risk of fraud and misconduct. Specifically, we address the components of an effective fraud and misconduct risk management approach: the assessment, design, implementation, and evaluation of controls, policies, and procedures for the prevention, detection, and response to fraud and misconduct as pictured in Figure PIV.1.

An effective fraud risk management approach aligns the appropriate organizational functions and activities to help manage risk in a manner consistent with

Additional contributor is Cassandra C. Cohen.

Figure PIV.1.
Source: KPMG International Cooperative, *Fraud Risk Management: Developing a Strategy for Prevention, Detection, and Response,* New York, 2006, p. 20.

the entity's business needs as well as marketplace expectations. Developing such an approach can be achieved in four steps:[1]

- *Assessing risk.* Assessing the needs of the organization based upon both the nature of fraud and misconduct risks and the adequacy of existing controls intended to mitigate that risk
- *Design.* Developing controls to help prevent, detect, and respond to identified risks in a manner consistent with legal and regulatory criteria and other leading practices
- *Implementation.* Deploying a process for implementing the new controls and assigning responsibility to individuals with the requisite level of authority, objectivity, and resources to support the process
- *Evaluation.* Evaluating the design and operating effectiveness of controls through control self-assessment, substantive testing, routine monitoring, and separate evaluations

Assessing Risk

The nature of fraud and misconduct risks facing an organization can be as complex as the organization itself. For example, the risks of fraud and misconduct for an automotive manufacturer that has experienced a rapid retrenchment in market size are different from those of a global energy company seeking to expand crude oil exploration in an environmentally sustainable manner. Accordingly, anti-fraud measures should be tailored to the unique risks of an organization and the conditions that give rise to those risks, while at the same time balancing risk and control. Determining what a company's fraud and misconduct risks are, how well the organization manages those risks, and the process to get started will be discussed in Chapter 7.

Design

Properly designed fraud and misconduct controls, policies, and procedures should help the organization operate effectively and efficiently while protecting the organization from the risk of fraud and misconduct. To be successful, these controls should be tailored to the specific risks and the unique business environment of the organization, and they should be planned in a manner that increases the likelihood that those controls will ultimately prove to be effective.

Implementation

Once fraud and misconduct controls have been designed, management should establish a strategy and process for implementing the new or improved controls across the organization. Meaningful and consistent implementation may require a substantial change in workplace culture and practices. Therefore, employees should receive clear and frequent communications with respect to when, how, and by whom the controls will be implemented, as well as the manner in which compliance with the new controls will be enforced.

Evaluation

Simply because a control exists does not guarantee that it is operating as intended. After a control has been operating for a period of time, it should be evaluated to determine whether or not it was designed and implemented to achieve optimal effectiveness. Such an evaluation should first consider those controls identified as "higher risk" before other, lower-priority controls are evaluated. However, it is important to note that simply because a particular control does not yet exist does not mean management should automatically conclude that the organization's risk management objective is not being met. In the absence of a specific control, other compensating controls may be operating effectively and mitigating the risk of fraud and misconduct.

When evaluating the design and effectiveness of a control, policy, or procedure, management can use a "gap analysis" process to determine whether or not the control in question incorporates the required design criteria. To evaluate the operational effectiveness of a particular control, management should focus on the extent to which the control's objectives have been achieved. However, in the end, the integrity climate will help determine the perceptions employees have of the organization's ability to prevent, detect, and respond to fraud and misconduct as well as provide a baseline for their own conduct.

We will now provide a look at preventive, detective, and responsive controls, policies, and procedures that are meant to reduce and mitigate the risk of fraud and misconduct. As described in Part III, mitigating fraud and misconduct risk unquestionably starts with leadership and governance, including oversight by the board or audit committee and by senior management. However, a truly effective approach requires coordinating numerous organizational functions and activities. As will be discussed in this section, these functions and activities include risk assessment; code of conduct; communication and training; employee and third-party due diligence; hotlines and other mechanisms for seeking advice; auditing, monitoring, and investigative protocols. The development and coordination of the aforementioned is critical to managing the governance, risk, and compliance challenge.

Chapter 7

Prevention: Risk Assessment

Timothy P. Hedley

fraud risk assessment is a step-by-step process for identifying the quantitative and qualitative nature of potential integrity breakdowns. When well executed, such assessments can help organizations identify the pressure points and incentives that give rise to some of the most salient integrity-related risks for organizations and their stakeholders. Importantly, a completed assessment can provide a foundation upon which an appropriate response can be constructed to mitigate fraud and misconduct risk and help management avoid losses due to fraud and misconduct. In this chapter, we will describe how to design assessments for identifying, measuring, and evaluating fraud risks facing an organization.

Design Considerations

Two major design considerations immediately present themselves when starting a fraud risk assessment. The first is determining whether or not the assessment will be performed as a separate evaluation or in conjunction with an enterprisewide or similar risk management initiative. Second, the organization should assign ultimate responsibility for conducting the assessment, including responsibility for the design, implementation, and evaluation of the assessment (known herein as the assessment team). Each of these is a decision that senior management typically makes depending upon considerations unique to the organization. For instance, has the board directed that management undertake an enterprisewide risk assessment? Is the organization working under a government

Additional contributors are Cassandra C. Cohen and Justin H. Snell.

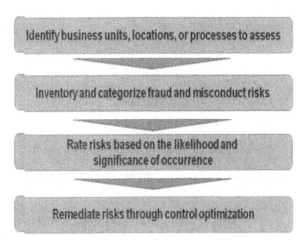

Figure 7.1.
Source: KPMG LLP, 2009.

settlement agreement? Has the organization recently experienced a major fraud? Are industry peers coming under government scrutiny?

Once these decisions are complete, the fraud and misconduct risk assessment typically follows four fundamental steps, as shown in Figure 7.1.

Harvey Pitt, a former chair of the Securities and Exchange Commission, said, "Management's most important job is identifying, assessing and managing risk; how well it's perceived to perform this role is often reflected in a company's share prices."[1]

Identify Business Units, Locations, or Processes to Assess

The assessment team's first task should be to decide upon those aspects or parts of the organization that will be subject to the risk assessment. More specifically, the team considers if it is going to conduct the assessment at the corporate level (entity level), the business unit level, or the business process or transactional level; or by geography (e.g., domestic and international); or with some combination of the above.

The corporate-level assessment typically provides a view of risk across all business processes, functions, and geographies. Such a perspective can provide the company with a comprehensive inventory of the types of fraud and misconduct risks it confronts with a good picture of the internal control infrastructure available to mitigate those risks. Of course, a broad, wide-ranging assessment of this type can be costly and disruptive.

To help control costs, many organizations opt to perform assessments at business units or geographies the team knows to be problematic or for which they have concerns. Those business units operating in areas of the world that are more susceptible to fraud and misconduct are likely to require more attention. For example, emerging markets such as India, China, and Eastern Europe that rank poorly on Transparency International's Corruption Perception Index[2] might present unique risk factors related to bribery and corruption.

Once it is determined at what level to perform an analysis, the team should consider who would provide input into the assessment. The involvement of personnel from across the organization, within the business unit, or in a geographic area—and at all levels (e.g., operations management, legal counsel, internal audit, senior management, and others with specific knowledge of the organization)—provides a diverse perspective that helps ensure that the broadest range of risks is being considered. Also, it helps ensure that the factors contributing to different types of fraud risks are identified and addressed.

Often, lower-level employees have firsthand knowledge of fraud and misconduct to which senior management might not have visibility. The assessment team may also want to consider, as appropriate, the participation of external sources such as industry experts, analysts, lawyers, or external auditors.

The assessment should also take into account the organizational and reporting structures, which can be significant factors in understanding the pressures, incentives, and opportunities for fraud and misconduct to occur. For example, autonomous divisional controllers may have greater opportunity to commit financial statement fraud by inappropriately booking manual journal entries to meet budgeted or forecasted results before they are reviewed by senior management.

The next area for potential examination includes the significant accounts and classes of transactions. The assessment team may include financial statement accounts that involve a high degree of subjectivity, including significant estimates made by management or classes of transactions that are material to the financial statements. Special reserves, certain asset valuations such as goodwill and intangible assets, may use models or assumptions at the discretion of management and have a greater inherent risk of being improperly manipulated.

Finally, management should consider the complexity of its business activities. Complex business activities or activities that result in transactions that require complex calculations, including derivatives, actuarial assumptions, or other calculations requiring a number of assumptions made by management, may pose an increased risk of fraud and therefore should be subject to the fraud risk assessment process.

Inventory and Categorize Fraud and Misconduct Risks

Developing a fraud risk inventory is simply cataloging the possible future scenarios under which the organization may be vulnerable to fraud and misconduct. The process of constructing an inventory consists of two balanced steps: input and analysis.

With respect to input, organizations may collect information by conducting market research, examining media reports, and reviewing internally reported incidents of fraud and misconduct. Also, there are numerous commonly known risks that the assessment team may consider for analysis, including theft of cash, financial misrepresentations, antitrust violations, violation of the Foreign Corrupt Practices Act (FCPA), commercial bribery, and conflicts of interest, among many others.

Importantly, some frauds are more prevalent in specific industries. For example, banks are vulnerable to check fraud, deposit fraud, and third-party mortgage fraud. Similarly, insurance companies face unique risks in claims fraud; software and telecom companies are vulnerable to revenue recognition schemes; and manufacturing environments face risks related to the theft and manipulation of inventory. Revenue recognition at some health-care organizations requires a significant amount of judgment by management associated with contractual allowances that are vulnerable to manipulation, while pharmaceutical companies face challenges with off-label promotions.

Nonetheless, a meaningful fraud risk assessment will require additional input around organization-specific risks and vulnerabilities; relevant policies, programs, and controls; tone at the top; upstream and downstream communications; organizational culture; training; enforcement; and comparison to competitors. Fortunately, numerous tools are available to an assessment team to help elicit such organization-specific information. A partial list of some of these input methods includes interviews, documentation reviews, perception capture surveys, focus groups, and benchmarking studies. We will now consider three of the most common input methods: interviews, documentation reviews, and focus groups.

Interviews

Risk assessment interviews are typically held confidentially with individuals who have particular subject matter, risk management, or operational responsibilities directly related to applicable areas of fraud and misconduct risk. The objective is to gain an overall understanding of the organization's culture and climate, internal control infrastructure, specific risk areas, and mitigation strategies.

An assessment team may consider interviewing individuals in the following types of roles:

- Chief executive officer
- Chief financial officer
- Controller
- Staff from accounting and finance
- Director or other members of internal audit
- Sarbanes-Oxley project manager
- Ethics and compliance officer
- Head or other members of human resources
- Director or other members of information technology
- Operations manager(s)
- Line managers and employees

When completed, interviews should be carefully recorded, documenting key issues identified that can be used during future interviews. Later in the assessment process, a content analysis of the interview notes will help form the overall assessment.

Documentation Reviews

In parallel with the interviews, the assessment team typically undertakes a documentation review to gain an understanding of and assess the organization's current policies and procedures, internal controls, and internal and external communication processes. In addition to assessing policy effectiveness, a documentation review can also help determine the availability, effectiveness, coverage, and completeness of existing documentation. This review should also help the assessment team ascertain specific types of noncompliance risks that arise from the organization's business activities. It is important to assess the degree to which fraud risk has been considered in developing policies, procedures, and controls. Documents to be reviewed may include the following:

- Code of conduct
- Reports of allegations of wrongdoing and irregularities
- Applicable job descriptions
- Internal audit programs and specific internal audits (where applicable)
- Corporate security policy and programs
- Hotline policy and logs
- Policies within financial operations
- Organizational charts

- Information and communication materials (e.g., company newsletters)
- Training and development materials (e.g., training plan, training modules for broad-based awareness training)
- Performance management systems (e.g., procedures on background investigations for new employees, goal setting, performance evaluations, disciplinary guidelines)
- Auditing and monitoring systems (e.g., compliance audit plans)
- Advice and reporting systems (e.g., policies and procedures for reporting misconduct internally or for seeking advice)
- Response and improvement systems (e.g., policies and procedures for conducting internal investigations or modifying management systems over time)

While performing the documentation review, the assessment team should consider the organization's industry to understand risk areas and trends affecting the industry, including key or changing areas of regulation, mergers, product diversification, and international expansion. It is also important to consider relevant stakeholder groups and the organization's ethical and legal obligations toward them.

Focus Groups

A focus group is comprised of selected individuals who are asked in a group setting about their perceptions and reactions toward specific topics. In a fraud risk context, such focus groups are conducted to gather firsthand employee views of fraud, misconduct, ethics, and compliance risks, as well as the strengths and weaknesses of key ethics and compliance program elements. Specific considerations for assessment teams include moderation, group size, timing, recordation, and demographics.

Once they have determined the 5 to 10 participants to include in a focus group, the assessment team should develop 5 to 10 questions that address the subject at hand. These questions should be asked by a moderator during a 60- to 90-minute session. Since this is essentially a group interview, it is imperative that all members participate as much as possible in answering each question. As with the interviews above, results should be carefully recorded and key issues identified. Later in the assessment process, a content analysis of the focus group notes will help inform the overall assessment.

Once the assessment team has completed gathering input, whether from interviews, documentation reviews, perception capture surveys, focus groups, or benchmarking studies, the next step is to use the fraud triangle, shown in Figure 7.2, to analyze the inputs in the correct organizational context. In other words, inputs

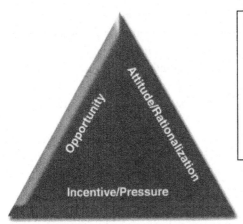

The Context

• Business goals and strategy
• Industry competitors
• Financial condition and performance
• Analyst expectations
• Nature of business operations
• Employee demographics
• Geography

Figure 7.2. The fraud triangle
Source: American Institute of Certified Public Accountants, "Consideration of Fraud in a Financial Statement Audit," Statement on Auditing Standards No. 99, October 2002, p. 8.

should be evaluated using the concepts of opportunity, pressure, and rationalization in the context of the organization's goals and strategy, competitors, financial condition and performance, analyst expectations, nature of business operations, employee demographics, and geography.

Use of the fraud triangle is best explained through example. Let us start with opportunity, the fundamental leg of the fraud triangle. Opportunity is created in the absence of effective internal control. KPMG LLP's *Integrity Survey 2008–2009* highlighted this clearly when it revealed that 47 percent of employees believe company policies or procedures were easy to bypass.[3] Case in point: At Koss Corp., the vice president of finance allegedly was able to embezzle more than $20 million by circumventing and overriding disbursement controls.[4]

As discussed in Part I, pressure is a major driver of financial reporting frauds as well as a driver of many asset misappropriation frauds. To understand this, we again can turn to the *Integrity Survey 2008–2009* conducted by KPMG LLP that found nearly 60 percent of respondents indicated they felt pressure to do "whatever it takes" to meet business targets, and another 49 percent indicated they feared losing their jobs if they did not meet targets.[5] These are indeed powerful pressures. This was exactly the situation at HealthSouth, where the pressure to meet market expectations resulted in revenue being fraudulently overstated by $3.8 billion to $4.6 billion.[6]

Finally, rationalization bridges the pressure to commit fraud and the actual fraudulent act. Rationalization describes the mindset of most fraudsters whose moral compasses do not allow them to commit fraud without being able to justify the act to themselves or others. Importantly, when assessing fraud risk, rationalization is generally the most difficult leg of the fraud triangle to take into account.

A practical way to use the concept of rationalization is to be alert for the rationalizing mindset—namely, when performing and analyzing interviews, walk-throughs, and other inputs, you should be constantly vigilant for individuals rationalizing beliefs and behaviors. For example, if during an interview in a sales function, you overhear a district manager say, "Everybody in this industry does what it takes to get numbers on the board," you have identified a prime example of a rationalizing state of mind.

As you can see, by using the fraud triangle, management can draw upon the collective knowledge of the entire organization to identify and understand the specific fraud risk factors that are unique to the entity's organizational structure, industry, and business environment.

However, prior to actually cataloging risks, it is helpful to organize risks into predetermined categories. This helps ensure that potential key risks do not fall through the cracks while bundling those risks with similar characteristics into common groups. Categories may include:

- Fraudulent financial reporting, such as improper revenue recognition, overstatement of assets, and understatement of liabilities
- Misappropriation of assets, including embezzlement, payroll fraud, external theft, procurement fraud, royalty fraud, and counterfeiting
- Other misconduct that may undermine management or business integrity, including conflicts of interest, insider trading, and employment discrimination

A sample may be seen in Figure 7.3.

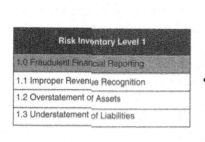

Figure 7.3.
Source: KPMG LLP, 2009.

Risk Rating

Once management has completed its inventory, the next step is to assess and rate each risk by its inherent likelihood and potential significance. The initial risk rating should be assessed prior to the consideration of any existing controls to clearly understand the risk without bias from the control environment. Identifying and evaluating controls subsequent to the rating assessment helps avoid the temptation of overestimating the effectiveness of related controls, leaving the organization vulnerable to unmitigated fraud risk.

We will begin with estimating the likelihood of occurrence. While there is no known method to predict with certainty the occurrence of fraud, there are many factors that may be used to help determine how likely it is that a potential integrity breakdown will occur. Some of these indicators include known instances or allegations of fraud, the complexity of the risk, the visibility associated with the risk, violations by industry peers, litigation trends, government enforcement actions, and media coverage.

To the extent that the above indicators or others are present, management can establish the likelihood of occurrence as low, medium, high, or any other scale that may be consistent with company practice. For example, if a company operates in an industry with many competitors and there has been little in the way of litigation related to a specific fraud risk, management might assess the likelihood of occurrence as low. Conversely, consider Medicaid and Medicare reimbursement claims made by health-care organizations. Billing Medicare or Medicaid for diagnostic procedures that were never performed (i.e., up-coding) is widely known to plague the entire industry. As such, management might assess the likelihood of occurrence as medium; or if the organization has had a history of up-coding, management then might assess the risk as high.

Weigh the Likelihood of Fraud Risk Occurrence

While estimating the likelihood of occurrence (see Table 7.1), the assessment team should also estimate the effect (i.e., significance) of such an integrity breakdown if it were to occur. This process requires consideration of both quantitative (typically measured in financial terms) and qualitative factors (often measured in reputational or similar terms).

Estimates of financial effect are based upon the potential monetary harm (i.e., loss or cost) to the organization. A high risk rating, for example, means the occurrence may exceed materiality thresholds and affect financial liquidity ratios or other key performance indicators for the organization. An example of low risk may be small-dollar, individual expense reporting violations.

Table 7.1.

Inherent Likelihood Factors	Rating
Known instances and allegations	**High/Probable**
Previous history	**(Score = 7–9)**
Pervasiveness of the risk across operations	
Complexity of the risk	**Medium/Reasonably**
Results of employee surveys and focus groups	**Possible**
Violations by other companies or industry peers	**(Score = 4–6)**
Industry and competitor litigation trends	
Government enforcement priorities	
Criticisms by the media or NGOs	**Low/Remote**
Other internal considerations	**(Score = 1–3)**

Source: KPMG LLP, 2009.

Additionally, what might be significant to a $100 million company may not be significant to a $50 billion company. Other measurable, quantitative risks may include loss of inventory, cash, or fixed assets; fines; settlements; and judgments.

Qualitative factors, on the other hand, are typically not directly measurable in financial or dollar terms. Examples of qualitative factors may include items such as negative media attention, reputational damage, the forced resignation or dismissal of C-level executives, financial restatements, regulatory intervention or probation, or hindered ability to meet market objectives.

Assessing the Potential Significance of Fraud Risk: An Example

Once the assessment team has estimated risk likelihood and significance (see an example in Table 7.2), it is helpful to plot risks on an axis representing their significance and likelihood of occurrence, as shown in Figure 7.4. Such a heat map enables management to visually represent identified risks and begin the process of evaluating compensating and mitigating controls.

Once the team has ranked each risk according to its estimated likelihood and potential significance, the next step is to reconsider each risk—taking into account the existence of mitigating controls. Organizations typically have a large catalog of entity-level and process-level controls in place designed to help ensure that operations are efficient, that financial statements are accurate, and that legal and regulatory requirements are met. Controls might also exist to help ensure safety standards or influence and set the tone for an organization's day-to-day activities.

Table 7.2.

Financial Significance	Nonfinancial Significance	Rating
> $50 million	Criminal investigation Major class action litigation Major change to corporate strategy Resignation or dismissal of C-level executives National media attention Financial restatement	High/Material (Score = 7–9)
$25 million < $50 million	Regulatory intervention and probation Complex litigation Major change to business unit strategy Resignation or dismissal of business unit executives Regional and trade media attention	Medium/More Than Inconsequential (Score = 4–6)
< $25 million	Regulatory sanction Isolated litigation Major change to functional strategy Resignation or dismissal of functional executives Ability to meet performance targets threatened	Low/Inconsequential (Score = 1–3)

Source: KPMG LLP, 2009.

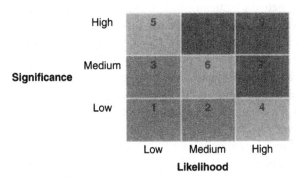

Figure 7.4. Inherent risk
Source: KPMG LLP, 2009.

Once the mitigating controls are identified, careful consideration should be given to evaluate the effectiveness of the controls as they relate to specific identified fraud risks. Many controls serve a dual purpose, and it is important for the assessment team to understand if the primary purpose of the control is to address the risk of fraud and misconduct and if the control is effective for that objective. Again, the assessment team should be mindful to avoid the temptation of overstating the effectiveness of these controls. To assist in avoiding this temptation, the team can look at the results from previous control evaluations performed by management or by the independent auditor. If such evaluations do not exist, the team may consider performing a test for those controls that they are heavily relying upon to mitigate the risk of fraud and misconduct.

The remaining exposure the organization faces, after controls have been put in place to mitigate the risk, is known as residual risk. In some instances, the residual risk may be minimal, and in other instances, it may still remain high or moderate. For example, suppose a relatively new company with few controls has scored the theft of inventory as a significant fraud risk. In addition, suppose that this company has high-valued, portable inventory that could easily be sold by an individual and that this risk is common in its industry. As a result, the company might implement periodic inventory cycle counts, restrict access to inventory, install security alarms, or even hire security personnel to help prevent and detect the theft of inventory. These measures might significantly reduce the risk of theft of inventory to a lower level, perhaps reducing the residual risk.

Let us suppose the same company operates in a number of foreign countries and identifies violations of the FCPA as a significant risk. As a result, management may institute a number of measures to help mitigate this specific risk, as well as include compliance programs, employee training, approvals for certain expenses, a whistleblower hotline, or even proactive forensic data analysis. However, if where the company does business is scored poorly on Transparency International's Corruption Perceptions Index, the team might still conclude that there is a high residual risk that the company could potentially violate the FCPA.

Having an accurate understanding of the residual risk assists management in prioritizing risks and devoting the right amount of resources to mitigating the salient fraud risks that still face the organization. So where do you devote company resources? There is no simple answer to this question, but prioritization may be an effective starting point.

Prioritization is the process of identifying the risks that need to be addressed immediately based upon the objectives of management and an understanding of the organization, including:

- Which highly rated risks have high residual risk and remain critical areas of concern?
- Does management have the ability to remediate the risk with the appropriate personnel, and do the personnel have the time to do it?
- What are the associated costs of remediating the risk in terms of time and money?
- Will remediation require days, weeks, months, or years? And likewise, what is the associated benefit of remediating the risk?
- Can that benefit be quantified in financial terms, and will the company realize immediate or future cost savings?

Remediate Risks through Control Optimization

Once the residual risk matrix is formulated, the organization can identify the processes, controls, and other procedures necessary to mitigate the identified risks based upon the assessment of the risks identified and the available resources to management, as shown in Figure 7.5. The assessment team's focus during risk remediation should be on strengthening controls for insufficiently mitigated fraud and misconduct risks. The team should begin with those risks that they have previously ranked as having a high likelihood of occurrence and a high risk of significantly impacting the organization.

Management may reduce or eliminate the likelihood or significance of certain fraud risks by making changes to activities and processes. An organization

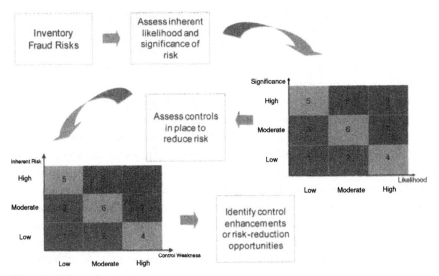

Figure 7.5.
Source: KPMG LLP, 2009.

may choose to sell certain segments of its operations, cease doing business in certain locations, reorganize its business processes, or institute specific preventive controls to eliminate unacceptable risks. For example, the risk of misappropriation of funds may be reduced by implementing a central lockbox to receive payments instead of receiving money at the entity's various locations. Likewise, the risk of corruption may be reduced by closely monitoring the entity's disbursement processes in high-risk jurisdictions.

Risk remediation focuses on strengthening controls for insufficiently mitigated fraud and misconduct risk. During the risk-remediation process, additional improvement opportunities may be identified. Accountability is key to helping ensure an effective risk remediation. Management should identify an individual with responsibility for helping to ensure that the control environment is improved. The results should be verified by internal audit and reviewed by senior management. In addition, there should be senior-level responsibility for communicating the results of the remediation to the audit committee, as well as for integrating the new or improved controls into the following year's risk assessment.

The assessment team then links specific controls, policies, and procedures to the identified risks and makes a determination about whether additional resources should be committed to enhance existing controls or to design and implement new programs and controls to mitigate the identified risks. For instance, consider where the team has identified price fixing as a fraud risk. Assume that, as part of the risk assessment process, it has been rated a high risk. After identifying that price fixing is associated with the sales process, management assigns specific individuals to identify the current controls in place, such as relevant policies regarding interactions with competitors, including codes of conduct and mandatory training. Additionally, these same individuals would be responsible for identifying improvement opportunities, such as equipping helpline operators to assist employees who are seeking advice on price-fixing issues or enhancing existing training for those individuals with discretionary authority to set prices. Once these observations are made, they are validated, evaluated, and adopted as appropriate.

Program elements to address fraud risk might include both entity-level and process-specific controls. Process-specific anti-fraud controls occur throughout the organization at all levels and in all functions. They may include preventive controls, detective controls, manual controls, automated computer controls, and management controls; and they may take many forms. Some examples of process-specific controls include authorization controls to approve transactions or access to assets or records, segregation of duties to help ensure appropriate custody and prevent individuals from being in a position to both perpetrate and conceal an error or irregularity, management review to provide an additional level of higher review, or reconciliation to check the consistency and accuracy of information within the organization. Process-specific controls might also include system access or physical controls to assets.

Process-specific anti-fraud control activities may also serve to reduce other business risks and, as such, may serve a dual role. Segregation of duties, authorization controls, account reconciliations, and management reviews can all be designed to target specific fraud risks. In addition, other control activities might include automated exception reporting, system access controls, physical controls, and monitoring of key performance indicators.

Conclusion

The effectiveness of a fraud risk assessment will be determined by the program's design and implementation. Specific design considerations that management should consider include:

- Is management effective in delegating responsibility for implementing the organization's fraud risk assessment (e.g., compliance function, line management, internal audit) and overseeing its success?
- Do qualified individuals carry out the risk assessment process?
- Has management obtained input on risks from external sources (e.g., industry consultants, analysts, lawyers, external auditors)?
- Has management obtained input on risks from internal sources (e.g., line personnel, control owners, senior managers, board and committee members, employee hotline reports, audit reports)?
- Does the fraud risk assessment consider risks at the entity level, during each business cycle, across all business units and operational divisions, and for all significant accounts or classes of transactions?
- Has management considered the changing conditions of the entity (e.g., changed operating environment, hiring of new personnel, implementation of a new information system, a period of rapid growth, the use of new technology, the development of new products, corporate restructuring, purchase of foreign operations) when carrying out the organization's risk assessment process?
- Does the risk assessment process take into consideration the likelihood of occurrence and significance of identified risks?
- Does the risk assessment process include a procedure to facilitate the immediate notification of appropriate parties (e.g., board members) upon the occurrence of a significant event?
- Are risk assessment reports provided in a timely manner to relevant individuals (e.g., CEO, CFO, board, audit committee chair)?
- Are results of the risk assessment process verified by internal audit and reviewed by the CEO, line executives, and the audit committee?
- Are results of the risk assessment process integrated into the subsequent year's program?

Chapter 8

Prevention: Codes of Conduct, Communication, and Training

Timothy P. Hedley
Ori Ben-Chorin

n the wake of significant loss of public confidence as a result of corporate scandals, many well-managed organizations have turned their attention to controls that help *prevent* the risk of fraud and misconduct. One such control—a code of conduct and related business standards—is especially important to large, geographically diverse organizations that seek to reinforce core values, ethical expectations, and other expected behaviors that impact day-to-day operations of the business.

This chapter provides guidance on important practice conventions for code style and context that have emerged among organizations with strong ethics and compliance programs and related anti-fraud programs and controls. As a code is often the centerpiece of an organization's communication efforts on preventing fraud and misconduct, this chapter also provides guidance on how organizational communication and training efforts build on and amplify the code.

Drafting and implementing a code is typically not a simple task. Companies that face considerable challenges, particularly those doing business worldwide with tens of thousands of employees, will find that it can be a demanding exercise. In

Mr. Ben-Chorin is a director in KPMG LLP's Forensic practice in Washington, DC. He provides Fraud Risk Management services to corporate clients.
Additional contributors are Jamie M. Faulkner and Jaime G. Jue.

fact, many companies realize that drafting and implementing universally applicable standards may possibly be one of the biggest communications exercises they ever undertake.

A well-crafted code communicates on issues relating to core principles, standards of business conduct, key risk areas, and the means by which employees can seek advice and report potential fraud and misconduct. It is through such a code and related principles, standards, and guidance that organizations convey to employees the behavior expected of them on the job. Many organizations find that effective communication and training on a code do bring about results—in fact, many companies have reported that as a result of their efforts, employees are aware of their code, with the awareness being attributed to document design, clear language, and engaging presentation.

A Continuing Evolution

While codes of conduct are commonplace today, this was not always the case. In the past, organizations did not see a need for, or publish, such documents. However, matters changed in 1991 when the Federal Sentencing Guidelines were passed by Congress into law.* Among other standards, the Sentencing Guidelines call for organizations that wish to seek leniency when sentenced for corporate misconduct to have in place standards of conduct and internal control systems. These standards and control systems need to be reasonably capable of reducing the likelihood of criminal conduct and otherwise promote a culture that encourages ethical conduct as well as a commitment to compliance with the law. Furthermore, the Sentencing Guidelines urge organizations to take specific steps to effectively communicate their standards to all employees.

This minimum requirement established by the Sentencing Guidelines has been widely acknowledged to be an expectation that organizations have a code of conduct as part of an effective compliance program. What once was a "nice-to-have" is now a "must-have" in a company's arsenal of fraud prevention controls. Such is their prominence that today, codes are frequently highlighted in evaluative frameworks and regulatory pronouncements. Examples include:

- *The Sarbanes-Oxley Act of 2002 (SOX).* SOX and related rules adopted by the SEC call on publicly listed corporations to implement a code.
- *The New York Stock Exchange and NASDAQ Listing Standards.* The NYSE and NASDAQ have both adopted corporate governance rules that

---

* In 2005, the U.S. Supreme Court struck down the Sentencing Guidelines in *United States vs. Booker* and *United States vs. Fanfan*, making them advisory, rather than mandatory. However, and for all practical purposes, federal judges still consider the Sentencing Guidelines in criminal sentencing.

generally require listed companies to have in place codes for directors, officers, and employees, disclose any code waivers, and adopt mechanisms to enforce those codes.

■ *The Committee of Sponsoring Organizations of the Treadway Commission (COSO).* COSO, an evaluative framework commonly used by publicly listed companies to evaluate internal control, specifically discusses codes of conduct, including the requirement for board monitoring of management adherence to the code, use of adherence to the code in performance evaluations, and employee acknowledgment of understanding and compliance with code standards.

As a result of this critical mass of regulatory pronouncements and requirements, codes are now a staple of corporate communication and training efforts on ethics and integrity, standards of business conduct, and organizational risk areas. Recent survey data show that most large organizations today indeed have in place a widely communicated code of conduct. For example, KPMG LLP's *Integrity Survey 2008–2009*, which draws on the firsthand experiences and perceptions of more than 5,000 employees in the United States, shows that the vast majority of respondents (82 percent) reported that their organizations have a formal code that articulates the entity's principles and standards.[1] In the same survey, the vast majority of respondents (90 percent) reported their organizations provided either formal or informal communications or training on the code, and almost half (49 percent) said they experienced some formal monitoring of employee compliance with their code's standards of conduct.

Design Fundamentals

Despite the widespread adoption of codes and the significant experience gained over the years in designing and implementing such documents, many organizations continue to publish ineffective codes. As such, it should not come as a surprise that ineffective codes do little to positively influence employee behavior. In fact, more than one-third (38 percent) of KPMG's *Integrity Survey 2008–2009*[2] respondents indicated that they did not rely on their organization's code to learn about standards of conduct, and more than half (51 percent) reported that if managers and employees violated company standards, it would happen because they did not take the code seriously. Such survey results suggest that companies can do much more to enhance the effectiveness of their codes, and the inquiry into what more can be done may begin with fundamental questions such as:

■ Who should design and implement a code?
■ What types of standards should a code contain?

- When and to whom should the code be communicated?
- Where should the code be rolled out?
- How should a code's effectiveness be evaluated?

Answering these questions requires introspection and a high degree of advance preparation as the risk of rolling out a code written in isolation and put into effect in a haphazard manner is that the document will not guide employee behavior effectively or prevent fraud and misconduct.

To meet the challenge of designing and implementing an effective code that fits an organization's culture, a working group should be convened, comprised of managers with compliance responsibilities from a variety of representative functions (e.g., compliance, internal audit, legal, and security). This working group should be tasked with overseeing the design and rollout of the code, and its responsibilities may include, among others:

- Developing and prioritizing a list of key risk areas to be addressed in the code (e.g., by using data from a risk assessment process) as well as policies around such risk areas
- Comparing provisions in the code with existing policies and procedures to ensure consistency
- Determining gaps where related policies and procedures do not exist for a particular provision in the code
- Testing the code with employees at different levels and in different functions to ensure that it is readable, realistic, and relevant
- Developing realistic questions and answers to illustrate key provisions of the code and policies, with input from rank-and-file employees
- Obtaining approval from senior management and the board on the final document

Relating the Code to the Organization

A code of conduct often serves as the starting point for an ethics and compliance program and related communication and training; therefore, it is essential for the document to be clear and meaningful to every person in the organization, taking into account varying roles and responsibilities. For example, when KPMG LLP sought to reinvigorate its existing code of conduct, it formed a content advisory panel that included 26 subject matter advisors from various functions across the business who worked to make the next iteration of the code more practical and to further demonstrate how the firm's principles and values apply in the everyday working environment.

Source: KPMG LLP, *The Road to a Model Ethics and Compliance Program: Ten Things We Learned on Our Journey,* Montvale, NJ, 2009, p. 3, https://www.amr.kpmg.com/facultyportal/NR/rdonlyres/F9F8536C-CF5F-4160-918C-7C9FBF14AC9E/0/ECwhitepaper_211.pdf.

Important style and content practice conventions have emerged among organizations with effective codes. While there is no single model or absolute requirement for drafting codes of conduct, a well-designed code typically includes many of the following features:

- *High-level endorsement.* The ethical tone for an organization typically starts from the top, and a well-designed code will often include a message from a high-level individual within the organization (e.g., CEO) that underscores a personal commitment to integrity and compliance and requires employees to do the same.

At One of the World's Most Admired Companies

Jeffery Immelt, chairman and CEO of the General Electric Company, consistently voted by *Fortune* magazine as one of the world's most admired companies,[*] introduced GE's code with a personal message that asks each employee to "make a personal commitment to follow our Code of Conduct . . . Do not allow anything—not 'making the numbers,' competitive instincts or even a direct order from a superior—to compromise your commitment to integrity."[†]

- *Mission, vision, and values.* A well-designed code will typically include guidance on values, principles, or strategies aimed at shaping organizational goals and guiding business decisions and behaviors. Such

---

[*] CNNMoney.com, "World's Most Admired Companies Top 50," money.cnn.com/magazines/fortune/mostadmired/2010/full_list.
[†] General Electric Corporation, *The Spirit & the Letter,* Connecticut, 2005, p. 1, www.ge.com/files_citizenship/pdf/TheSpirit&TheLetter.pdf.

guidance can take many forms, from a simple corporate mission statement that describes the business and how it should be conducted to Johnson & Johnson's famous one-page *Credo Values*, a cornerstone of the company's culture for 60 years, which begins with the following words: "We believe our first responsibility is to the doctors, nurses, and patients, to mothers and fathers and all others who use our products and services."[3]

- *Avoiding legalese and an authoritarian tone.* A code is typically read by employees with a variety of educational backgrounds and across the company's global footprint; therefore, its text should be written in simple and concise language. Tone is also important. Experience has shown that codes that use an authoritarian or negative voice are less effective in setting organizational expectations than codes that use a generally positive, authoritative tone with which employees can more easily identify.

- *Translations.* Codes should be translated into local languages that mirror the company's geographic structure. Importantly, organizations should take care to ensure that such translations correctly present the organizational standards in a manner that takes into consideration the values and cultural norms of each overseas location.

- *Practical guidance.* Many employees learn best by following examples, and code drafters therefore should introduce realistic question-and-answer sets, recognizable scenarios, hypothetical examples, and ethical decision-making tools to illustrate key code sections. In American Express's *Employee Code of Conduct*, for example, the company provides multiple question-and-answer sets that are specific to the company and assist employees in making the right choices.[4] One such set is reproduced in its entirety below:

> Q. I do business for the Company in various countries. In one country, when a shipment of supplies arrives at the customs warehouse, it is customary there to give a small amount of money to the shipping clerk to expedite the paperwork and receive the shipment. Otherwise, it takes months to get the supplies. What should I do?
>
> A. You should not make this payment. Contact your business unit's Controller and Regional Compliance Officer for guidance.

- *Visually inviting format.* To make it more readable, authors of a code increasingly take their cues from the professional publishing world. They use professionally designed formats, along with large page margins, colorful displays, and highlighted texts to illustrate specific topics. Such efforts promote readership, usage, and understanding.

- *Internal reporting mechanisms.* Because no document can anticipate and cover all situations that may arise in the workplace, the code should also include a clear explanation of mechanisms, such as telephone or Web-based hotlines, for seeking advice and reporting misconduct, along with guidance on the organization's policies for anonymous reporting, confidentiality, and protection from retaliation.

At Another of the World's Most Admired Companies

3M, another of *Fortune* magazine's top 20 most admired companies,* provides a wide range of options that employees can use to raise a concern or report misconduct. Employees may contact their direct supervisor or manager; the company's legal counsel; a Web-based reporting site operated by a third-party vendor; a toll-free, confidential, and anonymous reporting hotline; the director of business conduct and compliance; a local human resources manager; or the company's general auditor. To guide employees through these options, 3M also provides an interactive online training video, located on the same Web site as its conduct policies.[†]

- *Enforcement mechanisms.* Companies should also include within their codes an explanation of the means for enforcing the code through disciplinary measures, including management accountability for the misconduct of employees. For example, the *Code of Business Conduct and Ethics* at FedEx Corporation instructs that the company "will also discipline managers who fail to exercise appropriate supervision and oversight, thereby allowing such behavior to go undetected."[5]
- *Code content.* Companies should develop code standards based upon the organization's key risk areas, which can be identified through a risk assessment process. Although regulatory and evaluative frameworks provide little guidance on the specific standards that a code of conduct should contain, SOX Section 406 provides some direction in this respect. For example, Section 406 describes the standards that should be contained in a code of ethics for senior financial officers (which applies to the company's principal financial officer, controller or principal

---

* CNNMoney.com, "World's Most Admired Companies Top 50," money.cnn.com/magazines/fortune/mostadmired/2010/full_list.
† 3M, *Reporting a Business Conduct Concern*, 3M Web session, 2010, www.3m.com/busconducttrain.

accounting officer, and other persons performing similar functions) as written standards that are reasonably designed to deter wrongdoing and to promote:

- o Honest and ethical conduct, including the ethical handling of actual or apparent conflicts of interest between personal and professional relationships
- o Full, fair, accurate, timely, and understandable disclosure in reports and documents that a registrant files with or submits to the SEC and in other public communications
- o Compliance with applicable governmental laws, rules, and regulations[6]

Additionally, for SEC filers Form 20F[7] promotes:

- o The prompt internal reporting of violations of the code to an appropriate person or persons identified in the code
- o Accountability for adherence to the code

- *Code organization.* Experience has shown that organizing code standards into topical and stakeholder sections makes the content more readable, relevant, and effective for employees. The following serves as an example:
  - o Overview (e.g., CEO message, introduction, mission, vision, values, and questions to ask before acting)
  - o How to report concerns (e.g., seeking advice and reporting misconduct confidentially and anonymously by providing a hotline, ensuring no retaliation, and contacting compliance personnel)
  - o Commitments to customers and the marketplace (e.g., offering gifts and other business courtesies, and antitrust)
  - o Commitments to shareholders and creditors (e.g., safeguarding business records, safeguarding business resources, avoiding conflicts of interest, and avoiding insider trading)
  - o Commitments to employees (e.g., maintaining a workplace free of harassment and discriminatory behavior, maintaining a drug- and alcohol-free workplace, and providing for health and safety)
  - o Commitments to suppliers (e.g., fair competition and accepting gifts and other business courtesies)
  - o Commitments to the community and the public (e.g., interacting with government officials, doing business outside the United States, and protecting the environment)
  - o Available resources (e.g., Intranet Web site, telephone numbers, and e-mails of relevant resources)
- *Adjunct topical guidance.* Companies have also found that because some standards of conduct apply only to a small population of employees, it

makes little sense to include detailed discussion of such standards in the code. For instance, a manufacturing organization with little presence in overseas markets may not need to include detailed guidance on the anti-bribery provisions of the U.S. Foreign Corrupt Practices Act; such detail may cause employees who are in job functions that do not carry this kind of risk to disengage from learning about key risks in their own areas of responsibility. In such a case, the company's code should provide a brief description of the company's standards with respect to the risks at hand, adding links to additional resources where more detailed guidance can be found. The additional resources may include code companion policies or topical supplements that are distributed according to the needs of particular job functions.

- *Code distribution.* While some organizations choose to distribute the code only to certain managerial grades and above (e.g., companies that have a large hourly workforce where employee turnover is high), a well-communicated code is typically made available to all relevant employees, regardless of rank. At a minimum, a code should be provided to all who serve in management roles, have significant discretionary authority, or serve in compliance-sensitive functions such as accounting, finance, sales, procurement, or political affairs. Note that some organizations also choose to provide their codes of conduct to third parties, such as temporary workers, suppliers, subcontractors, agents, and joint venture partners. Moreover, organizations that are required to comply with SOX must now make their codes publicly available, for example, on their Internet Web sites or as exhibits to annual reports filed with the SEC.

- *Code certification.* As part of their implementation of the code, many companies also include a method for employees to periodically certify or acknowledge that they have received the code, agree to abide by the standards contained therein, and pledge to disclose any known or suspected code violations. Such a process can also help monitor distribution of the code and put employees on notice that they are required to read the standards contained therein. While code certifications have historically been paper-based, companies often seek to have their employees complete such certifications online, via the organization's intranet. A well-managed and documented certification process demonstrates an effort to implement the code. However, companies that do not accompany this process with well-designed and engaging communications run the risk of having their employees treat the certification process as an annual "check-the-box" exercise.

Evaluating a Code's Effectiveness

While many companies spend a significant amount of resources to design and implement a code of conduct, they typically expend considerably fewer resources in determining whether their code is actually effective in achieving its purpose. All too often, a code is rolled out with much fanfare, only to languish on a dusty workspace shelf. It is therefore important to periodically measure the impact that the code is having on employees in order to obtain critical data that can help enhance the effectiveness of the document in guiding employee behavior.

Such an evaluation can generally be accomplished using a variety of tools, including interviews, focus groups, and a statistically valid employee survey, and companies are typically well served by choosing several of these information-gathering methods to augment their assessment efforts. Regardless of the method used, the inquiry should center on determining, among others, the degree to which employees are familiar with, and rely upon, the code to guide them in their day-to-day activities, as well as their perceptions of whether the code is taken seriously by company managers and employees.

Surveys of employee perception and attitudes are especially helpful in substantiating and qualifying data gathered through interviews and focus groups. For example, the majority of respondents to KPMG's *Integrity Survey 2008–2009* indicated that they are familiar with their organization's code of conduct (83 percent).[8] A further 62 percent reported that they rely on the code to learn about their organization's standards of conduct, and 71 percent related that they have received information and guidance to help them understand their code.[9]

Communications and Training

Drafting and distributing organizational standards, policies, and procedures is typically not effective on its own in helping employees understand how they are required to comply with laws, regulations, and internal standards of conduct. As a result, companies often design and implement communication and training efforts to help enhance employee awareness of organizational risks and increase their ability to identify, assess, and report such risks, as well as enforce an appropriate tone across the organization that inappropriate behavior will not be tolerated.

Employee View on Communication and Training

The results of KPMG's *Integrity Survey 2008–2009* show that employees typically have favorable views on the communication and training they received on their organization's standards of conduct. In fact, the vast majority of respondents said that such communication and training were:

- clear and easy to understand (94 percent)
- effective in guiding their decisions and behaviors at work (91 percent)
- provided to them when they needed it (90 percent)

Source: Sarbanes-Oxley Act of 2002, Public Law 107-204, 107th Congress, 15 USC 7264 (July 30, 2002), www.gpo.gov/fdsys/pkg/PLAW-107publ204/pdf/PLAW-107publ204.pdf.

The remainder of this chapter sets out design and implementation considerations for organizations that seek to have in place effective communication and training programs.

The Organizational Imperative

One reason that communication and training, and particularly the latter, are sometimes seen as a low priority is that they can be expensive to design and implement.

The Cost of Training

In a recent benchmarking survey, two-thirds of respondent in-house corporate counsels said that their organizations spend up to $250,000 annually on ethics and compliance training, an increase of 17 percent from 2005. While smaller organizations may tend to spend much less, only 10 percent of companies with more than 25,000 employees spend less than $50,000 a year. In fact, most organizations that large spend at least $500,000, and more than a third spend more than $1 million annually on their ethics and compliance training.

Source: Robert Celaschi, "A Question of Compliance," *Boston Business Journal*, February 15, 2008, boston.bizjournals.com/boston/stories/2008/02/18/focus1.html.

In addition, communication and training are considered by some to be low priority because they do not provide readily apparent and direct productivity benefits and they take away time from day-to-day operations. However, training initiatives are crucial to the success of an organization's efforts to prevent, detect, and respond to fraud and misconduct. In fact, making employees aware of their obligations to control the risk of fraud and misconduct arguably *begins* with effective communication and training. Those organizations that do not provide employees with effective training run the risk of having a workforce that does not take fraud and misconduct prevention seriously. This was illustrated by the results of KPMG's *Integrity Survey 2008–2009* in which more than half of respondents (51 percent) reported that a driving factor for employee misconduct is a lack of familiarity with the organizational standards that apply to their jobs.[10]

The Legislative Imperative

Various sources of regulatory guidance and evaluative frameworks serve as critical points of reference for organizations that seek to communicate and train employees on the standards that apply to their jobs. For example, the COSO framework requires that an evaluation of internal control must seek to understand whether or not effective communication occurs in a broad sense—flowing upstream, downstream, and across the organization—with all personnel receiving clear messages from senior management that control responsibilities must be taken seriously. All personnel must also understand their own role vis-à-vis the organization's internal control system, as well as their individual activities in relation to the work of others. Such communication must be effective and must occur with external parties, including customers, suppliers, regulators, and shareholders.[11]

Moreover, the Sentencing Guidelines (discussed in greater detail earlier in this chapter) also call on organizations to take reasonable steps to communicate, periodically and in a practical manner, their standards and procedures, as well as other aspects of the organization's ethics and compliance program, by conducting effective training programs and otherwise disseminating information to the organization's relevant stakeholders, including:

- Governing authority[*]
- High-level personnel[†]
- Substantial authority personnel[‡]
- Employees
- Agents

---

* "Governing authority" means (1) the board of directors or (2) if the organization does not have a board of directors, the highest-level governing body of the organization.
† "High-level personnel" of the organization refers to individuals who have substantial control over the organization or who have a substantial role in the making of policy within the organization. The term includes a director; an executive officer; an individual in charge of a major business or functional unit of the organization, such as sales, administration, or finance; and an individual with substantial ownership interest.
‡ "Substantial authority personnel" means individuals who, within the scope of their authority, exercise a substantial measure of discretion in acting on behalf of an organization. The term includes high-level personnel of the organization, individuals who exercise substantial supervisory authority (e.g., a plant manager, a sales manager), and any other individuals who, although not part of an organization's management, nevertheless exercise substantial discretion when acting within the scope of their authority (e.g., an individual with authority in an organization to negotiate or set price levels or an individual authorized to negotiate or approve significant contracts). Whether an individual falls within this category must be determined on a case-by-case basis.

The Compliance Program Annual Report

Developing and publicizing to all relevant stakeholders an annual report on an organization's compliance and ethics program is one of the ways in which an organization can help fulfill the Sentencing Guidelines' criteria for communicating to stakeholders about standards, procedures, and other aspects of the compliance program. For instance, such a report can explain (or in some cases demystify) the various attributes of anti-fraud programs and controls. Consider a hotline reporting process that employees may not fully understand—they may want to know what happens when a report is made to the hotline. Are wrongdoers really punished? Do the actions of senior executives match their words?

KPMG LLP's annual *Ethics and Compliance Report* illustrates how such hotline issues are investigated and resolved. Among others, it discloses the number of reports that were received during the year by the firm's ethics and compliance function, ombudsman, and hotline; includes a section that describes how reports are handled from intake to resolution; and describes how actual reports have been handled and resolved. The report is distributed to all personnel and made available on the firm's internal and external Web sites.[*]

Importantly, such an annual report may also be especially helpful for organizations that find themselves in the unenviable position of having to demonstrate the effectiveness of their compliance program to government regulators or prosecutors (e.g., in order to avoid prosecution or receive "credit" for having an effective program in place). Because a government investigation into potential wrongdoing may happen years after the suspected offense, as a practical matter, substantiating the state of the program in years past may prove to be a difficult, if not impossible, task. As such, having on hand documented annual program reports, if sufficiently comprehensive, can help overcome the challenge of proving that the organization had an effective program at the time of the alleged offense.[†]

---

[*] KPMG LLP, *The Road to a Model Ethics and Compliance Program* (see note 6), 10; KPMG LLP, *Ethics and Compliance Report 2008: It Starts with You: A Continuing Conversation on Ethics and Integrity,* Montvale, NJ, 2009, us.kpmg.com/microsite/Attachments/2008/Ethics_and_Compliance_2008.pdf.

[†] Jeffrey M. Kaplan, "Earning Program 'Credit' in a Criminal Investigation-The Role of the C&E Annual Report," *Corporate Compliance Insights,* July 29, 2009, www.corporatecomplianceinsights.com/2009/role-of-compliance-and-ethics-annual-report-in-earning-program-credit-during-criminal-investigation.

However, it is important to note that communicating with and training individuals identically in all the above job functions will likely result in inefficiency, lack of focus, and poor understanding. Instead, organizations should tailor their communication and training efforts to individuals' respective roles and responsibilities. For example, directors and executives have different communication and training needs than current employees, who, in turn, have different needs than new employees:

- *Directors.* To help them practice their oversight responsibilities, members of the board of directors and its committees should receive regular and periodic information on the fundamental design, intended benefits, and efficacy of controls in place to prevent, detect, and respond to fraud and misconduct. They should also receive periodic updates on relevant regulatory frameworks and practices.
- *Executives.* An organization's executives should also receive much of the information provided to directors, but importantly, because they are expected to set the ethical tone at the top for the organization, they also should receive communication and training to help them succeed in the crucial job of fostering an organizational culture that values workplace ethics and integrity.
- *New personnel.* Starting with orientation, the organization has the ability to set the tone for a desired corporate culture, and management should take advantage of this window of opportunity. Specifically, the organization should help new employees understand the specific rules that apply to performing their jobs, as well as the resources available to them to answer questions or report problems.
- *Current personnel.* Existing employees may present a greater hurdle with respect to communication and training, as they are typically very familiar with the organization and have usually developed their own perceptions. Accordingly, communication and training should be frequent and regular, and may need to be introduced by senior management with explanations of why the topics discussed are relevant and important.

Communicating and training in such a focused way helps the organization ensure that the right individuals receive the right messages at the right time.

Leadership Education and Training

Ben Heineman, the former chief legal officer of GE and close advisor to Jack Welch and Jeffery Immelt, relates that at GE, the target population for leadership training is made up of the company's top 3,900 individuals: 200

officers, 400 senior executives, and 3,300 executives. The company's initial leadership training lasts at least a full day, and each person is also provided with a leadership self-assessment tool. Developed in-house, the tool asks leaders questions along six dimensions: their personal engagement, risk assessment, mitigation, reporting concerns, education and training, and high-performance-with-high-integrity communication strategy.

Source: Ben W. Heineman, Jr., *High Performance with High Integrity,* Boston: Harvard Business School Publishing, 2008, p. 85.

The Tone at the Top Also Comes from the Middle

There is little question that it is imperative for top executives to set the ethical tone for their organization, remaining knowledgeable about ethical issues and approachable if employees have questions or wish to deliver bad news. But although it is natural to look at the organization's efforts to prevent, detect, and respond to fraud and misconduct as originating "from the top," it is also very important to understand, and not underestimate, the impact that others such as frontline supervisors and middle managers have on setting the ethical tone of the organization "at the middle." After all, employees typically interact with front-line supervisors and middle managers far more than they do with senior executives, and therefore, the former have far more opportunity to drive ethical culture. Recent survey data bear out this premise, showing that the tone set by such middle managers is likely to be far more effective in influencing employees. For instance, the results of KPMG's *Integrity Survey 2008–2009* showed that:

- A majority of employees would be comfortable seeking advice and counsel from a supervisor (79 percent) or local managers (64 percent), rather than senior executives (47 percent).[12]
- A majority of employees would be comfortable reporting misconduct to a supervisor (78 percent) or a local manager (61 percent), rather than senior executives (43 percent) or board members (32 percent).[13]

Tone at the Middle

When KPMG LLP conducted a series of employee focus groups as part of the continual process of updating the firm's compliance program, feedback from the process indicated that immediate supervisors or peers were, in fact, the individuals most employees would turn to first in the event of a potential problem or ethical question. For example, feedback from the focus groups showed that the firm's third- and fourth-year associates were critical in setting the ethical tone and driving leadership's ethics and compliance messages through the organization. They may not have even realized that they play this role, demonstrating which behaviors were positive and which would not be tolerated. In fact, they created an environment that had no less impact than the messages coming from senior leadership. This insight changed the way KPMG thought about the structure of the firm's compliance training. The firm recognized that to create a culture of ethics and compliance, additional training and support had to be provided to middle managers so that they would be able to access more resources and become more effective role models.

Source: KPMG LLP, *The Road to a Model Ethics and Compliance Program: Ten Things We Learned on Our Journey,* Montvale, NJ, 2009, p. 5, https://www.amr.kpmg.com/facultyportal/ NR/rdonlyres/F9F8536C-CF5F-4160-918C-7C9FBF14AC9E/0/ECwhitepaper_211.pdf.

Developing an Effective Communication and Training Strategy

Organizations should consider developing a wide-ranging strategy and plan that calls for frequent, relevant, appropriate, and effective communication and training for all relevant organizational stakeholders in both general and topic-specific risk areas. Such a detailed strategy and plan often takes careful thought, planning, and coordination but, when done well, can help ensure that specific individuals receive communications and training in areas most relevant to their job functions, that gaps or overlaps in coverage are minimized, and that staff time and other resources are used more efficiently. In preparing such a plan, the organization should take into consideration, among others, the . . .

- results of a prioritized risk assessment effort that informs on key fraud and misconduct risks that are appropriate for communications and training
- various topics for potential communications and training (e.g., whistleblower mechanisms, standards of conduct, and related policies and procedures)
- training needs of specific individuals based upon their job function and risk areas

An important part of the organization's comprehensive communication and training plan is determining the types of actual training modules that should be developed. For instance, training modules can be developed in the following basic categories:

- *General awareness training.* All new and existing employees need to understand the organization's code of conduct and related standards, as well as resources, programs, and controls dedicated to preventing, detecting, and responding to fraud and misconduct (e.g., as embodied by the organization's ethics and compliance program and the resources available for promoting compliance with applicable laws and regulations). Such training should also be tailored to the group being trained to emphasize those areas most important to that group's particular job function and, to the extent possible, should be integrated into existing job skills training.
- *Topic-specific training.* Because it is not appropriate to train all employees on all risk areas, the organization should seek to develop topic-specific training events that are tailored to job function and individual risk areas. The applicable topics for such training, including its frequency and length, should be determined based upon the results of the organization's risk assessment, with functional areas that have relatively higher employee turnover rates receiving more frequent training throughout the year to help ensure that all employees are trained.
- *Refresher training.* Refresher training should be offered to employees in subsequent years and should be less comprehensive than the training event that was originally provided to employees. Organizations take a variety of approaches to providing such training, but the key to refresher training is that it occur each year and serve to remind employees of their responsibilities to adhere to the organization's standards of business conduct and relevant laws and regulations.

Developing Communication and Training Content

After an organization has developed its communication and training strategy and plan, it can then begin developing actual communication and training that more effectively engage employees. Although a one-size-fits-all approach is discouraged, certain leading practice conventions have emerged that are influential in helping stakeholders connect with the desired messages. These include, among others:

- *Integrating organizational values.* Communication and training efforts can often be enhanced by tying them to organizational core values and goals. Doing so can make messages less dry and improve crucial employee buy-in.

- *Publicizing reporting mechanisms.* To ensure that all relevant stakeholders know about the existence and purpose of the organization's internal reporting mechanisms, communication and training should frequently mention and describe the hotline and any other internal reporting mechanisms, including policies regarding confidentiality, nonretaliation, and acceptance of anonymous calls.

- *Using realistic examples.* One of the more important components of ensuring effective communication and training is the use of realistic examples and question-and-answer sections to illustrate key points. While some employees intuitively grasp how an abstract policy applies to their job responsibilities, others will not be able to do so no matter how well written the policy. Often, when an employee is provided with a realistic example of how a policy could be applied, the abstract words become meaningful for the first time. Training organizers should also encourage questions and provide ample time during training events for employees to ask them.

Getting the Message to Stick

The importance of providing realistic examples in a variety of formats cannot be overemphasized since, overwhelmingly, employees learn abstract concepts more effectively through such means. Individuals involved in designing communication and training should keep in mind the cognitive theory of multimedia learning, which is based on three central assumptions:

- There are two separate and distinct channels that individuals use to process all information: the auditory and the visual (in other words, using words and pictures together is more effective than using words alone).
- There is a limit on the amount of data that each channel can carry (in other words, trainees can only process a limited amount of data at any one given time).
- Learning is a process of filtering, selecting, and organizing, and its success is, at least in part, influenced by the individual's ability to integrate new information along with existing prior knowledge.

Source: Richard E. Mayer and Roxana Moreno, *A Cognitive Theory of Multimedia Learning: Implications for Design Principles*, Santa Barbara, CA: University of California, 1998, www.unm.edu/~moreno/PDFS/chi.pdf.

- *Tracking attendance.* In order to ensure that relevant individuals are indeed completing the training courses assigned to them, the organization should consider monitoring individual training requirements, tracking training attendance, and requiring all trainees to pass a subject matter test in order to complete individual training requirements.
- *Ensuring readability.* The downfall of many communication and training initiatives is that they are written in language that is too complex for an average reader to understand. As such, all key communication and training tools should undergo some sort of readability test to help ensure that they are readily understandable to their intended audience (for instance, a memo intended for senior management regarding compliance with tax laws should be written at a different level than a message on responding to government investigations that is intended for all employees). Examples of ways to assess readability include . . .
  - forming focus groups around the question of readability
  - soliciting employee feedback regarding comprehension
  - having employees ask their teenage children to read and explain the materials
  - utilizing a computer program to determine reading level
- *Providing translations.* Because some employees may not understand the local country's primary language fluently or may not be able to read because of illiteracy or handicap, efforts should be made to determine where such employees reside within the organization. For example, if a U.S.-based organization determines that employees whose primary language is Spanish are highly concentrated within a certain department, departmental meetings can be conducted in English and Spanish for each key communication. As such, the organization's training manager may . . .
  - identify non-English-speaking employees, possibly through the human resources department
  - alert department heads to any reading or language difficulties of such employees so that the department heads can accommodate their specific needs
  - provide interpreters to carefully explain the contents of key communications
- *Using multiple methods.* Employees have different learning styles and receptivity patterns, and good communication and training should employ creative and engaging methods to help keep the message fresh. Examples of types of communication that can be utilized include the following, among many others:
  - Internal and external mail
  - Group or town hall meetings

○ Articles in newsletters
○ Speeches by senior executives
○ Bulletin board postings
○ Voice mail messages
○ Letters and memos
○ Code of conduct
○ Paycheck stuffers
○ Videos, posters, cafeteria table cards
○ Wallet cards with the hotline number and core values

Examples of different types of training methods include live training, interactive computer-based modules, CD-ROMs, and workbooks. Also, different training techniques can be used to account for different learning patterns as well as to keep the training interesting and fresh. These may include role playing, case studies, and quizzes.

The Cutting (Digital) Edge of Training

Increasingly, organizations are seeking out advanced technologies to provide employees with new and more effective training environments. Because today's employees are typically comfortable in accessing digital media on the Internet (e.g., Facebook, MySpace, and YouTube), there are few barriers to moving employee training into the digital realm, beyond the now-common computer-based training module. Drawing on recent research, which shows that adults retain 10 percent of what is read, 20 percent of what is heard, and 80 percent of what is experienced, emerging and innovative training technologies include:

■ Epistemic gaming, which are complex and compelling computer games that encourage employees to reflect on chosen issues and engage in a decision-making process in an environment that creates an emotional connection in users and provides them with the sense that they are in control of the process (and the game). One organization that is reportedly leading the way in this educational technique is the U.K. Ministry of Defence, where games are often used to assign users to tasks in a simulated exercise that helps activate knowledge correctly.
■ Second ("Virtual") Life, where companies can train employees in a highly detailed virtual-reality world inhabited by "avatars,"

which are three-dimensional alter egos for computer users. Through using their avatars in prebuilt digital environments, companies can help employees gain knowledge in a variety of subject matters. Technically, there are no barriers to developing a virtual world. For instance, a large food manufacturer has recently created a virtual supermarket where employees can interact with suppliers to learn about relevant regulations and processes.

Source: LRN, *How to Effectively Leverage New Technologies and Approaches to Engage Your Workforce on Ethics and Compliance*, Los Angeles: LRN, 2008, www.lrn.com/docs/LRN-POV-technology-education-2008.pdf.

■ *Evaluating effectiveness.* After an organization has developed its communication and training strategy and plan, it can then begin developing actual communication and training procedures that are tailored to employees' respective roles and responsibilities and that engage them in an effective manner. To determine the effectiveness of the communications and training efforts, the organization can conduct . . .
   ○ a trend analysis of the number of hotline calls received immediately after a training session on the organization's code of conduct or after an article is published in the newsletter regarding the hotline
   ○ a survey to measure comprehension of communication and training messages
   ○ a survey to determine which communication and training vehicles employees utilize most frequently or find more helpful to facilitate the learning process

Conclusion

In summary, regulatory frameworks such as the Sentencing Guidelines and its recent revisions, as well as leading practices that organizations have found to be effective within the framework of the Sentencing Guidelines, have all added impetus to the need for organizations to have in place codes of conduct and related standards that define acceptable business practices, are built around the organization's core values, and provide employees with guidance on identified fraud and misconduct risks. Such codes should also be accompanied by effective communication and training that not only enhance the organization's efforts to prevent fraud and misconduct, but also provide a sound rationale for meeting the evolving needs of the business.

Chapter 9

Prevention: Corporate Intelligence

Laura E. Durkin

Effective prevention, detection, and response procedures share a common denominator—the requirement of information and intelligence as a basis for sound decision making. In the digital information environment, publicly available information via the Internet or third-party databases is a critical tool. Intelligence gathering requires the identification of relevant data, establishment of the facts, review of the applicability of these facts, and analysis of their implications. For purposes of our discussion, "corporate intelligence" will be used as the umbrella term for myriad applications related to research and information gathering, including background investigations; mergers and acquisitions (M&A) due diligence; reputation and integrity assessments; third-party, vendor, and employee reviews; know your customer (KYC) procedures; and competitive intelligence. No matter what term is used to describe the process, the bottom line is typically the same—the investigator-analyst seeks to answer such questions as who, what, when, where, how, and why.

Anyone with access to the Internet has the essential tool with which to obtain a universe of publicly available information emanating from all corners of the world. This boom in available information has made it possible for individuals and companies to identify data sources that offer personal, business,

Additional contributors are Nina K. D'Arcangelo and Joshua Riley.
Ms. Durkin is a managing director in KPMG LLP's Forensic practice in New York, NY. She leads our national Corporate Intelligence services and delivers Anti–Money Laundering services to corporate clients.

governmental, and political information in a large percentage of the world's countries. However, the spiraling number of online sources has created some issues: The sheer volume of information, misinformation, opinions, propaganda, rumors, and innuendo found on the Internet and in the media has often blurred the distinction between fact and fiction. In a world of white noise and potentially inaccurate information from thousands of inputs, the importance of credible intelligence gathering, adequate source assessment, and appropriate analysis rises exponentially.

This chapter will provide an overview of the elements and varying focuses of corporate intelligence, discuss the regulatory and business drivers in today's market, examine how intelligence may be applied to specific business decisions, proffer some guidance on where to go to obtain relevant information, and highlight considerations when conducting intelligence-gathering exercises in the United States and around the world.

Drivers

The transformative global events of the early twenty-first century—the internationalization of business, well-financed terror attacks around the world, and the economic implosion that laid bare fraud and misconduct—have resulted in the need for greater vigilance by governments, regulators, corporations, and individuals to protect borders as well as financial systems and to ensure the integrity of business transactions. The resulting global groundswell of legislative and regulatory mandates, internal investigations, corporate control reviews, and more stringent business policies aimed at increasing security and improving decision making has made corporate intelligence a critical part of a company's arsenal.

Sound business practices should impel a company to obtain and assess information about its employees, partners, vendors, distributors, customers, and government relationships. The type and the level of information required vary with the specific business need as well as regulatory mandate. Some regulations and laws are quite prescriptive about what information a company must obtain, while others provide more general guidance on what a company must do or understand about its transactions or relationships.

In addition to legal and regulatory mandates, a company should consider the level of risk associated with its critical business relationships. At the inception of a new relationship or during the course of an ongoing relationship, companies should continually assess the risks and consider the likelihood of economic or reputational damage stemming from new or hidden facts or events that could affect the integrity of its operations.

Legal and Regulatory Mandates

The main drivers behind the increasing need for effective corporate intelligence include:

- Federal Sentencing Guidelines
- USA PATRIOT Act
- Anti-corruption laws
- Sanctions and debarment laws and regulations
- Environmental, labor, and employment regulations

Federal Sentencing Guidelines. The Sentencing Guidelines cite an effective compliance and ethics program as a potential mitigating factor for an organization that has been convicted of a federal crime. Chapter 8, Part B2.1(a)(1), states that to have an effective compliance and ethics program, "an organization shall (1) exercise due diligence to prevent and detect criminal conduct."[1] Without defining or prescribing the due diligence to be undertaken, the Sentencing Guidelines state that under an effective program, the organization will conduct due diligence on senior personnel to ensure the individuals have not engaged in illegal or unethical activities.* In this context, due diligence refers to a background investigation.

USA PATRIOT Act. The USA PATRIOT Act imposes on regulated industries, such as financial services, broad new standards of scrutiny in accepting customers and business partners and in processing financial transactions. The act mandates proactive vigilance and due diligence requirements for banks and a broad array of other financial institutions, requiring that they "know" their customers: who they are, what they are transacting for, and where their money comes from.

Anti-corruption Laws. The U.S. Foreign Corrupt Practices Act (FCPA) is intended to prohibit U.S. persons, entities, and issuers from giving or offering to give anything of value to any foreign official. U.S. issuers, foreign nationals, and nonpublic U.S. companies, including managers, employees, and agents, cannot pay or offer to pay monies in order to obtain business or influence a foreign official. The law specifies the prohibition of payments to foreign

---

* Federal Sentencing Guidelines, §8B2.1(b)(3). "The organization shall use reasonable efforts not to include within the substantial authority personnel of the organization any individual whom the organization knew, or should have known through the exercise of due diligence, has engaged in illegal activities or other conduct inconsistent with an effective compliance and ethics program."

officials, political party members or candidates, and persons who thereafter would pay a foreign official on behalf of the U.S. company to secure business or other favorable action.

Sanctions and Debarment Laws and Regulations. U.S. and foreign companies that do business with and in the United States have obligations to be compliant with U.S. economic and trade sanctions. The Office of Foreign Assets Control (OFAC) of the U.S. Department of the Treasury administers and enforces sanctions based on U.S. foreign policy and national security goals against targeted foreign countries and regimes; terrorists; international narcotics traffickers; those engaged in activities related to the proliferation of weapons of mass destruction; and other threats to national security, foreign policy, or the economy of the United States.[2] Additionally, other U.S. departments and agencies, as well as those of other countries and supranational bodies, have their own sanctions or banned lists, and companies within certain industries or working within relevant jurisdictions must consult such lists to maintain compliance.

Environmental, Labor, and Employment Regulations. Around the world, there are a myriad of legal regimes that legislate and regulate how a business operates; a company incorporated and based in the United States with subsidiaries operating in Southeast Asia and transporting globally would need to be aware of a variety of laws. Environmental considerations can include emissions; waste production and storage; water usage, pollution, and treatment; erosion and runoff; chemical and toxin exposures; indigenous land rights; resource restoration; and historic damage, which could become a headache for successor owners. Local labor and employment practices should also be reviewed to see if a company's standards are consistent and compliant and are considered in context with the regulations of the company's home jurisdiction.

Risk Tolerance

Laws and regulations alone are not the only drivers of the need for corporate intelligence. The globalization of business and the risks associated with unfamiliar business relationships and remote locations are also key drivers of corporate intelligence. As enterprises entrust critical aspects of their businesses to factories, subsidiaries, back-office operations, suppliers, agents, and intermediaries that may be thousands of miles or continents away, their vulnerability and their risk rise concomitantly. Integrity assessments of important business partners very often include examination of the reputation, business history, and potentially related parties of a business partner. This can include a review of funding sources associated with a business relationship, as well as the way an entity and its managers conduct their business in a given jurisdiction.

As global markets and financial systems become increasingly intertwined, an enterprise should understand and be prepared for additional and, in some cases, potentially conflicting sets of laws and regulations in multiple jurisdictions. Companies seeking to obtain information from other jurisdictions or move that information across borders need to be cognizant of data privacy and data transport regulations. Companies often consider fresh legal input with each new cross-border business venture or data transfer.

Corporate Intelligence Techniques

Legal and regulatory drivers and risk considerations exist at all stages of a business relationship, including the period prior to entering a partnership or hiring an employee, through the full term of a business relationship, until the relationship has been severed. Consequently, there are applications of effective corporate intelligence in all phases of effective control: prior to the relationship, at the fraud and risk prevention stage; for the duration of a relationship, at the detection stage; and when a relationship is in crisis, at the response stage.

Subjects of Research

For each stage of a relationship, the type of intelligence that is gathered—and the depth to which a company will dig—will vary, and the focus of information gathering and analysis will often be quite specific to a company and the unique factors associated with its corporate intelligence needs. For example, a preacquisition integrity due diligence exercise in an emerging market would likely focus on an assessment of jurisdiction-specific risk factors including adherence to rule of law and risk of bribery and anti-corruption, whereas a preemployment screening for a U.S.-based national would likely involve a criminal and civil litigation background check and education and professional credentials validation. However, whether conducting a deep dive or a higher-level review, intelligence-gathering exercises typically seek the same outputs: identification of risk factors that can impact sound decision making by a company.

To successfully identify these risk factors, intelligence analysts use desktop research tools and, when warranted, conduct interviews, review e-mails and court and corporate records, conduct site visits, and use local resources to develop appropriate reporting.

The focus of a given corporate intelligence review will generally seek information about some or all of the following:

- Corporate activity, operations, and stability
- Senior managers and beneficial owners of an entity
- Source of funding for a transaction
- Reputation and integrity of an entity and its managers and owners
- U.S. and global regulatory compliance and violations or sanctions
- Prior or current investigations or inquiries into potential criminal conduct
- Civil litigation histories—both as plaintiff and as defendant
- Related parties
- Bankruptcies, judgments, liens, and liabilities
- Jurisdictional risk
- Intellectual property and patent claims
- Professional licensing, education, employment history, honors claimed, and business and personal associations
- Compliance with a specific goal, such as Shariah,* sustainability, or green initiatives

Such lines of inquiry can be applied to almost any subject, whether a natural person or entity, but only to the extent that information is available in a relevant jurisdiction, which can vary greatly. Common research subjects can include:

- Business partners
- Joint venture, private equity, or hedge fund investors
- Vendors and suppliers
- Third-party distributors or agents
- C-suite officers, directors, and new employees
- Subjects of investigative review, including employees and external parties

Intelligence-gathering exercises seek to focus on obtaining information that is relevant and appropriate, and a well-crafted exercise should go only as deep as is warranted for the task at hand. The following is an example of a situation where early intelligence gathering may have proved beneficial.

---

* Shariah is the fundamental religious concept of Islam; in addition to religious and other guidelines, there are guidelines for the conduct of business including lending and borrowing. "Shariah-compliant" finance adheres to the guidance of Shariah law to live within Islamic principles.

Thumbnail Case Study

In mid-2008, before the U.S. economy was traumatized by the "Great Recession," a real estate holding company reached out for investigative support when a Florida-based resort investment went belly-up and more than $100 million in loans evaporated. Subsequent investigative due diligence found that the owner of the resort property had created an intricate web of related entities and parties that had registered mortgage claims against the same property, shortly before the cash infusions of the holding company. The monies were used to "repay" earlier loans. The resort owner—not a U.S. national—disappeared abroad. Further investigation revealed he had been investigated overseas for arms trafficking to Syria, and he appeared on more than one country's watch list. An early background investigation of the resort owner would likely have identified these issues.

Source: KPMG LLP, 2010.

Scope of Corporate Intelligence

The scope of an information-gathering exercise is dependent upon the issues and risks associated with the relationship, executive position, jurisdiction of operation, industry, regulatory mandate, etc. The depth of research is also guided by the nature, importance, and closeness of the relationship. From this information, one can infer risk: the closer the relationship, the higher the potential risk associated with entering or maintaining such a relationship. For example, an entity based in Malaysia that provides piece goods for a U.S.-based brand-name manufacturer may be a small player in the supply chain, geographically distant and off the radar screen. But if the Malaysian entity carries the manufacturer's name, is partly owned by the manufacturer, and gets hit with accusations of severe child-labor violations in the global media, the reputational damage will likely accrue on the U.S. brand name.

Another factor to keep in mind when considering how extensive an information-gathering exercise needs to be is the volume of the data involved. For example, an organization that onboards several thousand new employees each year should balance its preemployment screening accordingly, placing greater emphasis on the C-level executives and others entrusted with critical and fiduciary responsibilities within the organization, and less on entry-level employees. Additionally, one should consider the distance of a relationship from company headquarters, either physically or through multiple layers of supply or reporting. A company setting up a manufacturing operation two continents away in a country where it has not previously operated should consider a broad review, ranging from deal specifics to the stability and corruption risk of local government, the integrity of the import-export structures, the security of the supply chain, and the possibility that related parties are acting in concert to defraud or take financial advantage of the new operation.

While a company should make a sincere effort to "know" all its relationships, there are reasonable limitations to the scope of information to be gathered, and these limitations have been recognized by regulators and other authorities. Above and beyond the mandatory and prescribed information points identified by relevant government agencies, companies should employ a risk-based approach to information gathering and analysis of a given relationship.

Technique

Before undertaking a corporate intelligence exercise, consider what and how much information is appropriate, relevant, and obtainable. Cost factors and time constraints may be as important to consider as regulatory and business drivers. An initial, risk-based assessment of the specific need of a project—whether a prospective relationship due diligence, periodic review, regulatory assessment, or investigation—will determine the focus, need, and depth of the corporate intelligence procedures to be conducted.

Investigators and investigative analysts will employ public records databases, the Internet, and proprietary data aggregators, in combination with well-defined search methodologies and research procedures, to extract as much data and value as possible from corporate registries, business directories, patent offices, industry journals, property records, voter and tax rolls, relevant criminal and civil courts, credit agencies,* regulatory agencies, and media. As needed, nonpublic information will be sought from relevant company books, records, and databases as well as document and e-mail reviews and interviews.

For the highest-level reviews, information requirements may be limited, such as in the case of a potential match against a sanctions list, which would require review and clearance or verification that the alert is a true hit. Thereafter, ever-deepening intelligence-gathering exercises require additional, more extended review and analysis.

At the deepest level, investigations and high-risk integrity reviews can involve hundreds of pages of material. Once sifted and reduced to relevant data

---

* Credit reporting with personal financial information is, in many jurisdictions including the United States, protected by local law. Consumer privacy laws often require permission of the subject for a third party to obtain a credit report. However, high-level information gathered by credit agencies, such as address histories and telephone numbers—often called "credit header information"—is available in the public record without subject permission in many jurisdictions including the United States.

only, a good analyst will identify any gaps in the facts, develop an understanding of the subject, and craft further procedures as needed. The plan will seek to fill out the "character sketch," identify facts associated with a person or entity, and bring to the surface potential inconsistencies and issues worthy of further study.

The analyst's toolkit includes interviews with associates, experts, and others with the experience and knowledge of a given subject's industry, business reputation, business practices, prior dealings and work experience, local market, particular expertise, and track record. Analysts may interview industry observers, competitors, partners, and colleagues of a subject. Such interviews, fieldwork, and site visits become particularly important in emerging market countries that lack centralized data storage or in regions where data privacy or other local regulation restricts the availability or transport of information.

Analysts generally combine and layer information and source material to obtain, as much as possible, confirmations of data points from two or more separate and independent sources. As previously stated, the enormous quantity of information to be accessed in the twenty-first century heightens the need for adequate assessment of information relevance and quality.

Assessment

Depending upon the nature of the risk assessment exercise, different facts will be sought; for example, internal investigation of an employee or group of employees in connection with an alleged theft would likely involve a review of the employees' assets and liabilities for potential financial stress factors, as well as a search for related parties to look for collusion, ghost parties, and fraudulent transactions. When assessing a prospective member of management, however, more relevant fact gathering would likely focus on the executive's business history, reputation, and credentials.

But regardless of the focus, the sources and research procedures associated with each exercise are basic and common to all information assessments. These sources become more numerous all the time, as more government bodies, academic archives, media, companies, and bloggers place information and documents into open, online access or into subscription data aggregation services. This section provides an overview of the many data points that can be relevant to intelligence-gathering exercises regardless of issue, industry, jurisdiction, or stage of the relationship.

Corporate Background

There are many excellent resources for information about corporations, which can be prioritized by the source's closeness to the original, firsthand source of facts and documentation. For example, the financial statements of a public company, filed with the Securities and Exchange Commission, can be considered a primary source, whereas the work of a financial analyst examining a company from the outside would be a secondary source. Corporate information can be garnered from self-reported statements of a company, business directories and industry or trade organizations, third-party data aggregators, the Internet, etc.

When harvesting information on companies, relevant information points can be:

- Names of senior managers, directors, principals, and ultimate beneficial owners
- Dates of incorporation, years of activity, or evidence of ongoing operations
- Robust, transparent, and informative company Web site
- Financial statements and credit history
- Competitor and peer comparisons
- Corporate structure
- Organization charts
- Business descriptions and history
- Related parties, subsidiaries, and branch operations (and where located)
- Authorized agents and distributors

But in the United States and around the world, the level of information that must be released by a corporate entity varies widely, and such corporate filings can be subject to scrutiny for factual basis. For example, corporate registries in the United States and elsewhere can contain minimal information, or even incorrect information, since they often are not subject to verification by the agency (such as a secretary of state) with which the entity is registered. Likewise, the information to be found on a company within some corporate credit libraries is self-reported—and therefore not necessarily factual.

Because of this, the corporate registries and archives can be, and have been, misused to facilitate fraud schemes. In April 2006, the U.S. Government Accountability Office (GAO) released a report that examined the incorporation of companies in the 50 states and the varying requirements for information provision among the states.[3] The GAO noted that most states do not require ownership information to be provided when a company is created; and when directors, officers, or managers are named in corporate filings, no state verifies the identities of these officials.

This lack of transparency, and the ease with which companies can be formed in the United States, has created an environment in which shell companies can be formed and utilized for illicit activities, according to the GAO report. Federal law enforcement officials told the GAO that increasing numbers of U.S. companies were being identified in connection with investigations in and outside the United States related to money laundering, tax avoidance, and sanctions evasion. The FBI told the GAO that U.S. shell companies were used to launder as much as $36 billion from the former Soviet Union. Immigration and Customs Enforcement officials reported that a U.S. citizen used Oregon-registered companies to move $1 million from Libya to a U.S. bank.[4]

In November 2006, the U.S. Financial Crimes Enforcement Network (FinCEN) released its own report examining the role of domestic shell companies in financial crime and money laundering.[5] FinCEN identified several schemes associated with shell companies, including:

- Credit card bust-outs
- Pump and dump
- Overinvoicing
- False invoicing
- Fraud

The lesson to be learned is that information from even official sources should be subject to validation or corroboration from a credible second or even third source.

Some, but not all, business directories and listing agencies undertake validation of information reported by companies that wish to list their business information, credit ratings, and other data for public reference and use. But much of the information in these listings is self-reported and therefore may not contain a whole, or truthful, story. More independent validation can be obtained from financial analysts, ratings agencies, financial media outlets, watchdog groups, and government agencies charged with oversight of particular industries or compliance sectors including labor, environment, antitrust, and consumer protection.

Sometimes, a company's Web site can be a valuable source of information, with the general caveat that it is likely to be mostly self-reported information. But for publicly traded or large private companies with global footprints, Web sites can provide robust information on financials, directors and managers, business focus, mission statements, ethics and compliance standards, markets of operation, clients, and business announcements.

Conversely, presenting a false face through creation of a Web site is simple and inexpensive. There are many off-the-shelf products with which a fraudster can build a Web site just a few pages deep—deep enough to convince a casual viewer. Further, the addresses associated with the entities can trace back to a virtual office service provider, which allows companies and individuals to receive mail or rent space in locations where they may just be starting business; such services can be used illegitimately to make a nonexistent business appear legitimate.

Related Parties

The identification of persons or entities associated with a given relationship is critical in a variety of corporate intelligence contexts: investigations, disputes and arbitrations, preacquisition due diligence, asset identification, third-party distributor, and vendor assessments.

Corporate records databases, registry offices, and business libraries can be accessed to research across several data points that can identify related parties:

- Names of subject individuals, spouses, and other family members
- Current and former addresses associated with subject individuals, which can be used to identify other entities or other addresses associated with an entity
- Variations on a known entity's name to identify previous or successor entities

Media, the Internet, regulatory bodies, financial analyst reports, and watchdog groups can be leveraged to identify other individuals who may be associated with, investing with, or joined in business relationships with an entity or individual who is subject to review.

Related parties can be used to facilitate frauds, divert assets, create off-balance-sheet vehicles, limit liability, and manage tax burdens; additionally, prior to an acquisition, companies should review related parties to make sure they understand the universe of relationships and potential obligations they are assuming with their acquisition.

Asset and Liability Information

Government units, including state and local clerks' offices (or provincial, canton, municipal, or other jurisdictional structures), can be researched, where permitted by local law, to identify property, vessels, aircraft, automotive vehicles, and equipment purchased or leased by an entity or individual. Depending upon the jurisdiction, information can be gleaned for the asset value, loan burden, and approximate purchase cost associated with the asset. Liabilities, including tax liens, can also be identified through such government bodies, where permitted by local law.

Judgments levied in connection with court actions can be accessed through local courts, where available in the public record. Where criminal and civil court proceedings are not captured in centralized databases, local media or trade journals can be a source of information with respect to judgments and penalties levied against individuals or entities. Bankruptcy filings should also be included in research through U.S. federal courts.

Financial information for individuals and nonpublic companies can be held private or be protected by relevant jurisdictional consumer protection laws. Bank statements, tax returns, loan applications, and such documents would therefore likely not be accessible through public records research. In some jurisdictions, permissions must be obtained from subjects prior to accessing additional financial information such as credit reports.

Asset and liability information can provide illumination on an individual's lifestyle, financial stress levels, and ability to manage personal finances. For example, a review of historic residential property ownership with repeated mortgage refinancing for ever-greater amounts could be a sign of financial stress.

Evidence of assets and liabilities can also be used to provide evidence of the active operations and ongoing status of a company and the size of an operation, and the evidence can be compared against similar information for peers or competitors. However, the same caveats that apply to corporate registry information can also be associated with registries of assets or liabilities.

Criminal and Litigation History

Criminal and litigation histories are appropriate baseline information points for nearly every corporate intelligence inquiry. In the United States, criminal histories are generally available for natural persons from local law enforcement authorities and can be ordered through online data providers if relevant local jurisdictions, dates of birth, and taxpayer identification numbers are available. For civil litigation, the federal, state, and local structure of the United States results in a patchwork quilt of investigative authorities, regulatory agencies, and courts with mandates in myriad areas. This can therefore mean that several sources will need to be accessed to be confident that relevant investigations and court filings have been harvested. An examination of a party from both the plaintiff and the defendant perspective can be illuminating: a prospective business partner with a history of breaching contracts and suing former business partners may not be a good candidate for a new venture. Similarly, a vendor that has been sued many times for failure to pay obligations may not be solvent or reliable.

Elsewhere in the world, the availability of criminal and civil litigation history varies widely; in many European countries, privacy regulations prevent the release of police or court records associated with individuals or entities. In these jurisdictions, such information might be found in local media, if released by an official source such as police or prosecutors. Assertions or rumors might be found in some online sources or local media if the items are sufficiently masked to avoid prevailing libel laws. However, masking such information also provides cover to media sources that might have their own agendas, and so the reliability of such information can be open to question and should be subject to validation from independent sources.

In other parts of the world, criminal and civil litigation may be available through local courthouses or government agencies, retrievable by local sources or authorized parties. In China, for example, where information is often held at the provincial level, local attorneys with authorization can be retained to retrieve corporate and, potentially, court information.

Curriculum Vitae, Professional License, and Education Review

Reviewing an individual's credentials generally involves multiple research stops and can require phone calls or written inquiries to relevant bodies, as well as desktop research. In many jurisdictions, individuals' employment history is subject to privacy laws and therefore cannot be confirmed through inquiries to current or former employers. In other jurisdictions, including the United States, the amount of information an employer will release is limited to such points as confirming if, and in what time period, an individual worked there.

Similarly, some institutions of higher learning will confirm degree grants and time periods of matriculation, while others will require permission of the student. In the United States, some universities and graduate schools provide their student information through the National Student Clearinghouse, which can be accessed via a Web site.

Professional licenses, from law degrees and engineering licenses to beautician certifications, can often be confirmed, depending upon jurisdiction, through relevant government or self-regulating bodies, usually through a Web site, a search through the relevant body's archives, or via phone or written inquiry. A check for violations, penalties, suspensions, or other disciplinary action can also usually be submitted.

Beyond the validation of professional claims, an individual's résumé should be reviewed for gaps of time between jobs or academia; reconciled for time periods of employment and education; and examined for the strength of its claims to positions, honors, and service to community or professional organizations.

Consider the case of the college student who was arrested and charged in May 2010 with having falsified his résumé so well that Harvard College accepted him. The CV was incredibly impressive and, in the end, incredible: Oxford, Georgetown, academic prizes, four languages including "Old English" and "Classical Armenian," lectures, and books in progress. The truth revealed that he was a young man who had been kicked out of Bowdoin College for academic dishonesty.[6] Perhaps the lesson is the bigger the claim, the more we tend to believe it, because who would falsify so outrageously?

In reviewing to corroborate, Web research and media archives that can identify company press releases, trade journal membership notices, or other local articles discussing job promotions, volunteer events, and service organization successes can provide a level of validation. Additionally, the growing number of job and social networking sites on the Web can provide information about where persons have worked, during what time periods they were employed, what their positions and responsibilities were, and, sometimes, how the experience ended. But information on these sites is self-reported by the people discussing their own credentials and, therefore, cannot be accepted as validation of a CV submitted for consideration for employment.

Similarly, there are growing numbers of blogs devoted to particular industries, career paths, or even specific companies. These blogs can provide some information, although the particular agenda of the given blog should be considered. A blog devoted to alumni of a defunct company who want to stay in touch may be quite different in content and tone from the blog of a disgruntled former employee.

Review of a candidate may also require conducting interviews and making phone inquiries, reviewing references provided by an individual, and contacting current or former associates identified through research, who may provide a more independent portrait of a candidate's capabilities.

Regulatory Violations, Sanctions, and Debarment Listings

Around the world, in local jurisdictions, and at the global and supranational level, a variety of entities track and report violations of laws and regulations. Additionally, a variety of governments, watchdog groups, and regulatory bodies publish and track entities and individuals that are under sanction or debarred from business transactions. Among the best known of these is the OFAC list published in the United States. It is against the law for any U.S. person or business, or any non-U.S. business that operates in the United States, to transact with OFAC-listed entities, countries, or individuals. Other countries and bodies maintain their own lists, including the United Nations and the European Union. There is overlap among the lists (for example, Osama Bin Laden appears on many countries' lists, and his name appears with multiple transliterations), as well as unilateral prohibitions (e.g., European nationals are not banned from traveling to or transacting with Cuba, as are U.S. nationals).

It is incumbent on companies to check all relevant lists; regulated industries in many countries, including financial services, are required to continually monitor transactions to see that monies moving through their institutions are not intended for or transacting through sanctioned entities. Other lists that are useful include commercial ban lists such as the U.S. Excluded Parties List

System, which names individuals and entities that have been banned from doing business with the U.S. government or named as violators by the Office of the Inspector General.

Additionally, several well-respected independent organizations, including Transparency International, provide guidance at the country level of commitment to anti-bribery and anti-corruption standards; the Organisation for Economic Co-operation and Development has articulated an Anti-Bribery Convention, which 38 countries have signed to date, that establishes binding legal standards to criminalize the bribery of foreign officials in international transactions.[7]

Further, there are regulatory requirements in many countries for industries, including financial services, to identify among their customers those that are politically exposed persons (PEPs), commonly defined as senior foreign political figures. Such parties, which have been identified by global law enforcement bodies as presenting an elevated risk, particularly with respect to bribery and corruption, should be subject to identification and heightened review by the financial institutions where they bank. But companies in other industries increasingly are making use of so-called PEP lists to help them identify potentially problematic relationships when they are using third-party agents or conducting business in jurisdictions where they are partnering with local resources.

Fortunately, in the United States and around the world, there are a variety of third-party services that will aggregate multiple lists and perform sanctions, debarment, and violations checks. These services can perform volume scrubs for large firms with huge vendor and customer databases, as well as provide access to their libraries of lists for Web-browsing or one-off checks. OFAC and other governmental sanctions offices update their lists often; U.S.-regulated entities will need to update their scrub lists to be current with such lists, and companies performing rolling reviews or periodic refreshes of their relationships should seek out current lists.

Information Gaps

Sometimes there is no information to be found where there should be information. These gaps can exist in corporate histories, professional résumés, media releases, professional licensing, financial statements, official registries, or the statements of individuals talking about themselves.

By itself, such a gap may signify nothing, but when gaps begin to accrue and research through multiple sources and for multiple data points yields little, the gaps can present a potential issue. In some cases, adding additional data sources or redoing research under different, related-party names can resolve the issue. Check the source data to make sure that the right names, addresses, and spellings have been received and input into the databases. In the current world of public records and information availability, an absence of information is increasingly rare and, therefore, by itself, can constitute or raise a red flag.

Reputational Risk

Examining an individual, entity, or transaction for reputational risk—involving fact gathering through public records, media, and the Internet as well as, potentially, through interviews and nonpublic information—can be a more complex undertaking than other assessments. A review for reputational risk will look for facts and indicators; therefore, it will assess existing risk based upon what has already occurred and signal potential future risk. A combination of any or all of the reviews mentioned previously—from corporate records to information gaps—can form part of a reputational risk analysis, which is generally accomplished through a holistic review of the subject party. Analysis and decision making on reputational risk could involve an examination of:

- Known facts from corporate records, court filings, business releases, CVs, and financial statements
- Unproved assertions by entities, individuals, journalists, and financial analysts
- Previous activity or conduct of an entity and its senior managers or an individual
- Risk factors associated with personal behavior, business style, or culture
- Industry
- Jurisdiction(s) involved
- Regulatory and legal histories of relevant parties
- Regulatory and legal climate associated with industries, jurisdictions, and transactions

Reputational risk assessment should involve identifying previous business and personal behavior, violations, sanctions, litigation, failures of compliance, community standing, ethics and compliance programs, commitments, and other factors. It is a worthwhile exercise that can help prevent surprises associated with what *could* have, or *should* have, been known—surprises that can result in regulatory or shareholder scrutiny, investigations, prosecutions or civil penalties, and unwelcome media coverage.

In recent years, companies involved in the global arena increasingly have requested assistance in assessing the reputational risk of parties that previously had been associated with high-profile investigations or failures, such as Enron, WorldCom, Statoil, and others for which there has been high publicity and reputational impact. Some of the issues associated with these assessments have included the closeness of a subject to the "flame," as it were, as well as such questions as "What did they know, and when did they know it?" While a good amount of information can be identifiable through public records, the media, the Internet, and blogs, this information will not, of itself, be definitive, and therefore, interviews and e-mail or other nonpublic document reviews should potentially be undertaken.

At the end of the intelligence gathering, risk factors should be enumerated, but reputational risk should not be quantified; an investigative analyst's report should not opine on potential damage to a company based upon association with a given party, nor should an analyst opine on the likelihood of future conduct based upon past issues. When assessing reputational impact, an entity must itself know its own appetite for risk, weigh the facts, and make decisions.

Corporate Intelligence Business Applications

The intelligence analyst's procedures, toolkits, and research methodologies may be applied across a variety of business needs. From the earliest consideration of a transaction through the acrimonious end of a relationship, information and intelligence will be sought and weighed to assist with the specific business application.

Intelligence for Prevention

Intelligence gathering prior to the initiation of a relationship is generally known as due diligence. Companies conduct due diligence across a variety of areas that, when compiled, can provide an understanding of a subject as well as the risks and opportunities of a relationship with such a business partner, C-level executive, director, or vendor, to name some typical subjects for due diligence reviews. Areas of focus can include business or personal finances, taxes, litigation, business and personal integrity, background and previous undertakings, related parties, regulatory standing, competitors, jurisdictions of operation and provenance, environmental issues, criminal and civil litigation history, patent ownership, and intellectual property rights. Such due diligence not only can illuminate past conduct and potential issues, but may highlight tendencies that could potentially resurface in future behavior, an example of which is described in the case study that follows.

Thumbnail Case Study: Chainsaw Al Dunlap

Albert John Dunlap was already known as "Chainsaw Al" and "Rambo in Pinstripes" when he was appointed CEO of Sunbeam Corp. in 1996, with a mandate to turn around the consumer appliance company. His methods, as indicated by his nickname, included widespread budget cuts and massive downsizing at such corporations as Scott Paper and Crown Zellerbach. When he was named CEO of Sunbeam, the market celebrated by boosting the company's share price to an all-time-high of $52 per share.

Within two years, however, Dunlap was the subject of an internal investigation by his board, which found evidence of accounting fraud with "bill-and-hold" schemes, through which Sunbeam goods were shipped to buyers and held in warehouses for future sale, but with sales booked immediately. Dunlap was fired, but eventually Sunbeam went into bankruptcy. Sunbeam shareholders sued Dunlap and won $15 million. In 2001, the Securities and Exchange Commission also sued Dunlap for fraud, and eventually he settled for $500,000 and a lifetime ban from serving as an officer of a public company.

But there's more: Not long after the SEC brought its suit against Dunlap, the *New York Times* reported that Dunlap had engineered a massive accounting fraud during his tenure as president from 1974 to 1976 of the Nitec paper mill company in Niagara Falls, New York. An external audit identified inflated inventory and nonexistent sales; Nitec's $5 million profit in 1976 was instead a $5 million loss. Nitec sued Dunlap, but eventually went out of business. Dunlap never mentioned Nitec on his résumé, although it was available in the public domain and was missed by the search firms.

Source: Floyd Norris, "The Incomplete Résumé: A Special Report," *The New York Times*, July 16, 2001. Jarden Corporation acquired the Sunbeam brand as part of its purchase of American Household Inc. in 2005. Neither Jarden nor any of its current management was affiliated with Sunbeam during the 1990s.

A well-considered integrity assessment—the pace of which can be at odds with a fast-tracked deal—might have provided cautionary insight into some of the ill-considered deals of the last decade.

This section examines several key areas within a company that can benefit from effective and proactive intelligence gathering. They include:

- Hiring: C-level and other new employees
- M&A
- Foreign agents and third-party providers
- Customers, clients, and higher-risk jurisdictions or corporate structures

Hiring: C-Level and Other New Employees

Conducting background reviews of the principals, founders, or directors of a target company can provide companies with an assessment of character, management, and likely leadership style and can reveal possible misrepresentations or other ethical issues. This can be done by examining business reputation, ethics and integrity, professional and educational credentials, leadership abilities and style, community involvement, other business relationships, and personal and financial backgrounds.

The depth of an intelligence-gathering exercise should be proportional to the risk associated with a potential failure of the relationship rather than the job level of the individual involved. When deciding what procedures to perform in connection with screening an executive or director, consider the proximity of the person to levels of power, the association of the person with a company brand, and the person's financial role in the company. Lower-level hires should be subject to screening for criminal background, sanctions-list filtering, and information that indicates a level of financial stress that could lead to theft, embezzlement, or other fraud schemes. Such indicators can include bankruptcies, judgments, liens, foreclosures, high level of personal debt, previous job losses, civil litigation such as acrimonious divorces, or personal injury lawsuits, which can drain and strain financial resources. The following sidebar contains a list of essential questions.

Essential Questions for the Decision Maker: C-Level, New Employees

- What is the reputation of your candidate? What is the candidate's business style? Does the executive's appetite for risk match your corporate culture? If a potential senior manager, how does that person lead and inspire?
- Have all the candidate's credentials and claims been verified? Are there gaps in the CV?
- Are there any pending litigation matters involving the candidate that could potentially harm the candidate or the company's ability to conduct business?
- Does the candidate have a criminal history?

Source: KPMG LLP, 2010.

M&A

All transactions bear risk, but a sound transaction is one in which the risks are recognized and understood from the start and balanced by controls that hedge or mitigate the risks. M&A due diligence generally includes reviews of an entity's finances; legal matters; environmental issues; and tax, pension, and human resources practices. Early evaluation of these factors informs the negotiation and can serve to alter the landscape of the deal. Such alterations to the deal can rise, for example, from the identification of potential liabilities with respect to environmental reparations. Ultimately, if the diligence reveals that the value of the target is not sufficient given the risks, the deal could be aborted. But findings from a well-executed due diligence often provide negotiating points that can help adjust terms, conditions, and pricing.

Increasingly, M&A due diligence on an entity in the current economic climate includes a review of its corporate governance policies, its ethics and compliance programs, and its global regulatory compliance and sanctions history; a jurisdictional or industry risk assessment; a sustainability review, including both environmental and social justice issues; labor agreements and executive compensation policies; corporate structures and related entities for accounting and tax purposes; business continuity planning; succession planning; intellectual property; and data security.

An important yet frequently ignored aspect of an M&A deal is management style and personality traits. The characteristics of a future partner, ranging from the positive—focused, realistic, loyal—to the negative—stubborn, indecisive, disrespectful—can be important considerations for a successful merger or acquisition.

An example is the downfall of Cendant Corp.'s $14 billion merger of HFS and CUC International in 1998, resulting from Cendant's failure to discover accounting irregularities in CUC's financials. While this is another instance that confirms the importance of pretransaction due diligence, media reports also highlighted a crack in the transaction's foundation that could have been uncovered in the early stages: internal feuding between HFS CEO Henry Silverman, a self-professed "control freak," and CUC CEO Walter Forbes, frequently referenced in the media as "blue-blooded." As described in one publication, "Well before they reached the altar, the two executives had developed a deep distrust of—even contempt for—each other. Their corporate cultures clashed horribly. Their rival management teams acted more like entrenched armies than merger partners."[8] As a result, where cooperating partners would have joined to mitigate the crisis by jointly handling the litigation, regulatory, and reputational consequences, the rift weakened the newly merged company even more.

Mining the media, Internet, and blogs and potentially conducting interviews of current and former colleagues and associates can provide insight into a business culture or an executive's leadership style that may involve an excessive travel and expense habit, a taste for risk or conflict, a disregard for regulatory mandates, or negative behavior toward colleagues or employees.

In emerging markets or countries with a weak legal, regulatory, or financial structure, corporate structures, controlling stakeholders, and sources of funding can be opaque. In such ventures, parties should seek transparency around potential shell companies, nested companies, offshore corporate and taxing structures, and shadow ownership. This often involves partnering with local resources that understand the territory and can gather reliable intelligence. The sidebar below presents a list of essential questions.

Essential Questions for the Decision Maker: M&A

- Who are the principals of the entity? Is it family-owned? Publicly traded? Does the local government hold a stake in the company? Is the ownership structure transparent?
- Is the industry in which the company is involved susceptible to corruption, bribery, or cash temptation? Is it subject to vagaries or radical change in the market, nationalization, or interference by local governments?
- How stable is the financial, regulatory, and legal infrastructure? Is this a high-risk jurisdiction for corruption, money laundering, gray markets, terrorist financing, IP theft, government interference, or instability?
- What are the assets, intellectual property, or patents claimed by the entity? Are they real and protected?
- What are the potential issues that could come back to haunt you? Unknown or pending litigation, environmental damage, insolvencies, market valuation, government takeovers, fraud, or corruption?
- How does the business or the principal operate? What is the word on the street?

Source: KPMG LLP, 2010.

Foreign Agents and Third-Party Providers

When a company relies on employees, agents, franchisees, distributors, or partners operating potentially thousands of miles away in countries with vastly different cultures and business histories, it is critical that the company have trust and confidence that these employees and agents will adhere to relevant laws and regulations as well as to the company's mission and values.

However, as identified in the KPMG LLP *2008 Anti-bribery and Anti-corruption Survey*, there are significant challenges for companies operating in foreign jurisdictions. At the top of the list of challenges was the difficulty in performing effective due diligence on foreign agents and other third parties, with 82 percent of respondents stating that effective due diligence was either "very" or "somewhat" challenging.[9] This challenge can increase in tandem with the perceived risk level of the jurisdiction for issues of corruption, money laundering, terrorist financing, political instability, organized crime activity, or drug running.

Some of the largest global companies have their own global security units that undertake field reviews or retain global or local investigation firms to gather information for due diligence purposes. Often, local attorneys, embassy staff, commerce officials, or journalists can also provide backgrounds or referrals.

But breaches of trust can occur even if due diligence has been performed, and companies with strong ethics and compliance programs can still be adversely impacted by investigations into business partners. For example, in 2007, the Department of Justice opened an investigation of Swiss freight-forwarding company Panalpina World Transport Holdings for alleged bribe payments to customs officials in Nigeria and other countries. Major oil services companies which reportedly had strong internal controls and anti-corruption policies, and which relied on freight-forwarding companies to negotiate customs, were asked to provide documents to the DOJ in connection with the investigation.[10]

Panalpina conducted a three-year internal investigation in coordination with the DOJ. As a result of this investigation, and with the oversight of outside counsel and the DOJ, Panalpina decided to close its Nigerian organization and restructure its operations in West Africa. Panalpina began settlement discussions with the DOJ in December 2009, and news reports indicate that the settlement agreement will be signed by the end of 2010.[11]

Intelligence gathering on entities or individuals—potential business partners or third-party agents or vendors—in foreign jurisdictions should seek to identify whether corrupt payments have been made to facilitate business or discourage competition. In addition, such reviews should consider whether the entities or the underlying shareholders or principals of the entities can be considered government officials. This consideration can be somewhat broad; in countries where hospitals and other health-care organizations are government-controlled or heavily invested in by government, doctors, nurses, and hospital workers can be considered to be government officials, and receipt of payment by them to test new drugs or medical devices could be subject to FCPA or other relevant anti-corruption and anti-bribery scrutiny. The following sidebar contains a list of essential questions to pursue.

Essential Questions for the Decision Maker: Foreign Agents and Third-Party Providers

- Is the industry in which the company is involved susceptible to corruption, bribery, or cash temptation? Is it subject to vagaries or radical change in the market, nationalization, or interference by local governments?
- What is the jurisdiction? Is it controlled by the rule of law? Is there a securities exchange commission? A monetary authority? Is this a high-risk jurisdiction for corruption, money laundering, gray markets, terrorist financing, IP theft, government interference, or instability?
- Do the agents or suppliers have reputations for integrity, or have there been issues of IP or supply chain theft, questionable relationships, business failures, or security breaches?
- What are the potential issues that could come back to haunt you? Unknown or pending litigation, environmental damage, insolvencies, market valuation, government takeovers, fraud, or corruption?
- How does the agent operate? What is the word on the street?

Source: KPMG LLP, 2010.

Customers, Clients, and Higher-Risk Jurisdictions or Corporate Structures

Within the financial services industry, the regulators charged with enforcement of the USA PATRIOT Act examine subject financial institutions, in part, for the level of information an institution maintains on its customers. The so-called customer identification program (CIP) requires regulated institutions to obtain and verify customer identifying information—name, address, date of birth (for individuals), and taxpayer identification number—and conduct additional review based upon a risk-based assessment of customers that considers customer type, bank product sold, jurisdiction, wealth, political or government rank, and other factors. This additional information—called customer due diligence or enhanced due diligence—is encompassed within an institution's overall KYC program. Specific to government officials, financial institutions must gather information to identify senior foreign political figures, their families, and their close associates among their client base in order to tag their status as PEPs.

In addition, certain jurisdictions have been identified as facilitating the creation of shell corporation structures that have been used by criminal enterprises to move or seemingly "cleanse" the proceeds of crime or to assist in the perpetration of fraudulent business schemes. While the supervisory intentions of the respective jurisdictions may be completely legitimate, a jurisdiction's enabling legislation may provide great privacy to incorporating entities and therefore help to hide beneficial ownership and business purpose. Some of these jurisdictions are offshore, such as the Cayman Islands or Bahamas. Others are countries such as the United Kingdom and Nigeria. And some are within the United States.

An analysis by FinCEN of suspicious activity reports (SARs) filed by financial institutions between 1996 and 2005 showed patterns of usage by U.S. LLCs in connection with wire transactions from foreign financial institutions—notably from Russia and Latvia—through U.S. correspondents and then back to another foreign institution, in which there appeared no genuine owner.[12] Bank personnel attempting to identify owners and operations of the named LLC companies would find only registered agents and postal addresses. In the absence of identifying either the originator or beneficiary of the funds or a business purpose for the funds transfer, they would file a SAR with FinCEN. The sidebar below contains a list of essential questions for the decision maker to ask.

Essential Questions for the Decision Maker: Customers, Clients, and Higher-Risk Jurisdictions or Corporate Structures

- Who is your customer or client, and what is the customer's or client's business? What is the source of funds?
- Where and how is the company incorporated? What is the level of transparency for the company? Do you know who the shareholders are? Have you received audited financial statements?
- What jurisdictions is your client dealing in? Is this consistent with the business? What is the risk associated with the jurisdiction?
- What is the credit standing or stress level of the customer or business? Is there a history of litigation, business failure, judgments, or liens?
- Will the customer deal with a high volume of cash or international wires?
- If this customer owns a business, how many locations does it own? Do daily deposits correspond with the locations of the business?

Source: KPMG LLP, 2010.

Intelligence for Detection

Information gathering should not stop once a relationship is sealed. As company managers, internal auditors, and corporate security personnel develop their compliance and monitoring programs and review schedules, they should consider scenarios in which information updates and reviews may assist their work. Areas of consideration for "refreshing" information, documents, and profiles can include vendors, clients, employees, and third-party agents. Triggers for review can include previous risk assessments or newly identified factors elevating risk; changes of circumstance, including contract renewals, business shifts, or employee promotions; regulatory mandates or changes; or a regularly scheduled audit.

Internal audit and corporate security departments around the world conduct periodic reviews of business operations, compliance, etc.; information gathering is a baseline tool for their work, which is planned based upon a variety of factors such as periodicity, risk, acquisition or sale, previous audit findings, or hotline reports. Alert monitors can be established with third-party data aggregators or Internet search engines to identify news events or other profile changes. Such material can be reviewed to assess the impact of news or events on a company's revenues, legal and regulatory compliance, reputation, competitive climate, business opportunity, or business operations. Some examples are discussed on the pages that follow; for additional information, see Chapter 7, "Prevention: Risk Assessment," and Chapter 11, "Detection: Auditing and Monitoring."

Risk-Based Reviews. In the regulated financial services industry, "refresh" reviews of third-party business relationships are conducted at frequencies associated with their risk: often annually, for the highest-risk entities; every two years for medium-risk entities; and every three years for standard, or low-risk, relationships. In other industries where operations are global or where industry-specific factors raise risk—such as product pipeline, distribution practices, joint venture partnerships, or clawback agreements—high-risk relationships (including third parties and employees) also can undergo annual or regularly scheduled reviews.

High-risk relationship reviews will likely cover a variety of areas, depending upon the specific concerns and regulatory obligations of the entity. Information points to be updated can include:

- Confirmation of the names of owners, directors, and managers of an entity, with subsequent research of the names against sanctions lists
- Public records research to update related-party and conflicts-of-interest information

- Research to identify potentially adverse reputational information
- Sanctions and debarment listing checks
- Civil or criminal litigation updates
- Ethics and compliance certifications and renewals
- Corporate structure, organizational chart, and reporting line updates and documentation

In the case of an FCPA due diligence exercise, investigative analysts should look both in the public record and inside an entity's books and records for indicators that payments were made to government officials either directly or through third parties. Such deeper dives into an entity, business operation, or individual are generally in direct correlation with the risk associated with the relationship. These exercises often involve fieldwork above and beyond the information to be garnered from desktop research, which forms the basis of information to develop fieldwork procedures and focus. For additional information, see Chapter 3, "Bribery and Corruption," and Chapter 14, "Response: Recovery, Presentation, and Analysis of Electronically Stored Information."

Database Scrubs. Additionally, a company's investigators sometimes employ forensic specialists or directly contract with third-party data providers to undertake risk-based reviews of a company's databases to validate information and potentially identify anomalies that could be indicative of fraud, misconduct, or regulatory noncompliance.

Through experience with risk indicators and fraud schemes, forensic technologists and investigators can sift through huge volumes of data and transactions to identify potential issues that might require further investigation, such as suspicious transactions or vendors, ghost entities, fraud indicators, and control failures. Public information, including corporate registrations, addresses, directors' and owners' names, and industry codes, can be matched against a company's internal information to bring changes and discrepancies to the surface. For example, assume ABC Company is listed in a company's payment systems at 123 Main Street. Through a third-party data review, three other companies are identified as being registered at 123 Main Street. These three companies are also listed in the company's payment system, but with payments going to another address. The commonality of the address for four companies is subject to a review, which identifies multiple payments and a collusive relationship.

As well, scrubbing a company's databases against third-party public records can identify ghost parties that are registered nowhere, post office box mail drops, virtual office addresses that can be utilized to create the appearance of active business operations, shell companies utilizing registry addresses, or previously unknown related parties. Such data scrubs can assist a company in cleaning and trueing up its data and can also assist a company in assessing and assigning risk to its various relationships. Potentially relevant public records information can include:

- Multiple addresses
- Multiple jurisdictions
- Owners, directors, and managers
- Sanctions and debarments
- Litigation

Intelligence for Response

Investigators from federal, state, and local police to internal auditors and forensic accountants rely on information and intelligence to support and inform their investigations. The ever-broadening availability of information on the Internet and through proprietary third-party data aggregators is a boon to investigators, but the unstructured, nonlinking, and sometimes unreliable state of some Web-based information can create labyrinths of potentially interesting data to sift through.

Information specialists can assist investigators in developing procedures; creating search methodologies through documents, e-mails, and hard drives; identifying previously unknown parties and relationships; tracing assets and money movements; unraveling complex or nested business structures; and monitoring media and the Internet for relevant investigative information and developments. Analysts can act as a central repository of information and leads—including suspect names, related parties, e-mail gleanings, dates, and addresses. Simple databases created by such analysts can assist with collecting and creating order out of the chaos of information overload. Investigative tools such as relationship mapping programs can identify related parties, plot events over time, and map transaction flows. Information gathered from public records sources, internal documents, e-mails, and hard drives can identify facts that fill in the portrait of a suspect entity or individual or that reveal inconsistencies that indicate red flags. Additionally, the analyst may discover other potential targets for investigation or facts that demand further inquiry. Documents and information found by the analyst may set time frames for events, identify relationships, show cause and effect of circumstances, and provide other relevant investigative facts. There should be a continuing information relay and loop, with investigators and information specialists working in tandem to accrue new facts, confirm or discard leads, and develop evidence relevant to the inquiry. For additional information, please see Chapter 12, "Response: Investigations."

Permissions and Restraints

An important consideration in intelligence-gathering work is prevailing law with respect to both what is considered publicly available information and what information is protected. Global regulations can create contradictory cross-border mandates, and there is increasing tension in the balance between the need to protect privacy and the need for information. Provisions of the USA PATRIOT Act, for instance, require that financial institutions identify and maintain documentation of who their customers are and from whence their customers' funds derive. But privacy regulations in the EU create challenges concerning the release of such customer information even to affiliated institutions.

Furthermore, analysts engaged in integrity due diligence must be aware of restrictions on retrieving material from certain jurisdictions; for example, the EU has legislation controlling the movement of personal information across borders. And some countries control what information can be released to or discussed in the media; for example, newspapers in some countries cannot report on criminal cases that are being tried in the courts unless the appointed authorities release information directly to the public for reporting.

In jurisdictions where a great deal of information can be identified through public records, including the United States, the Fair Credit Reporting Act (FCRA) protects consumers' personal information and privacy. Under the FCRA (15 U.S.C. § 1681 et seq.), "any consumer reporting agency may furnish a consumer report . . . to a person which it has reason to believe . . . intends to use the information for employment purposes."[13] The scope of information that can be considered as a "consumer report" can be broad, including records of civil and criminal proceedings, assets, bankruptcies, and personal identifying information. The FCRA broadly defines a consumer report to include "written, oral, or other communication of any information by a consumer reporting agency bearing on [an individual's] credit worthiness, . . . character, general reputation, personal characteristics, or mode of living which is used or expected to be used or collected in whole or in part for the purpose of serving as a factor in establishing the consumer's eligibility for . . . employment purposes."[14,*]

This permission carries obligations, including the employer's obligation to certify that:

- The information provided will only be used for employment purposes (or another statutorily enumerated permissible reason) and for no other purpose.

---

* The term "employment purposes" reaches both current and prospective employees, as it is defined as "the purpose of evaluating a consumer for employment . . . or retention as an employee." 15 U.S.C. § 1681a(h). (Emphasis added)

- The information provided will not be shared with or given to anyone else other than the subject of the report or a joint user having the same purpose.
- The information provided "will not be used in violation of any applicable Federal or State equal employment opportunity law or regulation."[15]
- The user has made a "clear and conspicuous [written] disclosure"[16] to the individual that a report may be procured for employment purposes before the report is procured.
- The user has secured the relevant individual's authorization in writing.
- The user will comply with additional disclosure requirements that arise if the employer elects to take "any adverse action based in whole or in part on the report."[17]

Skilled advisors, legal counsel, and corporate security or human resources executives familiar with local laws, regulations, and more should be consulted to help comply with relevant laws and reconcile potentially conflicting regulations.

Conclusion

Clearly, not all intelligence-gathering exercises are the same. The depth to which an investigator or analyst will drill varies, based upon regulatory mandate, specific data need, volume, and risk. Nonetheless, a company engaging in any intelligence exercise should have confidence that its investigators and analysts are properly trained, certified, and bonded, as necessary, and are able to develop and implement research and intelligence-gathering procedures that are responsive and relevant to the need at hand. Investigators and analysts also must be conversant and compliant with relevant laws and regulations.

Managing the risk of fraud through intelligence gathering is a cyclical and continuing exercise. Due diligence may begin prior to entering a relationship, but vigilance should continue throughout the relationship. To quote former President Ronald Reagan, "Trust but verify." The foundations of transparency and fact are laid through holistic examination of a subject for soundness, stability, integrity, credibility, professionalism, and adherence to the laws and regulations. With adequate information, the potential risk or reward associated with a relationship can be assessed, and sound decisions can be made.

Chapter 10

Detection: Mechanisms for Reporting Fraud and Misconduct

Timothy P. Hedley
Ori Ben-Chorin

When employees witness misconduct in the workplace, they have a decision to make. They can remain silent about what they have seen, and many do exactly that. In such cases, the misconduct often continues unabated or takes longer to uncover, likely causing additional damage to the organization. However, employees can take a different route; they can report the misconduct. In fact, it is precisely through such reporting that major fraud and misconduct is frequently uncovered, as was illustrated by a recent survey that showed that tips and complaints accounted for the detection of more than 42 percent of all million-dollar frauds.[1] Those organizations that have a better chance of detecting misconduct early are the ones that have built a culture where employees believe they have a stake and responsibility to raise their hands and report misconduct, where they feel comfortable doing so without fear of retaliation, where they believe that management will be responsive, and where there are multiple and accessible means for reporting.

Since employees are so critical in uncovering major fraud, organizations should develop and publicize a number of ways for employees, agents, and other

Mr. Ben-Chorin is a director in KPMG LLP's Forensic practice in Washington, DC. He provides Fraud Risk Management services to corporate clients.

third parties to report suspected wrongdoing and to seek advice and clarification on laws, regulations, and company standards of conduct. We will devote this chapter to providing the reader with practical guidance on designing and implementing mechanisms that encourage employees and other third parties to come forward, as well as help ensure that management is able to properly handle such allegations. Although we will offer guidance on a number of mechanisms, we will focus a great part of the discussion on the popular telephone "hotline," because it is in such wide organizational use and because a large number of tips and complaints (31 percent according to a recent survey[2]) are received through this reporting channel.

Warren Buffett on Hotlines

Warren Buffett, CEO of Berkshire Hathaway, Inc., and one of the country's most celebrated businessmen, perhaps put it best when he said, "Berkshire would be more valuable today if I had put in a whistleblower line decades ago."

Source: Warren Buffett to the Shareholders of Berkshire Hathaway Inc., February 28, 2005, p. 22, www.berkshirehathaway.com/letters/2004ltr.pdf

---

A Change in Popular Culture

When *Time* magazine named Sherron Watkins as "Person of the Year" for blowing the whistle on Enron Corporation in what was one of the decade's most publicized scandals,[3,*] it showed just how far the nation had come in valuing those who step forward to reveal corporate misconduct. But such recognition was not always the case. Too often, employees were valued more for their perceived loyalty; reporting misconduct, and thereby raising an alarm, was seen as "snitching" or a betrayal of trust.[4] All too often, reporting misconduct resulted in retaliation and other negative consequences for the reporting individual.

It is little coincidence, then, that many employees are reluctant to report fraud and misconduct due to both the perceived and, at times, actual high personal cost their actions might exact. A 2008 study of alleged corporate frauds found that in 82 percent of cases where a reporter's identity was known, the reporter was fired, quit the job under duress, or continued to work, but with significantly altered responsibilities. Moreover, scores of such individuals have

---

* Sherron Watkins, Enron's vice president of corporate development, sent the company's CEO, Kenneth Lay, an anonymous seven-page letter raising alarm over accounting manipulations. In her letter, Watkins prophetically wrote, "I am incredibly nervous that we will implode in a wave of accounting scandals."

reported having to move to new towns or work in new industries to avoid harassment, with some saying, "If I had to do it over again, I wouldn't."[5]

Now More Than Ever Before

The importance of providing employees with an environment where they can feel comfortable seeking advice and reporting misconduct without the fear of retaliation cannot be overstated. This becomes even more of a corporate imperative due to the Dodd-Frank Wall Street Reform and Consumer Protection Act (Dodd-Frank Act), which enhances the SEC whistleblower bounty program by allowing the SEC to award whistleblowers who provide "information relating to a violation of the securities laws"[6] (including violations of the FCPA), anywhere between 10 and 30 percent of a recovery of $1 million or more in a successful enforcement action. As such, the Dodd-Frank Act makes it critical that organizations not only have effective whistleblower mechanisms in place, but also encourage whistleblowing, make it easy for employees to do so, and respond properly to allegations by conducting internal investigations and preventing retaliation.

However, to ensure that companies remain the first port of call for employees who seek advice or wish to report misconduct, they must also ensure that their overall compliance program and other related anti-fraud programs and controls are effective in managing risk in light of escalating market complexity; enhanced scrutiny by shareholders, regulators, and the media; and increased globalization.[7] Today, an organizational culture that actively encourages employees to step forward and volunteer their concerns can reap the benefits of having employees act as the company's risk management engine.

Employees who report misconduct not only serve as an organizational early warning system, but also act as catalysts for creating organizational change and a culture of high ethics and integrity. Increasingly, regulatory frameworks call for management to encourage employees to report fraud and misconduct and safeguard these employees from potential harm when they do so.

Incentives for Blowing the Whistle

In 1986, Congress amended a little-used Civil War–era law, the False Claims Act, in an effort to deter fraud against the federal government. These amendments strengthened the act's *qui tam*, or whistleblower, provisions, which are a unique mechanism whereby private citizens who have evidence of fraud against the government can sue private companies, on behalf of the government, to recover the stolen funds. This powerful private-public partnership for uncovering fraud does have its rewards.

In compensation for the risk and effort of filing the *qui tam* lawsuit, the private citizen whistleblower is typically awarded a proportion of the funds recovered, often between 15 and 25 percent.* Although it may take many years for a whistleblower to collect a financial award, the award may be very large indeed—a recent study showed that a sample of successful *qui tam* whistleblowers collected an average of $46 million each.[†]

As an example, the largest fraud settlement in history against a pharmaceutical company actually came about as a result of a whistleblower's *qui tam* lawsuit. Pharmaceutical giant Pfizer Inc. and its subsidiary Pharmacia & Upjohn Company agreed in late 2009 to pay a total of $2.3 billion in combined criminal fines and settlements,[‡] including payments to six individual whistleblowers totaling more than $102 million. One of these whistleblowers, John Kopchinski, a former Pfizer sales representative, waged a six-year legal battle against the company and will reportedly earn more than $51.5 million for his troubles.[§]

The total recoveries under the False Claims Act since it was strengthened in 1986 is more than $24 billion, an astonishing amount of money by any account.[**]

Evolving Standards

The need for organizations to have in place mechanisms for seeking advice and reporting misconduct became more palpable when Congress passed the Federal Sentencing Guidelines in 1991. The Sentencing Guidelines established minimum compliance program requirements for organizations seeking to mitigate penalties for corporate misconduct and, among others, called for organizations to put in place a "system, which may include mechanisms that allow for

---

* Taxpayers against Fraud, the False Claims Act Legal Center, "What Is the False Claims Act & Why Is It Important?" www.taf.org/whyfca.htm.
† Corporate Executive Board, "Enhancing Compliance Risk Detection Unlocking Information Traps, Risk Management in Crisis?" presentation at the 2009 ECOA Sponsoring Partner Forum, Compliance and Ethics Leadership Council, facilitated by Ronnie Kann, managing partner, 2009.
‡ U.S. Department of Justice, "Justice Department Announces Largest Health Care Fraud Settlement in Its History, Pfizer to Pay $2.3 Billion for Fraudulent Marketing," press release, September 2, 2009, www.justice.gov/opa/pr/2009/September/09-civ-900.html.
§ Bill Berkrot, "Pfizer whistleblower's ordeal reaps big rewards," Reuters, September 2, 2009, www.reuters.com/article/newsOne/idUSN021592920090902?pageNumber=1&virtualBrandChannel=11604.
** U.S. Department of Justice, "Justice Department Recovers $2.4 Billion in False Claims Cases in Fiscal Year 2009; More Than $24 Billion Since 1986," press release, November 19, 2009, www.justice.gov/opa/pr/2009/November/09-civ-1253.html.

anonymity or confidentiality, whereby the organization's employees and agents may report or seek guidance regarding potential or actual criminal conduct without fear of retaliation."[8] But while organizations were encouraged to design and implement reporting mechanisms, the discretionary nature of the Sentencing Guidelines made it impossible for those mechanisms to be used to provide legal protections for employees who reported misconduct.

Beginning in the 1970s, some federal and state laws were enacted to safeguard employees from retaliation for reporting their concerns. However, these safeguards were mostly applicable to organizations doing business with the government. Few provisions were extended to private-sector employees, and many reporters continued to experience serious retaliatory consequences. More recently, in direct response to the large corporate scandals of Enron, WorldCom, and the like, Congress mandated, for the first time, significant protections as part of the Sarbanes-Oxley Act of 2002 (SOX). Specifically, Section 806 of the SOX Act made it a criminal offense for a company to "discharge, demote, suspend, threaten, harass, or in any other manner discriminate against an employee" who has acted as a whistleblower by providing information or assistance related to potential fraud while working in a publicly traded company.[9] Importantly, the SOX Act also directed audit committees to establish procedures to receive, retain, and deal with complaints from employees and others about accounting, internal accounting controls, or auditing matters. Such procedures must provide a means for "the confidential, anonymous submission by employees . . . of concerns regarding questionable accounting or auditing matters."[10]

The Sarbanes-Oxley Act of 2002 includes federal protection for corporate whistleblowers, and the U.S. Labor Department's Occupational Safety and Health Administration (OSHA) enforces these provisions. But how protected are the whistleblowers? You make up your mind: a recent study showed that the government has only ruled in favor of whistleblowers 17 times out of 1,273 complaints filed since 2002. (Another 187 cases have been settled.) Of these complaints, 841 cases have been dismissed, many on the technicality that the whistleblowers were employees working at a corporate subsidiary and thus were not protected by the act's "plain language," which protects only those working for a publicly traded corporation. SEC. 929A of the Dodd-Frank now provides protection for employees of subsidiaries and affiliates of publicly traded companies.

Source: Jennifer Levitz, "Whistleblowers Are Left Dangling," *The Wall Street Journal*, September 4, 2008; The Wall Street Reform and Consumer Protection Act of 2009, HR 4173, 111th Cong., 1st sess. (December 2, 2009), Sec. 929A.

Mechanisms for Seeking Advice and Reporting Misconduct

With the oversight and guidance of senior management, organizations can provide employees with multiple channels for reporting concerns about fraud and misconduct. Many typically request that employees follow a process that begins with alerting their own supervisors or managers, if possible, or a designated human resources or compliance officer. While telephone hotlines are often made available and can be used at any time, they are usually intended for use when the organization's normal channels of communication are impractical or ineffective. (See an expanded discussion on telephone hotlines in the section "Challenges to the Effectiveness of Reporting Mechanisms" later in the chapter.)

It is therefore important to note that a variety of alternative means exist to uncover potential issues and capture risk data. These other mechanisms can operate contemporaneously with a telephone hotline and include, but are not limited to:

- *Workshops or focus groups.* Such facilitated meetings can be designed to elicit employee feedback on misconduct witnessed in the workplace, encourage employees to brainstorm about hypothetical issues that could come up on the job, and suggest how the organization can best prevent, detect, and respond to such potential misconduct.

- *Employee surveys.* Confidential and anonymous employee surveys can help management spot potential risks based on employee attitudes, perceptions, or behaviors. Management might find such insights useful as it considers the organization's vulnerabilities to fraud and misconduct and the effectiveness of programs and controls to mitigate such risks.

- *Third-party interviews or surveys.* Soliciting information from customers, vendors, regulators, creditors, analysts, or others who come into routine contact with employees can provide critical insight into typical business practices and risks for misconduct.

- *Auditing and monitoring.* Auditing and monitoring in high-risk areas are important tools that management can use to help determine whether the organization's controls are working as intended, and can often identify issues that may have otherwise escaped management's attention. Such auditing (evaluating past events) and monitoring (evaluating events in real time) can be conducted in, but not limited to, areas where there is a specific concern, a history of fraud and misconduct, high employee turnover, or organizational change.

- *Exit interviews.* Management can also identify potential issues of concern by conducting exit interviews with employees who are leaving the organization to debrief them on issues they perhaps did not want to voice while still employed.

- *Management by walking around.* This philosophy encourages managers to adopt a hands-on management style of visiting employees in their work-spaces, listening to their concerns, asking them questions, and listening to their suggestions about the potential issues they face on the job.

- *Open-door policy.* A managerial open-door policy allows all employees to have direct access to senior executives without having to go through multiple layers of bureaucracy. An open-door policy can help identify issues that may have otherwise escaped management's attention.

- *Web-based reporting system.* A dedicated Internet reporting system typically provides 24/7 access for employees to report fraud and misconduct in a candid and anonymous manner. Many large organizations combine a Web-based reporting system with their telephone hotline.

Using Organizational "Ethics Champions" for Early Warning

Geographically dispersed organizations should not presume that their telephone hotlines will be successful at surfacing fraud and misconduct across all organizational levels and locations. Such organizations may wish to consider designating local resources to serve as points of contact for transmitting concerns and allegations from the field directly to leadership. Like a long-distance communications network, such a system can be especially effective for large organizations with multiple local offices in dispersed geographies. In such local offices, locally designated ethics champions can serve as the focal point for both communicating messages from leadership and receiving inquiries and reports of potential misconduct from the field. This system puts a familiar face to another potential reporting mechanism, making it yet more likely that employees will feel comfortable in expressing their concerns.

Challenges to the Effectiveness of Reporting Mechanisms

Modern organizations are implementing reporting mechanisms more than ever before, as was illustrated by a recent survey in which the vast majority of respondents reported that their organizations provide a means for employees to report suspected misconduct (81 percent).[11] A dedicated telephone hotline is the most common among the reporting mechanisms typically employed by large organizations. In fact, KPMG's *Integrity Survey 2008–2009* of more than 5,000 U.S. employees across a variety of industries, job responsibilities, and geographies showed that a full 65 percent* of respondent organizations use such hotlines.[12] Because of the prevalence of telephone-based hotlines in modern organizations, they are the primary focus of the balance of this chapter. However, one should note that many of the same practice conventions used with telephone hotlines apply to other reporting mechanisms, such as the ones described earlier in this chapter.

But despite the fair abundance of hotlines as reporting mechanisms, companies are increasingly finding out that it is not always easy to convince employees to give voice to their concerns using this method, as was recently illustrated by KPMG's *Integrity Survey 2008–2009* data, which showed that:

- Too few employees would call a hotline to report misconduct in the first place—only a disappointing 44 percent of employees surveyed said they would do so.
- Employee comfort level in calling a hotline generally is not high—only a slim majority of respondents said they would feel comfortable reporting misconduct to a hotline (57 percent).

Arguably, the low number of employees who feel comfortable reporting misconduct is a consequence of the distrust they often feel with respect to the manner in which their employers are likely to respond to a report. In fact, the results of KPMG's *Integrity Survey 2008–2009* show that a significant number of employees are:

- Not confident that their employer will keep a report confidential (36 percent)
- Not confident that their employer will take appropriate action as a result of a submitted report (34 percent)
- Not confident that their employer would protect a whistleblower from retaliation after a report had been made (47 percent)

Is Management an Obstacle?

Recent survey data show that management may be acting as an impediment to the capture of risk information. Of those compliance executives surveyed, 43 percent identified managers as a significant obstacle (25 percent

---

* This figure represents a statistically significant 11 percent increase from KPMG's 2005–2006 survey results (54 percent).

of managers not recognizing and reporting employee concerns and 18 percent of managers not escalating employee concerns). While an organization's tone at the top is important, the "tone at the middle," or the commitment and behavior of middle management, may be equally important, because middle management commitment is the one typically most visible to employees. Organizations that seek to have in place effective whistleblower mechanisms and, indeed, effective anti-fraud programs and controls should therefore communicate to, and convince, middle management that a commitment to ethics and compliance does matter, and that for the organization to maintain an appropriate ethical culture, their direct involvement and buy-in is required.

Source: Enhancing Compliance Risk Detection Unlocking Information Traps, Risk Management in Crisis? Compliance and Ethics Leadership Council, Corporate Executive Board, presentation at the 2009 ECOA Sponsoring Partner Forum, facilitated by Ronnie Kann, Managing Partner, 2009.

Enhancing the Effectiveness of Whistleblower Mechanisms

To help mitigate potential employee concerns and increase the likelihood that employees will use a hotline, management should focus on designing this reporting mechanism in a way that helps to surface employee concerns effectively. In this respect, formal guidance is lacking. Regulatory frameworks that call on organizations to have hotlines in place recognize the need for organizational flexibility and, therefore, typically do not mandate strict guidelines on how such mechanisms should be designed and implemented.

The Employee's Perspective

As can be expected, a "one-size-fits-all" hotline solution is typically not effective, and management should therefore keep in mind the organization's size, business structure, geographic footprint, and available resources when designing and implementing a telephone hotline. However, certain conventions have emerged that are influential in helping employees feel comfortable voicing concerns. These include, among others:

- *Confidentiality.* Employees who do not believe that the confidential nature of their report will be protected are less likely to call the hotline. Management should therefore seek to include, as part of the organization's reporting protocols, relevant safeguards to protect caller confidentiality, such as limiting access to personal information (if volunteered). Safeguards put in place should be publicized to increase confidence and trust in the hotline. However, hotline operators should disclose to callers any limitations the organization may have in preserving caller confidentiality (e.g., callers should have no expectation of confidentiality if the call leads to a government investigation).

- *Anonymity.* Many hotline callers choose to raise concerns anonymously (and perhaps would not do so otherwise). In fact, recent survey data have shown that a majority of individuals who report to a hotline prefer to do so anonymously (54 percent).[13] As such, management should consider designing a hotline process that allows anonymous reporting and communicate this fact. For example, anonymous reporting can be achieved by letting callers know they do not have to identify themselves, programming the hotline such that it does not register or keep a record of the caller's telephone number, or providing callers with a case tracking number they can later use to check the status or outcome of the call. However, it is worth noting that it can be difficult to follow up on anonymous reports.

- *Nonretaliation.* Perhaps one of the biggest obstacles to hotline reporting is employee fear of retaliation. Management should therefore seek to design and publish protocols that prohibit retaliation against employees who make a good faith hotline report. Such protocols should also include following up with callers periodically after the hotline case has been closed to monitor whether the caller had, in fact or perception, experienced retaliation.

- *Prominent communications.* If employees are not aware that a hotline exists, they cannot use it to seek advice or raise concerns regarding potential misconduct. As such, management should seek to inspire trust in and awareness of the hotline by publicizing it in a prominent manner. For example, this can be accomplished by illustrating the hotline within the organization's code of conduct and other key publications, using hotline case studies in training events, describing the hotline in management "town hall"–type meetings, and featuring the hotline number on workplace posters and signs. In fact, survey data show that the largest percentage of respondents who called a hotline likely became aware of it by seeing a workplace poster or sign (34 percent).[14]

- *Toll-free service and 24/7 availability.* Employees are more likely to use a hotline when it is easily accessible. Management should therefore seek to make available to employees a toll-free number that is accessible from outside the organization. The hotline should also be available at all hours for those employees who work in different time zones or for individuals who may wish to make calls after hours when they are away from their normal working locations.

■ *International availability.* For geographically diverse organizations, management should keep in mind that potential hotline callers may be located in any of the organization's operations around the globe. The organization may therefore wish to consider providing hotline services that are appropriately accessible to employees wherever they may be (e.g., by using toll-free call routing; by providing real-time foreign language translation; or by implementing separate, local hotlines in specific countries or regions).

The Organization's Perspective

Many of the design considerations discussed in previous pages are intended to assist management in creating an organizational culture in which employees feel comfortable reporting concerns. But once a report has been made, the organization is still not assured that it is in the best position to accrue the potential benefits of the report, which are typically realized only if the report is handled properly. To help ensure that reports are handled appropriately, management should consider designing the hotline to incorporate the following features:

■ *Appropriate oversight.* Management should consider carefully which function is best suited to providing oversight for the hotline. While a hotline can be "owned" by any one of many organizational functions (e.g., human resources, legal, internal audit, compliance, security), arguably, the compliance function is often singled out as the one best suited to the task of managing a hotline. This is often the case because the compliance function typically maintains the desired attributes of a direct reporting relationship with the board or the audit committee. With the compliance function providing oversight, the remaining functions can be tasked with offering close support and expertise in dealing with specific hotline reports (e.g., human resources assisting with investigating reports of wrongful termination).

■ *Appropriate protocols.* Management should seek to put in place appropriate call triage and data intake protocols that describe procedures for handling the call as well as provide for subsequent management review and resolution of allegations. Such intake protocols may also vary depending upon the type of hotline call received. For instance, calls may include:
  ○ Concerns regarding questionable business practices or plans
  ○ Warnings about particular risk areas that are unchecked

○ Questions about what organizational standards or the law permits under certain circumstances

○ Allegations of fraud or misconduct

Management's review process should be undertaken as a precursor to determining next steps (e.g., classifying the report, closing out a report that is not actionable, conducting appropriate follow-up with the reporter or other witnesses, launching a formal internal investigation, etc.).

■ *Experienced personnel.* To help ensure that reports are handled properly, management should invest in staffing the hotline with skilled personnel who can manage the hotline in a professional and consistent manner. Such personnel can provide callers with the opportunity to both report a concern and seek advice and guidance (e.g., skilled staff can answer a question such as, "Will I be violating our company's code of conduct if I accept this expensive gift from our supplier?"). Although hotline operators who work for third-party vendors are typically not able to provide employees with guidance, management can design and implement protocols whereby the operators are trained to either refer the caller to an appropriate company resource during regular business hours or forward a request for guidance to the company for later response.

■ *Case management system.* Ensuring that hotline calls are handled appropriately also requires maintaining an effective case management system that provides details on hotline calls, from initiation to resolution, as well as automated formats for reporting to senior management and the board. Such a system is often electronic, consisting of a database containing indexed, retrievable, and searchable information about an organization's entire caseload.

■ *Data management procedures.* The hotline should include protocols that operators and company personnel can follow when gathering report facts, managing and analyzing call data, and reporting key performance indicators to management and the board. These procedures should provide guidance on how to identify trends and measure key performance indicators that can subsequently be reported to senior management and the board. One of the more common types of analysis that companies perform in connection with a hotline is the categorization of incoming reports, which can help management better deploy scarce compliance resources. An example of such category-style reporting includes:

○ Personnel Management (49.6 percent)

○ Company/Professional Code Violation (16.8 percent)

○ Employment Law Violation (10.8 percent)

○ Corruption and Fraud (10.6 percent)

○ Environment, Health & Safety (5.2 percent)

- ○ Other/Unresolved (3.6 percent)
- ○ Customer/Competitor Interaction (2.2 percent)
- ○ Misuse of Assets/Information (1.2 percent)[15]

    Other hotline metrics that organizations typically monitor and share with the board or the audit committee include:

- ○ Number and nature of calls requesting advice
- ○ Number and nature of calls reporting misconduct
- ○ Number and nature of substantiated allegations
- ○ Number and nature of call resolutions
- ○ Number and nature of open or unresolved cases
- ○ Levels of caller satisfaction

- ■ *Notifications.* The hotline should include protocols for various notifications to management and the board with respect to sensitive reports, including:
    - ○ *Emergency notification.* Providing emergency notification to designated individuals, particularly if the caller relates an immediate threat to life, public safety, or property
    - ○ *Audit committee notification.* Escalating allegations to the audit committee (especially important for companies that must comply with the requirements of SOX)
    - ○ *Knowledge sharing.* Sharing the nature of allegations with the disclosure committee and executives who sign certifications required by Section §302 of SOX (for those companies that must comply with the requirements of SOX).

- ■ *Identification of financial reporting concerns.* The hotline should include protocols whereby qualified individuals (e.g., from the organization's internal audit or legal functions) can determine whether an allegation may trigger a financial reporting risk. Other factors exist, and individual companies may find different guidelines appropriate for their particular circumstances. For example, Table 10.1 shows potential criteria for notification protocols.

Table 10.1.

	Handling	Audit Committee and External Auditor Notification	§302 Certifiers and Disclosure Committee Notification
Low materiality/ Low-level employee	Internal investigation	Next scheduled meeting	Next scheduled meeting
Medium materiality/ Mid-level employee	Internal investigation	Within 72 hours	Within 72 hours
High materiality/ High-level employee	Third-party investigation	Within 72 hours	Restricted case-by-case (72 hours)

Source: KPMG LLP, 2009.

Implementing the Hotline

In implementing a hotline, management may grapple with making a decision about whether such a reporting mechanism should be administered internally or externally. In some organizations, for example, a hotline can be administered by a dedicated internal resource, while in others, the best solution is often an external third-party vendor operating on a fee-for-service basis. While many companies do operate in-house hotlines (38 percent, according to a 2007 ACC survey), an even larger percentage outsources the system to an independent service provider (43 percent) or employs a blend of both (17 percent).[16] Each model has its advantages and disadvantages.

While typically more costly than an in-house service, an outsourced hotline can usually provide around-the-clock operator service and may inspire greater trust in the promise of anonymity. Both these features are important, as survey data show that almost half (45 percent) of calls typically happen outside of regular business hours, and many callers would be more willing to make a report if they could remain anonymous (39 percent).[17] Around-the-clock service and the promise of anonymity may be harder to support with an internal hotline operated by a company insider who is available to answer calls only during conventional working hours.

Conversely, a hotline that is staffed in-house can more easily provide real-time advice to callers, while a third-party vendor hotline may only offer callers guidance on a referral basis, significantly delaying employees in obtaining what may be crucial information to guide their actions. In deciding whether to opt for an internal or external hotline, management should weigh carefully its decision in light of the organization's risk profile, specific circumstances, and compliance needs.

Table 10.2 on the following page outlines some typical advantages and disadvantages that are often considered when deciding whether to outsource the hotline.

Testing a Hotline for Effectiveness

To help ensure that the hotline is operating effectively, organizations should periodically seek to measure the tangible impact that this reporting mechanism is having on employee behavior. Such an evaluation can generally be accomplished using a variety of tools. For example, a review of documents such as a hotline log, communications on the hotline, and reports to the board on key performance indicators can confirm that these exist and are used appropriately. Moreover, employee surveys and structured interviews with selected employees can also be conducted to assess knowledge of the hotline and confidence in using this reporting mechanism. In addition, by surveying or interviewing past hotline reporters, data can be gathered with respect to the effectiveness of the company's efforts to monitor the work environment of these individuals for potential retaliation.

Table 10.2.

Feature	In-House	Third Party
Can provide toll-free telephone service	Usually	Usually
Can provide 24/7 service	Sometimes	Usually
Can provide access to international callers	Usually	Usually
Can access real-time interpreters	Sometimes	Usually
Can provide real-time advice and guidance to callers	Usually	Rarely
Can staff the hotline with trained professionals	Usually	Usually
Can understand the company lingo likely to be used by callers	Usually	Rarely
Can provide staff that will never recognize the caller's voice	Sometimes	Usually
Can invest in technology-based call and data management protocols	Sometimes	Usually
Can apply confidentiality and anonymity protocols	Usually	Usually
Can forward cases to appropriate departments and monitor resolution	Usually	Usually
Can instill confidence in the quality and integrity of the mechanism	Sometimes	Sometimes
Can operate a hotline cost-efficiently	Rarely	Usually

Source: KPMG LLP, 2009.

Finally, a "staged" call to the hotline can be a useful way to determine whether operators are handling calls effectively. For instance, the chief compliance officer of the County of Orange Health Care Agency (HCA) conducts three staged calls a year to determine whether the third-party vendor's hotline operators are doing a good job at call intake, management, and response. Members of HCA's compliance committee volunteer to place the fake calls, and operators are evaluated on how accurately they capture a caller's complaints and whether company procedures are followed during the call.[18]

Third-Party Use of a Hotline

A growing trend among organizations that seek to enhance the effectiveness of their hotlines is making this reporting mechanism available to third parties such as agents, customers, vendors, or suppliers. One advantage of doing so is that this practice facilitates reporting by those outsiders who are often in the very best position to observe employee misconduct. Moreover, organizations with large customer bases (e.g., consumer-oriented companies) may further benefit from opening up their hotline to third parties in that customers may choose to first report potential fraud or misconduct directly to the company, rather than reach out to regulatory authorities or consumer protection agencies.

Implementing Reporting Mechanisms Internationally

Although an impressive array of reporting mechanisms has sprung up in the United States, encouraged and often mandated by regulatory frameworks such as the False Claims Act and the Sarbanes-Oxley Act of 2002, other nations of the world have arguably been slower in adopting such mechanisms.[19] The challenges inherent in rolling out a hotline internationally begin with local laws and regulations that may be in opposition to the hotline, and end with deep-rooted cultural bias and reluctance to report on fellow colleagues.

Setting Up an International Hotline

When Bombardier Inc., the manufacturer of business aircraft such as the Learjet, attempted to set up a hotline in Europe, many of the company's managers and employees were uncomfortable with the idea. As Bombardier's compliance officer remarked, "People in the EU often have reminiscences of the Second World War or the Communist era—they associate this [hotline] with denunciation."* Such anecdotal explanations, however, may not always be accurate in expressing prevailing cultural norms, as a recent Conference Board study has shown. The study's results suggest that the reluctance of Western Europe to use a hotline may simply reflect their preference for using other channels, such as work councils, labor unions, or face-to-face conversations with management.†

---

* Tiffany Kary, "International Whistleblower Hotlines Present Cultural, Language Challenges for Companies," *Dow Jones Newsletters*, January 19, 2005, info.ethicspoint.com/files/PDF/resources/ Dow_Jones_Corp_Gov_newsletter_article_011505.pdf .
† The Conference Board, *Ethics Programs, the Role of the Board: A Global Study, 2003*, New York, 2004, p. 24, available by subscription at www.conference-board.org.

From a regulatory perspective, certain European data privacy laws, such as the EU Data Protection Directive, make it more difficult for U.S. organizations to implement a hotline in Europe. Such laws typically regulate the collection, storage, transfer, and release of personally identifiable data of the citizens of the relevant jurisdictions. For example, the EU directive prohibits EU nations from transferring employee personal data to non-EU countries that do not meet a European "adequacy" standard for privacy protection, for example, the United States.[20]

And from a cultural perspective, reporting mechanisms may not be accepted in every nation of the world. For example, Italy, Mexico, Russia, and Spain offer no whistleblower protections to public-sector employees. And while some countries such as Canada, Japan, France, and Germany have legally mandated whistleblower protections, these have notable differences from comparable U.S.-based legislation. For instance, a hotline in France must comply with the criteria of the French government privacy agency (CNIL) that limits the type of events that can be reported, and requires companies to refrain from encouraging employees to submit reports in an anonymous manner. A hotline in Germany, on the other hand, has a broad scope and can cover a wide range of issues, beyond the limited scope of financial and accounting issues contemplated by the French CNIL.[21]

Table 10.3 provides a summary of laws and regulations governing hotline usage in a number of counties in North America, Europe, and Asia.

Table 10.3.

Country	Resources
Canada	Multilateral Instrument 52-110 (not effective in British Columbia) requires that an independent audit committee of the board have oversight of the receipt, retention, and treatment of complaints received regarding accounting, internal accounting controls, or auditing matters. The whistleblowing process must allow for the confidential, anonymous submission by employees, customers, or other third parties of their accounting or auditing concerns. Public servant whistleblowers are also protected by the Public Servants Disclosure Protection Act (Bill C-11) (passed October 2005).
European Union	The Charter of Fundamental Rights of the EU (2000/C 364/01) establishes a right to personal data privacy. The EU directed each member country to enact data privacy legislation and establish a governmental agency for its enforcement. Organizations that seek to operate a hotline in EU member countries should ensure that they are in compliance with EU principles that govern data privacy and hotline usage. The EU Article 29 Data Protection Working Party

(continued)

Table 10.3. (*Continued*)

	opinion provides guidance to member states on the matter, and although not binding, is considered very persuasive.
United Kingdom	The Public Interest Disclosure Act 1998 protects whistleblowers in specific situations in order to allow employees to raise concerns outside of the company without the fear of retribution. The U.K.'s data privacy protection agency operates without formal guidelines on hotlines, but the U.K. generally follows the EU with respect to data privacy principles. The Combined Code on Corporate Governance (July 2003) states that audit committees should review arrangements by which employees can, in confidence, raise concerns about possible improprieties.
France	The Commission Nationale de L'Informatique et des Libertes (CNIL) issued guidelines in 2005 offering a comprehensive view on hotlines and how data should be collected, stored, and transferred. Organizations that seek to establish a hotline in France must apply to the CNIL for authorization and certify compliance with the CNIL guidelines, with any departures from the guidelines justified. Adherence to French rules on hotlines will typically comply with guidelines set by other EU states.
Spain	The Agencia Espanola de Proteccion de Datos (AEPD) has not issued guidelines for the implementation of a whistleblower hotline. It has, however, issued an opinion that provides a basis for future rulings, generally following the CNIL guidance and the EU Article 29 Data Protection Working Party opinion. The AEPD, however, in a departure from the two, prohibits, rather than discourages, anonymous reports.
Germany	The German Ad Hoc Working Group opinion, as related to employee data protection, follows the guidelines set by the EU Article 29 Data Protection Working Party opinion and the CNIL. It discourages anonymous reporting in all but exceptional cases, and all whistleblowing schemes must serve as a supplement to traditional reporting channels. It also follows the established protocol for data storage, collection, transfer, and protection. It expands the CNIL and Working Party's guidelines in its scope of reporting topics, allowing for reporting beyond financial or accounting topics.
The Netherlands	The Dutch Data Protection Authority guidelines promote confidentiality over anonymous reporting but will accept the latter. It is generally similar to EU and CNIL guidelines and requires that the whistleblowing system be supplemental to other internal reporting channels.

Table 10.3. (*Continued*)

Japan	Japan enacted the Financial Instruments & Exchange Law, commonly referred to as J-SOX. It does not provide any guidance on an employee complaint process. Japan has, however, passed a Whistleblower Protection Act, which affords employment protection to employees, impacting both the public and private sector. The Whistleblower Protection Act requires a complaint be investigated properly, but offers no penalties for failure to do so.

Source: Adapted from *Best Practices in Global Ethics Hotlines, a Guide to Navigating Hotline Compliance Guidelines Worldwide*, The Network, 2009.

While different cultures may have their own reasons for why whistleblowing is unpopular, the reality is that some discomfort regarding blowing the whistle is fairly universal. In dealing with this challenge, organizations should first understand country-specific laws and potential cultural reluctance to accept a reporting hotline and then work to create an international "philosophy" of compliance that is sensitive to local norms and nuances, yet encourages reporting of improper conduct through dissemination of shared goals and implementation of effective reporting mechanisms.

Conclusion

Increasingly, reporting mechanisms are catalysts for creating organizational change and a culture of high ethics and integrity, and regulatory frameworks are encouraging organizations to design and implement such mechanisms. However, organizations should adopt such mechanisms not just because they are required by regulations or suggested by evaluative frameworks, but also because reporting mechanisms are indispensable tools in the effort to detect fraud and misconduct and to bring potential issues to light before they become significant—or public—legal problems.

The importance of equipping a reporting mechanism with the right features cannot be overstated. It can make a drastic difference in whether management can effectively surface compliance-sensitive information. And in this context, some of the more critical features of a reporting mechanism are the ability to receive reports in an anonymous manner and keep the reports confidential, as well as an organizational promise—one that must not be broken—that employees who report in good faith will not be subject to retaliation.

Chapter 11

Detection: Auditing and Monitoring

Timothy P. Hedley
Barbara M. Porco
James R. Littley

Auditing and monitoring are oversight activities that provide a systematic, disciplined approach to evaluate and help improve the effectiveness of risk management and governance processes. In this context, auditing is a formal process that provides independent, objective assurance regarding how well the organization or select organizational functions comply with applicable laws, rules, regulations, policies, procedures, and controls. An example may include an objective review of how well the organization handled employee complaints that came in through its hotline. Namely, did all allegations eventually move to disposition? Did, for example, the HR function properly follow up to ensure nonretaliation? Were investigative protocols followed?

Monitoring is typically less formal than auditing and normally part of the day-to-day activities of those involved in compliance and similar functions. For example, the hotline administrator may execute an effectiveness survey at the end of a hotline call. Another example may include following up at a future point with individuals who have made hotline calls to ensure nonretaliation. Organizational pulse surveys that measure employee attitudes are a third example.

Barbara Porco is an assistant professor in the accounting department at Fordham University.
Jim Littley is a principal in KPMG LLP's Forensic practice in Philadelphia, PA. He leads KPMG's national Continuous Auditing and Monitoring services.
Additional contributors are Peter J. Bradford, Cassandra C. Cohen, and Christopher H. Hunt.

Auditing and monitoring are carried out to provide information about the operation of controls and to provide evidence to support an assessment of the operating effectiveness of a control system. The processes embedded in auditing and monitoring help organizations identify anomalies indicative of internal control failures and may reveal potential misconduct, breakdowns in controls, and company and employee malfeasance. Once these failures are identified, organizations can address control weaknesses and can improve the reliability and integrity of financial information, the safeguarding of assets, and the compliance with corporate policies, programs, and controls.

This chapter further defines the nature of auditing and monitoring functions to help provide a framework for the development, design, and implementation of such programs. We will also detail the key considerations of auditing and monitoring oversight, with particular emphasis on the critical elements typical of successful procedures to prevent, detect, and respond to fraudulent activities. Finally, the chapter will offer insight into the use of technology to enhance the oversight process.

Defining Auditing and Monitoring

Auditing is a systematic methodology for analyzing specific business processes to evaluate an internal control system and is commonly established as an objective appraisal function (e.g., internal audit) within an organization to analyze business processes, procedures, and activities. The goal of such independent functions in this context is to highlight organizational problems and recommend solutions to management. Internal auditors, for example, evaluate the design and operational effectiveness of control processes and assess the extent to which managers have reasonable assurance that business objectives will be realized.

Effective audit functions report to top management and generally have direct communication with the audit committee and the board of directors. The communication and reporting structure for the internal audit process infers objectivity; however, auditors should not be perceived as truly impartial. Since an unbiased perspective is critical in an audit function, auditors typically perform assessments in areas where they do not have a vested interest and where they are insulated from individual consequences resulting from their findings. Coupling the direct reporting process with objective evaluation, auditing can offer an invaluable contribution to the corporate oversight process.

Unlike auditing, monitoring is a generalized system of oversight providing an organization with an appraisal or self-appraisal of its control system's performance. Monitoring programs are implemented to help ensure "that internal control continues to operate effectively."[1] Typically, effective monitoring programs are built into a company's normal operations and do not function as a separate exercise occurring outside of regular operations.

The two general surveillance objectives of monitoring and auditing are determining that components of internal control are operating as designed and that any deficiencies revealed are resolved in a timely manner. To help accomplish these major principles of oversight, the following three broad elements should be embedded in an organization's framework of internal control.

First, an organization should design its activities for auditing and monitoring around overall priorities for compliance-related activities based upon both short- and long-term organizational objectives. These objectives may include the following:

- How leadership's commitment to compliance is integrated into business goals, strategies, decisions, and day-to-day practices
- What methods are used to promote, reward, and enforce a culture committed to the company's core values function
- How specific compliance policies, programs, and controls are intended to operate
- How authorities and accountabilities are delegated for various functions in achieving compliance and integrity objectives
- How budgeting and compliance resources are allocated
- How challenges faced in the implementation of compliance activities are addressed
- How key performance indicators (KPIs) are used to measure the effectiveness of compliance activities
- How priorities, professional standards, industry practices, and regulatory expectations are adhered to

These foundational considerations should be matched to an appropriate organizational structure that assigns roles to personnel with appropriate capabilities, objectivity, and authority. The design specifics will be driven by the organization's particular operational structure.

Second, the effective implementation of these surveillance and oversight programs is essential. Effective implementation will help ensure that the oversight function is focused on acquiring persuasive information regarding the operation of key controls that address meaningful risks to organizational objectives. Every organization is different, with different structures, policies, programs, and controls, and, importantly, different tolerances to risk.

Nonetheless, there are certain key implementation considerations:

- Is there clear support from the board of directors and senior management?
- Are there well-established objectives for auditing and monitoring?

- Are reporting lines well established with unfettered access to the board if applicable?
- Has an assessment been performed to identify the barriers to success?
- Is there a remediation plan to overcome identified barriers?
- Have sufficient resources been provided to help ensure that such efforts are not merely window dressing?
- Are there personnel available who have the requisite skills and training? Will it be necessary to train professionals?
- Have organizational structures been taken into account? For example, is the organizational structure so highly decentralized that it may make it difficult for highly centralized auditing and monitoring functions to succeed?
- Have all key stakeholders been consulted during planning? For example, have all stakeholders responsible for compliance, investigations, and operations (e.g., HR, legal, security, finance, and accounting) provided meaningful input?
- Is there an established time line for implementation?
- Is there a process for evaluating the success of the implementation efforts?

Third, reporting the results of auditing and monitoring should be structured to help ensure necessary communication to corporate stakeholders. For example, reports should include evaluating the severity of any identified deficiencies and reporting the monitoring and auditing results to the appropriate personnel and the board for timely action and follow-up, if needed. Three key elements to successful evaluation and communication processes include the prioritization of findings, policies for reporting results to the appropriate level, and remediation actions required.

While the assessment process focuses on both the likelihood and magnitude of potential fraud and misconduct (see Chapter 7 for more information), oversight activities should consider the entire organization, including the entity's significant business units, operational divisions, and significant accounts. Controls that are not periodically assessed for relevance and practicality tend to deteriorate over time. Consequently, regular auditing and monitoring practices can lead to organizational efficiencies and reduced costs associated with public reporting on internal control. Accordingly, identification of control deficiencies should be addressed proactively, rather than reactively, to help ensure efficient resolution.

When procedures for monitoring and auditing functions are well designed and implemented, organizations can benefit. These benefits may include the following:

- Identification and correction of internal control problems on a timely basis
- Identification of fraud and misconduct risk

- Deterrence of corporate malfeasance
- Production of more accurate and reliable information for use in decision making
- Preparation of accurate and timely financial statements
- Preparation of periodic certifications or assertions on the effectiveness of internal control

Auditing and monitoring procedures can also facilitate an effective governance process through the evaluation of other characteristics, including ethics and values, performance management, and the assessment and communication of risk. An effective auditing and monitoring structure can help a corporation to direct resources to protect against misconduct.

Auditing and Monitoring Imperatives

Although not the sole drivers, auditing and monitoring processes have been significantly influenced by the Sarbanes-Oxley Act of 2002 and by the Federal Sentencing Guidelines. Specifically, the requirements of Sarbanes-Oxley have mandated the development of corporate internal control systems, while the Sentencing Guidelines have contributed to the heightened importance of organizational oversight procedures aimed at protecting company resources as well as preventing and detecting fraud. Both necessitate the creation of an effective compliance and ethics program, including auditing and monitoring functions as a critical component.

Section 404 of Sarbanes-Oxley requires companies to adopt an internal control framework that is developed, documented, and monitored. The requirement states that management should formulate assertions of internal controls based on the application of "a suitable, recognized control framework."[2] In compliance with Section 404, publicly held corporations are required to issue these assertions with their annual SEC filings, including management's report on its assessment of the organization's internal controls over financial reporting.

Within the report, company management will state that it is responsible for establishing and maintaining adequate internal control over financial reporting. The report requires specification that the internal control system contains monitoring mechanisms and procedures that appropriately respond to identified deficiencies or system breakdowns.

Although Section 404 does not specify one particular internal control structure, the Committee of Sponsoring Organizations of the Treadway Commission (COSO) offers a recommended internal control framework that provides a standardized method to define and assess corporate control environments.[3] The COSO framework is often recognized as a global benchmark for providing guidance on critical aspects of organizational governance, business ethics, internal control, enterprise risk management, fraud, and financial reporting.

According to COSO, an effective internal control framework includes a well-developed control environment, secure information systems, and appropriate monitoring and auditing activities. The prescribed framework consists of five key interrelated components of internal control:

1. The control environment
2. Risk assessment
3. Control activities
4. Information and communication
5. Monitoring

Although monitoring is specifically represented as the fifth element of the framework, the internal auditing function is also construed to be a component of the oversight procedures. Both activities provide an element of ongoing self-assessment that helps prevent, detect, and deter fraud and unintended errors. While auditing and monitoring are not control activities, they contribute to the success of an effective internal control system. The linkage between these two processes forms an integrated system of corporate oversight that reacts dynamically to changing conditions and reveals potential lapses in controls.

Testing and evaluating entity-level controls has been a challenge for compliance professionals since the Sentencing Guidelines became effective in 1991. Although the 2004 amendments to the Sentencing Guidelines provide more insight for defining an effective program, they do not specify how to measure or otherwise determine if a particular program element is indeed operating effectively. The amended directive states that elements of an effective control should "promote an organizational culture that encourages ethical conduct and a commitment to compliance with the law."[4] Unfortunately, a generally accepted measurement framework to assess an organization's internal control system does not exist.

The Sentencing Guidelines do suggest, however, that an "organization shall take reasonable steps to ensure that the organization's compliance and ethics program is followed, including monitoring and auditing to detect criminal conduct and to evaluate periodically the effectiveness of the organization's compliance and ethics program."[5] The ability of an entity to demonstrate efforts and resources directed to such a program can provide the organization consideration that may be used in determining sentencing in the event of a breach.

Compliance with the Sentencing Guidelines suggests that an organization's compliance and ethics program should include both monitoring and auditing as an integral process to help prevent and detect criminal behavior within a corporation. The guidelines further suggest that an organization should periodically assess the effectiveness of the corporation's compliance and ethics program. While the guidance is not specific, the institutionalization of monitoring and auditing procedures provides corporations with the ability to demonstrate assurance efforts to maintain a culture that prevents as well as detects malfeasance.

The creation and assessment of an effective compliance program can offer different aspects of a holistic approach to fraud risk management. According to the Sentencing Guidelines, the Department of Justice looks favorably upon corporate self-regulation. Ultimately, the Sentencing Guidelines encourage corporate management to create and monitor an internal control structure that helps ensure that the organization's practices are in accordance with applicable laws and regulations.

Furthermore, government regulations and technical requirements are continually maturing, and as a result, individuals assigned monitoring and auditing roles are responsible for not only understanding current system challenges but also preparing for future changes.

Key Considerations

We will now turn our attention to key considerations when conducting oversight activities. Specifically, we will look at ensuring professional competency, applying professional skepticism, incorporating fraud and misconduct risks, embedding risk assessments, and reporting results.

Ensuring Professional Competency

The organization's chief compliance officer and director of internal audit should work to ensure that all employees responsible for performing auditing and monitoring functions have the necessary knowledge and experience to adequately perform an assigned oversight process. Competency is a critical element to auditing and monitoring practices. Oversight personnel should possess adequate training and experience, as well as an understanding of the organization, which can allow them to evaluate proficiently specific risks associated with any area being assessed. Ideally, individuals performing an internal assessment should recognize how management typically interacts with its employees, how the organization communicates its standards, and how it trains personnel to help ensure they understand their responsibility for complying with laws, regulations, standards, and policies governing their job functions.

Procedures to monitor and measure future compliance or improvement in compliance are imperative to help insulate the organization from potential unlawful conduct. Therefore, the ability to distinguish between normal and abnormal employee behavior can be achieved by interacting with members of the company on a regular basis. This familiarity informs the oversight process, enabling identification of irregularities and potential wrongdoings. All this, however, is dependent upon those charged with oversight and surveillance exhibiting the proper mindset—namely, a skeptical mindset.

Applying Professional Skepticism

Professional skepticism, or a doubting state of mind, is an attitude that includes questioning and a critical assessment of findings. An objective, skeptical auditor or compliance professional neither assumes that management or employees are dishonest nor assumes unquestioned honesty. In auditing and monitoring employees, management, or organizational activities, exercising professional skepticism is a top priority. Inadequate professional skepticism is frequently cited as one of the main reasons why significant fraud or misconduct has not been detected. Internal auditors and others charged with oversight play a critical role in the success or failure of fraud risk management.

With their intimate knowledge of the workings of an entity, such professionals are often in a unique position to identify many of the indicators of fraud and misconduct. When those charged with oversight act with skepticism and focus upon the effectiveness of internal controls, the likelihood that they will recognize the common characteristics of integrity breakdowns is increased. Professionals who do internal auditing and monitoring should perform and carry out their responsibilities trusting, but always verifying, the source of evidential material supporting the efficacy of the internal control system.

Incorporating Fraud and Misconduct Risks

In addition to understanding the corporate environment, professionals performing auditing and monitoring functions should possess a knowledge of fraud and misconduct schemes. This background serves as a crucial element in identifying red flags indicative of malfeasance. Oversight can be enhanced if assessors understand the characteristics of fraud and similar acts, are knowledgeable about the techniques used to commit fraud, and have fluency with various fraud schemes and scenarios associated with the activities being reviewed.

Having insight into fraud and misconduct provides employees responsible for an organization's oversight with the ability to identify opportunities that could enable fraud as well as address methods to reduce future corporate exposure to fraud. For example, if significant control deficiencies are detected, additional procedures should be conducted to specifically identify whether fraud has transpired. This will also help determine additional auditing and monitoring mechanisms to assist a company's compliance with laws, regulations, and policies that govern its business operations.

Professionals responsible for internal auditing and monitoring should consider several key issues while performing monitoring and auditing functions. Fraud and misconduct risks should be considered in the assessment of internal control design and the determination of oversight steps to perform. Although internal auditors are not expected to detect fraud, individuals assigned the role of internal auditor are expected to obtain reasonable assurance that business objectives for the process under review are being achieved and material control deficiencies—whether a result of simple error or intentional effort—are detected.

As discussed previously in this book, a successful fraud risk management approach focuses on three objectives—prevention, detection, and response. Each of these objectives is a critical consideration in designing an auditing and monitoring approach and in training. Prevention controls are designed to reduce the risk of fraud and misconduct from occurring, while detection controls are designed to discover fraud and misconduct when they occur. Equally important is the third type of control that is designed to respond with timely action to remediate potential damage resulting from corporate errors or misconduct.

Once key controls within these areas are determined, monitoring and auditing procedures identify information that will support a conclusion about whether those controls have been implemented and are operating as intended. Identifying this information requires the ability to gain insight into potential control failures as well the ability to determine the type of information needed to assess whether or not the control system is operating properly. The persuasiveness of such information is important and refers to the "degree to which the monitoring information is capable of providing adequate support for a conclusion regarding the effectiveness of internal controls."[6]

Embedding Risk Assessments

As discussed previously, designing an effective assessment begins with understanding and prioritizing risks to achieve important organizational objectives. Once risks have been assigned their relative order of importance, key controls are noted and the available persuasive information is identified. At the culmination of the risk assignment process, the organization's implementation of surveillance procedures should evaluate the effectiveness of the internal control system's ability to manage or mitigate those identified risks. Although monitoring and auditing activities cannot be conducted for every facet of an organization's compliance system, it is imperative that oversight procedures are based on carefully prioritized risks, and those functions revealed as areas vulnerable to fraud should be identified for routine internal review.

In addition to a company's practices identified through the normal risk-profiling process, areas that should receive precedence should include functions that legally require compliance audits or business practices that governmental agencies have targeted through enforcement efforts. Other areas of concern may include departments that have high employee turnover, unresolved issues regarding specific personnel, and regulations or procedures that have changed significantly. Organizational transition or organizational stress should also be included in the risk assessment process. Individuals performing monitoring and auditing roles should review the company's performance management systems to help ensure that employees are appropriately incentivized for compliant behavior and disciplined when they commit compliance violations.

When conducting auditing and monitoring procedures, it is also important to consider that they should be varied in nature in that the number of transactions and activities examined should be selected through a rotation of different departments, divisions, business units, and geographies. This unpredictability can help ensure that oversight activities are not circumvented.

Reporting Results

Once monitoring and auditing procedures have been completed, the results should be compiled and reported to the appropriate personnel. Conclusions will indicate whether or not established expectations about the effectiveness of internal control have been achieved and highlight identified deficiencies for achievable corrective action.

At this point, company executives should evaluate whether or not timely and sufficient corrective measures have been taken with respect to any noted control deficiencies or weaknesses and whether the plan for monitoring the business infrastructure continues to be adequate for the institution's ongoing success. Additionally, management may consider if it needs to increase auditing and monitoring activities for identified areas that are susceptible to fraud and misconduct.

Using Technology for Continuous Auditing and Continuous Monitoring

Continuous auditing and continuous monitoring (CA/CM) allows audit functions and operational employees to shift their focus and review from traditional retrospective and detective activities to proactive and preventive activities. Many of the indicators of fraud and misconduct—both actual and potential—reside in an organization's financial, operational, and transactional data and can be identified using

CA/CM tools and techniques. Such tools and techniques use sophisticated analytical tests, computer-based cross-matching, and nonobvious relationship identification to highlight potential fraud and misconduct that can remain unnoticed by traditional review techniques. Some benefits of forensic-based CA/CM may include:

- Identification of hidden relationships between people, organizations, and events
- A means to analyze suspicious transactions
- An ability to assess the effectiveness of internal controls intended to prevent or detect fraudulent activities
- The potential to continually monitor fraud threats and vulnerabilities
- The ability to consider and analyze thousands of transactions in less time, more efficiently, and more cost-effectively than using more traditional forensic sampling techniques
- The ability to consider a company's unique organizational and industry issues

Financial and operational data can be continuously audited or monitored by using either less frequent, retrospective-based methods or more real-time, frequent, proactive methods. Retrospective-based continuous CA/CM applied in the detection of fraud and misconduct, for example, can allow organizations to analyze financial transactions in monthly, quarterly, or annual increments, enabling organizations to discern patterns that are not visible with shorter-term analyses. In addition, more real-time monitoring can help an organization identify potentially fraudulent transactions on a daily, weekly, or monthly basis.

CA/CM Objectives

The goal of pursuing CA and CM is to provide greater transparency, effectively manage risk (including fraud and misconduct risk), and improve performance. Table 11.1 highlights the objectives of each discipline.

The Choice: CA or CM or Both

Organizations that work to draw the maximum value from CA/CM tend to use a combination of both CA and CM throughout the business. While neither CA nor CM needs to be present for the other to be implemented, companies that combine CA and CM tend to coordinate the efforts of internal audit with management to avoid duplication of efforts and unproductive use of resources. Some organizations that have successfully implemented CA without having a CM

Table 11.1.

Continuous Auditing (*Performed by Audit Function*)	Continuous Monitoring (*Operational Responsibility*)
• Gain audit evidence more effectively and efficiently • React more timely to business risks • Leverage technology to perform more efficient internal audits • Focus audits more specifically • Help monitor compliance with policies, procedures, and regulations • Become more valuable to the business	• Improve governance—aligning business and compliance risk to internal controls and remediation • Improve transparency and react more timely to make better day-to-day decisions • Strive to reduce cost of controls and reduce the cost of testing and monitoring • Leverage technology to create efficiencies by identifying opportunities for performance improvements

Source: KPMG LLP, 2010.

process in place have deployed CA to better understand risks to the enterprise, assess control effectiveness, support compliance efforts, and better manage and utilize their internal audit resources. Often, CA techniques can lead to management ultimately adopting select procedures as CM.

Three Dimensions of CA/CM

In order to monitor their fraud and misconduct risks, leading organizations tend to use a combination of three dimensions of CA/CM based on a number of factors, including current IT systems, fraud and misconduct risk areas to be monitored, ease of implementation, and cost:

- *Continuous controls monitoring* (CCM) includes monitoring a system's global configuration settings, access controls, and rules that define the parameters of how an event or transaction can be initiated, processed, and recorded. CCM primarily focuses on monitoring for unauthorized users trying to perform authorized activities. An example is monitoring controls that limit a plant manager responsible for purchasing materials from creating a fictitious vendor and processing fictitious or inflated invoices.
- *Continuous transaction monitoring* (CTM) includes the creation of rules and tests run against the actual flow of transactions—identifying exceptions, anomalous patterns and trends, or other outliers that represent risk or are

contrary to expected measures of performance such as KPIs. CTM primarily focuses on monitoring for authorized users performing unauthorized activities. An example is monitoring trade accounts payable for possible violations of the Foreign Corrupt Practices Act.

- *Macro-level trends and results monitoring* relates to "seeing the forest through the trees" and requires evaluation of analyses measuring historical or emerging trends in identifying potential fraud and misconduct issues with underlying changes in the organization's people, processes, and technology. Examples include trends and patterns in manual journal entries to reserve accounts substantially impacting quarterly earnings.

Leveraging Technology Tools

CA/CM technology tools provide users a means to structure, document, and manage business risk; monitor internal control effectiveness and performance; and detect and correct controls gaps while making timely performance improvement adjustments. These tools can be directly integrated into the enterprise resource planning (ERP) or operate as a separate bolt-on solution.

The value of the tools lies in their ability to translate a business rule to a configurable control and assess the performance of transactions against expected results. When a configurable control or transaction does not conform to a predefined risk-based, business-rule pattern or trend, an alert can be automatically generated. Such an alert could be as simple as an e-mail notification to the business user and a supervisor, or it could be a summary dashboard by control points, process area, and operating unit, thus providing tactical and strategic business insights.

Together, CA/CM can bring greater insights and transparency for continuous assurance and performance. The success of CA/CM is dependent upon the effective use of technology tools, and organizations should carefully evaluate the features, functions, and capabilities most appropriate for their needs before engaging a tool provider.

Drivers

Many organizations are considering the value of a CA/CM discipline in reducing fraud and misconduct risk, along with the value of the technology tools and techniques that enable such programs. Their efforts are driven by a number of business imperatives that also shape and influence the road map for CA/CM:

- Increased regulatory compliance requirements
- Increased fraud and misconduct risk including recent exposure to fraud
- Recent merger or acquisition

- Cost pressures including downsizing, outsourcing, and offshoring
- Shareholder and audit committee expectations

Areas that tend to have the greatest return of investment in an initial implementation include procure to pay, for example, procurement cards; travel and entertainment expense; and manual journal entries.

Conclusion

Monitoring and auditing practices are essential features of every compliance program. Although internal control systems encompass one of the most valuable protections from theft, error, waste, and abuse, they have inherent shortcomings, including the potential for management override, that should be considered in appraising their contribution to reducing the risk of malfeasance and increasing operational efficiency. Organizations should recognize that practical compromise exists between the costs of maintaining controls and the value of what they protect. Although no defense against entity risks is guaranteed, the protection afforded through monitoring and auditing procedures cannot be understated. Surveillance and timely revision to ensure against the degeneration of controls increase the level of fortification. When designing monitoring and auditing processes, the following considerations are paramount:

- Focus on high-risk areas
- Validate policies and procedures
- Properly qualify reviewers
- Take corrective action in response to audit results
- Assess the potential of management override
- Monitor and report the audit efforts

Management has primary responsibility for establishing, implementing, and maintaining monitoring and auditing procedures. Their synergistic performance represents critical elements of a comprehensive system that can help protect an organization from corporate fraudulence and corruption. Regular compliance evaluations can provide optimal risk assessment and prevention activities.

The monitoring and auditing functions are intertwined oversight procedures that can provide corporate leadership with information critical in preventing, detecting, deterring, and responding to entity malfeasance. Reducing potential fraud and errors and enhancing operational activities can help institutions successfully attain organizational goals.

Chapter 12

Response: Investigations

Richard H. Girgenti

Despite the best efforts to prevent misconduct, most organizations will face wrongdoing by employees, management, or outsiders at some point. The misconduct may vary in size and scope. While there is no one "right" way to respond, it is important to respond effectively and in a proper and timely manner. A poorly conducted response will almost certainly make a potentially bad situation worse.

Organizations that respond quickly and with proper planning can be in a better position to get the investigation right the first time. This is particularly true because unintentional missteps can limit the organization's ability to discover important facts, fail to identify those involved in the wrongdoing, and inadvertently destroy or contaminate potential evidence. A mismanaged investigation can lead to additional costs, result in failing to properly calculate losses, result in denial of potential insurance claims, and increase the chances of damaging a company's reputation and the morale of its employees. It can also open an organization to lawsuits resulting from wrongful termination, shareholder actions, and regulatory actions and penalties.

An organization does not want to be in a position in which some of its actions in conducting an investigation are scrutinized later by regulators and law enforcement agencies and determined to be inadequate or, worse

Additional contributors are Joseph P. Dooley, Thomas P. Keegan, Marc L. Miller, Philip D. Ostwalt, Nicole Stryker, and Nimna Varghese.

yet, illegal. This was the result of an internal investigation by a global technology company to determine who within the boardroom had leaked inside information to local media. State and federal law enforcement agencies determined that some of the actions taken by the investigative team, which included subcontracted investigators, were illegal. In particular, the investigation was faulted for using an improper technique known as "pretexting," or posing as someone else to obtain phone records of reporters and board members suspected of involvement in press leaks. The adverse attention from media, law enforcement, and Congress may have been avoided if there had been an appropriate investigative plan in place that adhered to appropriate investigative techniques.

Source: David Lazarus, "HP's Investigation Broke State Laws, Attorney General Says," SFGate.com, September 8, 2006, articles.sfgate.com/2006-09-08/business/17309775_ 1_phone-records-board-members-hp (accessed August 17, 2010); Damon Darlin, "House Panel and U.S. Attorney Join H.P. Inquiry," *The New York Times*, September 12, 2006, www.nytimes.com/2006/09/12/technology/12hewlett.html?_r=1&ref=hewlett_packard_ corporation (accessed August 17, 2010).

Organizations should be prepared to make important decisions in the early days of an investigation, as these decisions will put the investigation into motion and affect its future direction. Each investigation presents a unique set of challenges that require the investigator to tailor the approach and scope.

This chapter is intended to assist organizations in:

- Determining when an investigation is needed
- Assessing the initial and interim actions that need to be taken
- Determining who must be notified of the allegations and investigations
- Deciding who should oversee and who should conduct the investigation
- Identifying the conduct in question and the person(s) responsible
- Assessing the legality and propriety of the conduct
- Understanding the techniques, tools, and methodologies for conducting a proper investigation and managing investigative records
- Determining when an investigation is complete
- Evaluating when and how the results of an investigation should be reported
- Making informed decisions regarding when, how, and what corrective action should be taken, including enhancements that may be required to improve the organization's controls and compliance program
- Determining whether or not the conduct that is the subject of the investigation needs to be disclosed to government authorities

Preinvestigation Preparation

Once an allegation is raised, an organization should decide whether a particular matter warrants investigation and, if so, who will be involved. Adding to the challenge is that these initial decisions need to be made when the extent of the wrongdoing, or the identity of those involved, may not be fully known.

Organizations that have an established response plan can be a step ahead. These plans typically delineate key decision points and general procedures and protocols that the organization can follow in deciding to conduct an investigation and outlining what needs to be done and by whom should an investigation become necessary.

These protocols typically include:

- Procedures for receiving and recording allegations
- A process that delineates who is responsible for deciding whether an investigation is warranted and what criteria should be applied to decide on an appropriate response
- An escalation process for appropriate notification to the board and audit committee
- A process for planning and managing the investigation
- A standardized evidence collection method (e.g., how to deal with witness statements and how to collect and record physical evidence)
- Guidelines for properly preserving electronic evidence, conducting interviews, and analyzing evidence
- Guidelines on what is acceptable for investigations at international locations, consistent with the laws of the nations where the organization operates
- Guidelines for notifications and communications that might need to be made to auditors, analysts, media, regulatory bodies, shareholders, and others who have reason to be informed

Establishing such protocols can help management and, as warranted, the audit committee and the board to guide a well-run investigation. Without such protocols in place, an organization is more likely to spend the first few, often chaotic, days or weeks after learning of an allegation trying to determine what to do under very challenging circumstances.

Initial Considerations

The initial considerations can be broken into six steps.

Step 1: Assessing Whether an Investigation Is Needed

Allegations can arise from a variety of sources. For example, a whistleblower may file an anonymous tip, a vendor may call the organization's ethics and compliance hotline, or an employee may walk into a manager's office or the human resources department. Shareholder litigation can also spark an investigation.

Often, before launching an investigation, an organization may conduct a preliminary inquiry. This may include an assessment of the reliability of an allegation. Factors that organizations should consider in making a determination to initiate an investigation include:

- The nature of the allegation
- The credibility of the allegation and the source
- The potential consequences if the allegation is accurate
- The duration, complexity, and cost of conducting an investigation
- Additional facts that may be needed
- Resources needed to conduct a proper investigation
- Subject matter expertise that may be required

After an initial assessment, it may be determined that a formal investigation is not required because the complainant misunderstood the facts and circumstances at issue, no other facts or resources are needed to resolve the issue, or the issue lends itself to an informal resolution.

As a good practice, organizations should document and retain the analysis used to establish whether a formal investigation was warranted. Such a confidential record should supply sufficient detail to identify the allegation, the date it was announced, and the steps and dates of actions taken to resolve it.

During the first few days of an investigation, organizations should also consider the scope of the investigation to be undertaken. In responding to allegations, an investigation can prove inadequate when an organization takes an approach that is too narrow; or the investigation can be overly expensive and disruptive when an approach is too broad.

Step 2: Decide if Interim Actions Need to Be Undertaken

Depending on the allegation and its severity, an organization may need to take necessary steps to protect employee safety or company property. This could include removing the accused from the workplace (or placing the accused on leave) if there is concern that evidence may be destroyed, potential witnesses may be reluctant to cooperate, or attempts may be made to obstruct the investigation.

Step 3: Determine Who Must Be Notified of the Allegation and Investigation

Investigations should be conducted with sufficient confidentiality to help ensure the integrity of the investigation, help avoid reputation damage to those who might be wrongfully suspected, enlist full cooperation of witnesses, and help ensure evidence is neither compromised nor destroyed. It is important to recognize that all those who may be involved in a particular wrongdoing may not be identified at the outset of an investigation. Often, the subjects of an investigation will evolve as more is learned and uncovered. As a result, an organization should be very selective about who is notified and who is involved in the investigation. In addition, the organization should consider whether the allegation needs immediate disclosure to government authorities.

Step 4: Decide Who Will Lead and Oversee the Investigation

An important consideration at the outset of an investigation is determining who should oversee the investigation. In many instances, when there is a suspected illegality, investigations will be overseen by management. This could be the head of internal audit, a special investigative unit, company counsel, the head of compliance, or another C-level officer. More minor allegations, such as theft of property or creation of a hostile work environment, may be overseen by security or HR. However, instances of misconduct should be addressed as part of an overall compliance program in which top management and the board have responsibility for overseeing and ensuring that there is an effective investigative process. Other allegations, particularly those concerning senior management, financial reporting fraud, or potential illegal acts that are not inconsequential, will require direct board and special or audit committee oversight. In those instances where the allegations involve management, it is important that board members overseeing the investigation be independent. Some investigations are also directed or initiated by counsel, in-house or external.

The primary party designated to oversee the investigation should be sufficiently involved in:

- Ensuring that adequate resources are available
- Determining whether the scope of the investigation is adequate
- Consulting on any changes to the investigation scope, time frame, or resources
- Analyzing whether the investigation is appropriately focused and progressing toward the organization's desired outcome

- Reviewing the work plan, the work standards, and the time estimated for various steps
- Communicating with the investigative team and other stakeholders, including employees and regulators, with the frequency tailored to the severity and materiality of the allegation and the length of the investigation
- Creating an appropriate environment in which employees feel comfortable coming forward as needed to assist with the investigation

Step 5: Decide Who Will Conduct the Investigation

After determining who will oversee the investigation, the next critical decision is who should conduct the investigation. In making this determination, the objectivity of the investigative team should be assessed. At times, this assessment may result in an external investigation team being engaged. At a minimum, the investigative team should be removed enough from the target of the investigation to be objective. In no instance should the investigative team consist of employees who are involved in any of the suspected events, report to persons potentially involved in the events under investigation, or are evaluated by persons suspected of being involved. When assessing whether or not team members are capable of being objective, an organization should consider:

- The nature of the allegation and who is potentially involved
- The potential impact on the business unit or division suspected of improper activity
- Other geographies or departments of the company's operations that could be affected
- The individuals and functions likely involved based on the specific allegations and the possible individuals who have responsibilities that may be related to the allegations

Generally, internally performed investigations will have the benefit of institutional knowledge and can quickly get up to speed. However, there are circumstances when an organization may benefit from external investigators to coordinate and carry out an investigation. An independent external investigative team generally provides the most impartiality to an investigation. An external team may include one or more of the following: a law firm, a forensic accounting firm, corporate intelligence specialists, private investigators, and subject matter specialists. When the allegation involves financial or accounting fraud (e.g., matters that may be indicative of fraudulent financial reporting), forensic accountants will ordinarily be required. Allegations of illegal activity such as corruption and bribery, misappropriation of assets, or money laundering may also benefit from forensic accounting and other subject matter experts. These matters will often require specialized skills in financial analysis, account and transaction restructuring, analysis of accounting records, hidden assets discovery, calculation of losses, and preparation of proof of losses for insurance claims.

When independence is required, care should be taken to help ensure that outside firms or other service providers have no relationship with the organization that could bring into question the independence or objectivity of the investigation. When selecting an external party to conduct the investigation, organizations typically consider the amount and nature of prior work the prospective investigative firm has done for the organization and the likelihood that work may be done in the future. Depending upon the allegation and its visibility, the selection of a law firm or other advisor will be examined by such parties as external auditors, regulators, or state and federal law enforcement.

Step 6: Assess Special Considerations

Areas deserving of consideration include legal privileges, interaction with regulators, and cross-border investigations.

Legal Privileges. Given the myriad scenarios in which counsel may be engaged, there is an inherent assumption that documents and other materials will be discoverable in the event of a lawsuit. With that in mind, certain legal issues around documentation and communications between members of the investigation team need to be clarified at the outset. Two legal concepts that are to be considered in this respect are the attorney-client privilege and the attorney work product doctrine.

Attorney-Client Privilege. This privilege protects confidential information (including electronic information) disclosed to an attorney in the process of obtaining legal advice or assistance. The privilege applies to communications between the attorney and the client. State and federal evidence and procedure laws as well as relevant case law precedents will govern the applicability of this privilege. During an investigation, forensic accountants and other subject matter experts team with attorneys; and in such circumstances, it is important that the investigation team discuss issues that may be covered by privilege and clarify any related questions.

Attorney Work Product Doctrine. This privilege applies to "tangible material or its intangible equivalent"[1] collected or prepared in anticipation of litigation or a trial. The work product doctrine extends to analyses prepared by the investigation team to support findings.

A noteworthy point of distinction between the two concepts is the inclusivity of each. While the attorney-client privilege applies to communications between an attorney and a client, the work product doctrine applies to all documents, either prepared by the attorney or prepared by a third party for the same purposes.

Interaction with Regulators. When a company uncovers a fraud or an illegal act, it often has to consider voluntary disclosure to the relevant regulatory or government authorities. In other cases, federal and state authorities may have already commenced a formal or informal investigation on an individual or entity. For instance, the Securities and Exchange Commission may have issued a Wells notice, which informs persons involved in preliminary or formal investigations about the nature of an investigation and requires a statement within a prescribed time frame. Under circumstances where there are considerations of voluntary disclosure or parallel government investigations, advice of counsel is recommended.

Cross-Border Investigations. The investigation of cross-border fraud and misconduct involves differences in rules and regulations, legal requirements, business customs, accounting principles, general ledger systems, and cultural interpretation of evidence resulting in unique resource needs and constraints. It may be helpful to involve a local in-country practitioner in cross-border or multijurisdictional investigations to help ensure that appropriate jurisdictional considerations are being addressed. In international investigations it is important to understand different business customs and confirm that those customs do not violate local or international laws no matter how prevalent or accepted some customs may appear. A well-known issue of cultural differences in a cross-border investigation can be found during the interview. Certain behavior during an interview can be considered a sign of guilt in one culture and normal behavior in another culture. The successful conclusion of a cross-border investigation depends on several factors, including knowledge of local language, customs, laws and local governments, officials, and law enforcement.

When the need arises for a cross-border investigation where language barriers may cause difficulties, a key consideration in selecting team members is to ensure that communications within and with the team are clear and understood. In particular, when interviewing a witness or a suspect, it is important that the interviewee is comfortable during the interview and that the investigator has confidence that both the questions and answers are clearly understood. Working with local governments and law enforcement can pose difficulties for an entity. For example, in some countries, it may be considered normal to pay a "fee" to conduct business, whereas in others, such an act is considered to be illegal and may have serious consequences. In particular, this is an issue for consideration by U.S. multinationals, who are required to comply with the U.S. Foreign Corrupt

Practices Act (FCPA) in every country in which they operate. (For a discussion of the FCPA, see Chapter 3, "Bribery and Corruption.")

Organizations that have global operations have an additional dimension to consider during their investigations. They must bear in mind the laws and regulations that govern any country where information will be gathered or transported, recognizing that a legal investigative procedure in one country may be illegal in another. Some common differences among countries include:

- Access to and transportation of electronic data in compliance with local laws and regulations
- Access to and transportation of information in compliance with state secrecy laws
- Use of gathered data as evidence
- Evidence required to secure a successful civil outcome or criminal prosecution
- Data privacy regulations and laws

The Investigation in Process

Once the organizational focus has decided who will oversee and lead the investigation, the emphasis should shift to how the investigation will be conducted. In this phase, attention should turn to:

- Drafting and updating an investigative work plan
- Preserving evidence, including a document preservation notice
- Gathering information and evidence, including documents and electronic information
- Conducting interviews
- Analyzing investigative results
- Drafting a written or oral report of investigative findings

The Investigative Plan

A thoughtful work plan can assist team members in understanding investigative objectives and the tasks required to achieve them, as well as provide measures to gauge progress of the investigation. In preparing a work plan, the investigative team should begin by developing a hypothesis that suggests how the fraud or other illegal conduct might have occurred and who might be responsible. Development of a hypothesis, which may be altered during the investigation, can help the team to understand where the investigation may head, outline actionable steps to be completed in a work plan, and enable team members to consider efficient and effective investigative techniques.

Work plans will vary depending on the type of scheme or allegation investigated and should allow for changes as the investigation evolves. However, in general, an investigation work plan should contain the following elements:

- Investigation goals and strategies
- Preliminary scope and action items, including the electronic and paper documents to be gathered and reviewed, the people to be interviewed, potential accomplices who may be involved, and the analysis to be conducted
- Estimated time and resource requirements
- Reporting procedures

The investigative team may also need to take into account any jurisdictional differences that may limit the type of information that can be transferred across borders. For example, if an investigation is likely to involve data collection in the European Union, the work plan should address the fact that the EU does not permit certain electronic data to leave its borders due to restrictive data privacy laws; if the investigation involves data collection in China, the work plan needs to recognize that in China many businesses are state-owned, and, therefore, there is a very broad interpretation of what might constitute a state secret. So for the EU, the work plan will need to address the requirement that the analysis of relevant data should be conducted within the EU; in China, procedures will need to be in place to ensure that information that might be viewed as state secrets is not collected, viewed, or transported across borders.

Gathering Information

Information can be gathered from multiple sources, e.g., documents (in hardcopy form), digital information, public data, and interviews. Each of these sources of information requires different considerations. This section will discuss those considerations and how organizations and investigators can address them.

In the early hours of an investigation, one of the most important considerations is the securing of evidence that will need to be gathered and analyzed. Whether potential evidence is in the form of hard copy or digitalized documents, the first order of business should be to maintain the integrity and completeness of records.

Documentary Evidence

As early as possible, investigators should identify the types of documents to be preserved and collected and note which employees or other third parties may have such documents. Hard-copy documents may include everything from memoranda, correspondence, personal diaries, and handwritten notes to spreadsheets, calculations, charts, and tables. Often, hard copies are produced and stored electronically in digital form as well. However, although there will be much duplication, it is not uncommon for employees to make notes on hard copies that can often be critical in understanding intent and the employees' interpretation of information contained in the document. Locating, organizing, analyzing, and preserving information, whether hard copy or electronic, can be a complex undertaking.

To start, an organization should consider whether or not to issue a preservation or retention notice to all affected employees or departments. This is a legal judgment and is critical if there is any risk of alteration, destruction, or deletion of needed documentation. Often the decision to preserve documents is made as soon as there is any reason to believe that the documents might be relevant to an investigation or potential lawsuit. Many companies include in the organization's compliance program the responsibility for understanding and adhering to preservation policies and notices. Proper preservation and collection calls for maintaining a chain of custody over relevant documents and records and ensuring the integrity of information from notice of retention to final storage.

The method the investigative team uses to schedule and collect desired information should be incorporated into the investigation work plan. Often, documentary information can be gathered from employee worksites. Investigators should keep a log of each document collected and where it was obtained. It is important to consult counsel before gathering documents to ensure that the investigation is being conducted in accordance with all local laws and regulations. Both the organization's work plan and its protocols should address how the organization will ensure proper document control over the recording, tracing, and retrieval of the investigative documentation.

During an investigation, an organization may need to search and seize the property or documents of a potential target. Search and seizure is the process of locating and securing documents or other property, but also preventing the subsequent removal or destruction of the documents or property. Employees have been known to store important documents at their desks or elsewhere in their offices, and an investigator might find those documents useful. As always, local laws apply to the search for, and seizure of, such property.

Digital Evidence

Perhaps one of the most significant differences in conducting an investigation today as opposed to a decade or so ago is the amount and variety of electronic data. The challenge of a digital era has changed dramatically the manner in which investigations are typically conducted. Electronic media allow massive amounts of information to be transmitted and stored in multiple ways. Electronically stored information (ESI) can include e-mail, word documents, text messages, financial data, phone messages stored by digital voice mail systems, faxes that are sent and received digitally, proximity card readers that authenticate and log employee comings and goings, digital surveillance from cameras that monitor physical plants, and automobile fleet GPS systems that log vehicle location and routes.

ESI can also be found on a variety of devices, including office computers, servers, PDAs, mobile phones, or portable media such as thumb drives and discs. All this information may be relevant to an investigation and contain evidence of improper conduct. A more detailed discussion of ESI may be found in Chapter 14.

When a digital file is created, it leaves a trail that can be tracked; and in most instances, the trail remains even after the original files are deleted or overwritten on computers, laptops, or other storage devices. It is vital in many investigations that this data trail is followed.

The availability and accessibility of electronic data often present challenges in investigations. Yet there are certain practices that organizations can implement when digital evidence needs to be collected. To begin, the investigative team should evaluate the organization's IT environment as it relates to initial steps in obtaining and preserving electronic information. For example, the team should consider what types of electronic data exist and where the data may reside. The team should move swiftly to preserve and retain the data it will need for its analysis. The goal is to preserve the integrity of the data and to avoid any tampering. For instance, capturing forensic images of data rather than merely copying data is preferred should the investigation lead to a court proceeding. Forensic imaging allows one to understand the history around the creation and modification of a document by preserving necessary content from the hard drive including the dates of creation, the modification of a document, and the identity of those who may have accessed the content.

Since today's investigations increasingly involve digital evidence, teams should become familiar with digital evidence recovery, which is the process of identifying and preserving digital evidence in a manner that is acceptable in legal proceedings. Such data differ from other physical forms of evidence in that the data are:

- Often intangible in nature
- Often volatile and transient in nature
- Susceptible to manipulation
- Often located on any technology system in any country in the world
- Often "belong" to more than one person
- Reliant on computer technology for examination

The electronic discovery process should be tailored to the size and scope of the investigation. For larger investigations involving many electronic documents and e-mails, a variety of forensic software applications can help. These applications use keyword searches to isolate targeted documents or messages. As with any search, organizations will likely have to see how broad or narrow to make their keywords in an attempt to yield the most effective results.

Similar to paper-based discovery, any electronic document or e-mail that directly implicates an individual or offers clues in an alleged fraud should be set aside and used to further the investigation. In doing so, the organization should take care to preserve these materials for potential use in criminal or civil proceedings or by law enforcement or government agencies. This type of evidence must be retained in its original form to ensure that it cannot be manipulated or altered. Transactional data obtained from relational databases are often a significant component of internal investigations. The investigative team should give special consideration to the types of information that may be available within these systems. Log files, access rights, and permission levels are examples of several valuable pieces of information that can help an investigative team determine the key questions of who, what, and when. While every system is different, the investigation team should incorporate the following steps in its collection of data: document the methodology for extracting the data (including the programming syntax), validate between the source and the extracted data sets, and compare with existing business records to substantiate the veracity of data.

Physical Surveillance

Under appropriate circumstances, an investigative team may also use surveillance procedures that may yield important evidence. Surveillance activities may be useful particularly when the alleged misconduct involves the theft of assets such as cash or inventory. It may also be useful to verify the existence and location of residences or businesses that establish relationships and also to verify the scope and nature of a person's activities or assets. Surveillance may be conducted in person or through the use of video cameras.

Publicly Available Information

Public data, whether located on the Web, social networks, or government sites, can help uncover critical pieces of intelligence. Professionals experienced in accessing publicly available information, commonly referred to as corporate intelligence, can be a valuable investigative aid in locating and recovering assets and in uncovering information about individuals or entities.

Fact gathering in an investigation combines the identification of internally available information (from interviews, computers, e-mails, etc.) with information that can be gleaned from public records databases and the Internet. Such information can help the investigative team support or enhance its hypothesis; provide additional investigative leads; identify potential assets and previously unknown relationships; and "fill in the blanks" around events, persons, timelines, and trends.

At the early stage of an investigation, timely review of public records can provide background information for interviews and internal fact gathering through cost-effective research. Integrating corporate intelligence procedures into an investigation can assist with:

- Obtaining background information on individuals or entities
- Identifying related parties
- Identifying red flags such as financial stressors, criminal history, etc.
- Creating search-string terms for e-mail harvesting
- Preparing for interviews with targets and witnesses
- Identifying ownership of assets for determining the net worth and lifestyles of individuals for attachment or recovery in a lawsuit or for filing insurance claims

Intelligence analysts should understand what material is available in the public record, as well as what information is protected by U.S. or local jurisdictional mandates. For example, in the United States, credit information is subject to the Fair Credit Reporting Act, which has several requirements around the collection and distribution of information on individuals. See Chapter 9 for more information on corporate intelligence techniques used in an investigation.

Interviewing

Many, if not all, investigations involve interviews of individuals who have knowledge relevant to the allegation at hand. In an investigation, interviews have one of two objectives—gathering facts or seeking admission. Typically, interviews should be designed to achieve the first objective of gathering information and are a rudimentary tool in an investigator's toolbox. Admission-seeking interviews are typically less frequent and should generally be conducted by more experienced investigators. Regardless of the objective, encouraging interviewees to cooperate is one of the most important aspects in the investigation process.

As a first step, an investigation team should develop an interview strategy. Such a strategy should include a list of individuals who should be interviewed, along with the order of the interviews, specific issues to discuss in each interview, and notice of the interviews—whether they will be impromptu or scheduled in advance. The interview strategy should be informed by the allegations, the position and level of the interviewee, documents and digital information collected during earlier stages of the investigation, and information developed from earlier interviews and public data searches; the strategy also should be informed by whether the interviewee is viewed as the subject of the investigation.

An interview has, at times, been described as a conversation with a purpose and is critical in identifying details that pertain to the allegation, collecting new information, or determining additional issues that need further review. Depending on the allegation, those managing the investigation may elect to first interview individuals not directly related to the incident or allegation in question in order to gather facts and background information before interviewing the potential targets of the investigation. Regardless of who is to be interviewed, investigators should focus on the information they want to acquire by either drafting in advance some of the questions to be asked or creating a list of key points to be covered. These questions or bullet points are meant to guide interviewers during the meeting but should not drive the interview or restrict the conversation. The interviewer should adjust the questioning based on what the interviewee says. It may be that the interviewee reveals information that leads to a new hypothesis or moves the investigation in a different direction.

The interviewer should give thought in advance to the best location for the interview since the setting can influence whether a candid, open discussion will occur. Typically, interviews are conducted in conference rooms or other locations where there is a sense of privacy and the door can be closed—but never locked. This is because an interviewee should never feel unable to leave the interview. Interviewers can also help minimize such feelings by explaining to the interviewee when the meeting begins that the interviewee is free to leave at any time. Depending on the circumstances, the interviewer may verbally remind the interviewee of this at specific points in the discussion.

To further encourage open dialogue, an interviewer will usually meet with one person at a time. Depending on the situation, an investigator may schedule the meeting with very little notice to the person to be interviewed. This is particularly helpful when the investigative team is concerned that critical documents may be destroyed or that other witnesses may be alerted about the course of the investigation and inappropriately tailor what they say at the interview. Little notice may also be critical when the violation is ongoing or when there is a threat to the safety of others.

It is also generally advised to have at least two interviewers—one to ask questions and the other to take notes. An organization may also consider having a representative from the human resources department present during the interview, depending on where the investigation is taking place or on other particular circumstances. In some countries, local laws, regulations, or customs require the presence of HR representatives. Having an HR representative present can be particularly advantageous if the interview is in a foreign country, because the HR professional may be able to explain country-specific information and any rules on the types of questions that may and may not be asked.

While each interviewer will have an individual style, many effective interviewers project a proper demeanor of objectivity, patience, and cordiality. Skilled interviewers are typically even-tempered and nonjudgmental. An effective interviewer should be aware of any cultural issues that may affect how questions should be asked and answers interpreted. It is also critical that the interviewer engage in effective listening by:

- Being alert for content and detail
- Observing nonverbal behavior and the form of verbal responses, particularly indications of deception such as nonresponsiveness of answers or protest statements that are designed to convince rather than convey information
- Using silence to gather further information
- Not interrupting or completing interviewees' sentences
- Avoiding personal and external distractions
- Using positive verbal and nonverbal gestures
- Asking questions to clarify
- Repeating or summarizing key points

Interviews should begin with introductions, an appropriate level of background information, and guidance around confidentiality and honest disclosure. Investigative teams should consider what types of warnings to provide to an interviewee, which will likely vary depending on the jurisdiction. For example, interviewers—especially if an attorney—should inform the interviewee that they represent the company and do not represent management or the interviewee. Depending on local or labor laws, the interviewer may be required to inform the interviewee of the right to have counsel or a union representative present. The employee may also be informed that any information that is provided will be treated as confidential, but it will be at the discretion of the company to disclose it to law enforcement or other regulatory agencies as required.

A case in point is *Upjohn Co. et al. v. United States et al.,* where it was held that communications between a corporate plaintiff's lower- and middle-level employees and the plaintiff's counsel acting at the direction of corporate superiors in order to secure legal advice from counsel would not be covered by attorney-client privilege. This was held to be so since the "client" was the corporation and not the employees.[2]

Key in any interview is to solicit as much detail as possible from the interviewee. This can be accomplished by asking open-ended questions. It is often helpful to repeat or rephrase questions. Sometimes just rephrasing a question can elicit a much different answer. Depending on the investigation, it can also be advantageous to shift away from a question and then return to it later on, particularly if the interview is not progressing.

Interviewers should present questions in a logical sequence and should close by reconfirming the facts usually in the form of summarizing the information provided by the interviewee. More effective questions typically seek agreement and avoid confrontational language.

Ordinarily, interviews will be documented and memorialized in an interview memorandum. An interview memorandum should include:

- An introduction that, at a minimum, documents the witness's name and contact information
- Details of what the interviewee said during the interview, including all documents shown to the witness, explanations regarding these documents, and all information provided
- Any evidence collected from the interviewee
- The date of the interview
- The names of the interviewer and note taker, if applicable
- The manner in which the interview was conducted (e.g., in person, phone call, video conference call)

As a good practice, the interviewer should draft the memorandum as soon as practicable after the interview.

Interview memoranda will likely form the bulk of the final investigative report. Moreover, any memoranda or informal notes written by an investigator could also be subject to discovery orders or even treated as exhibits in potential legal proceedings.

Analysis of Information

Throughout the course of an investigation, those managing the inquiry should analyze the information gathered to determine whether the original hypothesis has been proved or whether the investigation needs to be refocused, expanded, or closed. After new information is obtained, the investigator should compare that information with previous interviews, electronic evidence, or corporate intelligence in order to look for a developing theme in the investigation.

Analytic procedures are particularly important in detecting a variety of financial frauds. An investigator may want to consider an organization's historical financial data, financial trends, and ratios to identify anomalies and potential risk areas, particularly when the allegations involve potential financial reporting fraud.

Investigators possessing financial analysis skills can help unearth a financial fraud, because fraudsters are generally unable to manipulate all the information necessary to produce the expected financial relationships one would expect to see in a normal financial report. Areas to consider when designing financial analysis procedures for financial fraud investigations are:

- The areas of impact on the issuer's balance sheet and income statement
- The effect of the transactions and the execution thereof on the balance sheet and income statement
- The risks associated with the transactions to the business of the issuer and the interests of stakeholders in the business of the issuer
- The expected disclosure of such transactions in the balance sheet and income statement of the issuer

One of the critical aspects of an investigation is the analysis of electronic evidence. As discussed in this and other chapters in the book, this evidence may include unstructured data such as e-mails or documents, which usually represent the majority of electronic data collected during an investigation, or structured data such as databases or financial systems. The analysis of unstructured data is usually accomplished through a variety of tools that permit keyword searches to identify e-mails and documents relevant to the investigation. Structured data, which organizations routinely collect in the normal course of business, are more highly organized than unstructured data and, therefore, more amenable to data-mining techniques. By performing a series of comparisons, summaries, and aggregations, the experienced investigator can analyze structured data sets to identify patterns, trends, and anomalies that are indicia of fraud and various forms of misconduct. Various types of fraud, such as financial reporting fraud, purchasing and payroll fraud, and time and expense abuses, are particularly amenable to discovery through the use of preprogrammed or custom-programmed data-mining techniques.

Concluding the Investigation

When is an investigation finished? An investigation into one area of fraud or misconduct may identify others that require further investigation. For this reason, determining when an investigation is over becomes one of the most important decisions an organization must make.

An effective way to avoid the never-ending investigation is to periodically return to the investigative team's work plan to assess progress against the goal. When the original goals of the work plan are fully accomplished and all individuals potentially involved have been identified, the investigation should be deemed concluded. At a high level, the fraud or suspected wrongdoing should have been discovered to exist or not, and any potential accomplices should have been fully investigated. If any new wrongdoing was identified during the investigation, further review of this activity should be spun off into a new and distinct investigation.

Reporting

Reporting the results of an investigation in a concise, unambiguous way is an important part of the process.

Overseers and investigators should decide whether the report will be written or oral. The choice will typically depend on the purpose of the report, the length and complexity of the issues and facts uncovered during the investigation, and the ultimate audience. There are different considerations when reporting to management or the board of directors than when issuing a report prepared for a government regulator. A benefit of a written report is that the findings are memorialized in writing. The written report may take several forms. It can be formatted as a letter, a full report memorandum, or a presentation. An oral report is sometimes requested over a written report to avoid creating documents that may become discoverable in the course of litigation and could potentially provide a road map for opposing counsel. Whether written or oral, key elements of a good investigative report are that it tells the story of the investigation by detailing:

- The nature of the alleged misconduct
- Critical issues investigated
- Documentation of investigative decisions
- Uncovered facts—those agreed upon and those disputed
- Factual conclusions
- Names, roles, and conduct of implicated individuals
- Persons interviewed and documents collected
- Recommendations for control enhancements

Closing the Investigation

If misconduct has occurred, the organization should consider taking the following steps, where appropriate:

- Remedying the harm caused
- Examining the root cause of relevant control breakdowns to help mitigate risk and strengthen controls

- Disciplining those implicated in the action, as well as potentially those in management who failed to prevent or detect such events
- Communicating to the wider employee population that management took appropriate and responsive action
- Considering voluntary disclosure of the results of the investigation to the government or another relevant body, such as a regulator

According to a survey done in 2005 by *Directors & Boards* magazine, the most common actions taken at the conclusion of an investigation were termination of an employee or employees (71.1 percent), private settlement (23.7 percent), and criminal prosecution (22.7 percent). In 17.5 percent of the instances detailed in this survey, the organization concluded there was no wrongdoing.[3]

One of the most important decisions during and at the end of an investigation is whether an organization needs to make a disclosure to the government of any wrongdoing uncovered. Clearly, these considerations can only be made under the advice of counsel. Since the issuance of guidance by the U.S. Attorney General's Office on charging organizations with a crime (the Holder Memo, the Thompson Memo, the McNulty Memo, and, most recently, the Filip Memo), organizations may weigh, among other things, what regulators and the courts will consider to be attorney-client privilege and how much cooperation with the government will be considered for leniency, as well as the work product itself.

Conclusion

To help increase the effectiveness of an investigation, organizations should pre-plan the inquiry and devise an investigative work plan that is tailored to the needs of the investigation. This requires patience and deliberation. Through gathering information, in paper or electronic format, domestically or cross-border, as well as interviews and document analysis, organizations can gain an understanding of the misconduct. This can assist the organization in applying the lessons learned during the investigation and help it to move forward once the investigation ends.

Chapter 13

Response: Government Settlement Agreements

Richard H. Girgenti
Glenn E. Moyers

When an organization becomes aware of potentially serious misconduct, its management and directors may face a number of decisions that could steer the organization to very different outcomes. The stakes are often high, potentially including substantial fines and penalties as well as harm to the corporation's reputation or relationships with clients and customers. The spin-off effects of leaders' actions are difficult to predict: How will markets react if the news goes public? How will shareholders respond if the company is dragged into court? Faced with these and similar questions, organizations may try to mitigate such uncertainty by seeking government leniency through cooperation. Doing so can pay dividends in the long term, because generally speaking, the government rewards cooperative behavior. The Siemens AG case is illustrative.[1]

In late 2008, Siemens admitted to violating the U.S. Foreign Corrupt Practices Act (FCPA) and was forced to pay over $800 million in fines and profit disgorgement to the U.S. government, in addition to similar-sized penalties levied by the German government. Even though this represented the largest FCPA settlement to date, the punishment could have been much greater had it not been, in part, for Siemens's "extraordinary cooperation in connection with the investigation of its past corporate conduct."[2]

Mr. Moyers is a partner in KPMG LLP's Forensic practice in Atlanta, GA. He leads KPMG's national Healthcare Regulatory service line.
Additional contributors are Adam K. Bowen, Aaron Grieser, and Nimna Varghese.

In testimony given before the Criminal Law Subcommittee of the Senate Judiciary Committee, Lanny Breuer (assistant attorney general, Criminal Division of the Department of Justice) stated, in the context of Siemens AG, that the company was indeed "providing us [DOJ] with almost unparallel cooperation."[3] The company hired law firms and forensic accountants to conduct extensive investigations into suspect transactions, created document collection sites to process documents related to the violations, and shared information freely with German and U.S. regulators. The company even created an amnesty program, permitting certain employees to disclose any information associated with the violation of anti-corruption laws without the threat of termination or other retaliation. Siemens is credited with establishing document collection sites in Germany and China and spending more than $100 million to collect, review, and process these documents.[4] Siemens's level of cooperation showed the government that it was willing to atone for its past mistakes and take steps to help ensure that illegal behavior would not occur in the future. As a result, Siemens received substantial leniency from the government through a reduction in fines and penalties, and the company was able to walk away from the settlement in a relatively positive light.

Not all organizations go to such lengths. Some, in fact, take the opposite approach. By way of example, in 2006, the class-action law firm Milberg Weiss Bershad & Schulman chose to fight the DOJ's stipulations for a settlement agreement. The firm was accused of a long-running conspiracy of paying kickbacks to class-action plaintiffs. After being approached by U.S. attorneys and attempting initial settlement negotiations, the firm did something hard to imagine in today's regulatory environment—it walked away from the bargaining table. The firm declined to admit to the alleged illegal activity, claiming that the government wanted the firm to make "unfounded statements accusing its own partners of crimes" and waive attorney-client privilege as a precondition to avoiding indictment.[5]

The result of Milberg's failure to reach an initial settlement with the government to defer prosecution illustrates the risks of taking a defiant stance during negotiations with the government. Once the government's indictment was announced, the firm saw several top partners and clients defect. In the end, 4 former partners received prison sentences, a total of 11 individuals were convicted of felonies, and the firm ultimately agreed to pay $75 million to settle the case, to employ a compliance monitor, and to enact a "best practices" program for two years.[6] While it is difficult to predict what the outcome may have been had Milberg decided to go along with the government's demands, it is hard to imagine it being any worse.

It could be argued that the difference between the results of these two scenarios is the concept of cooperation. Cooperation between government enforcers and private-sector organizations has changed the way the government prosecutes organizational fraud and misconduct. The Federal Sentencing Guidelines, the

DOJ's guidelines, and recent court cases are milestones in the sometimes rocky evolution of this cooperation. These and other guidance give organizations incentives to cooperate with regulators and, in so doing, have altered the dynamics of U.S. regulatory enforcement. Effectively negotiating the nuances and subtleties of whether, when, and how to cooperate can significantly alter the outcome of government enforcement actions.

For the purposes of this chapter, the term "government settlement agreements" (GSAs) is used as an umbrella term to describe the family of agreements that include, for example, deferred prosecution agreements (DPAs), nonprosecution agreements (NPAs), settlement and corporate integrity agreements (CIAs), and similar arrangements between alleged wrongdoers and government enforcement entities. (In this context, GSAs refer to DPAs, NPAs, and CIAs specifically, while including other similar agreements generally.)

These agreements have evolved over the last two decades, but key questions have endured. For example, what level of cooperation is sufficient to garner government leniency? Or alternatively, how much can or should the government exact in exchange for forbearing prosecution? The answers to these questions, like a pendulum, have swung back and forth over the last two decades. Typically, regulators enjoy significant leverage and broad discretion as to whether or not an organization, for example, should be offered a GSA and whether or not it has complied with the terms of a GSA. The cost of being convicted is generally so large that it has been likened to a corporate death sentence.[7] Thus, although a corporation, like any other accused, has a Sixth Amendment right to trial by jury, corporations often cannot afford to exercise their rights to jury trials. As a result, there is typically tremendous pressure to cooperate with regulators, particularly if the target is publicly traded, highly regulated, or dependent on government procurement or licensing.

In theory, where there is evidence of corporate wrongdoing, a GSA should be good for all concerned. GSAs meet the government's goals of notice to the corporate community, deterrence, full disclosure, restitution, and reform of corporate culture, without inflicting undue "collateral consequences"[8] on an organization, its employees, and shareholders. But perhaps more importantly, the organization maintains its professional standing, avoiding the most serious reputational harms—prosecution or conviction.

Although organizations entering into GSAs may be saved from prosecution, they should nevertheless be prepared to spend time and money. Cooperation has its costs, and these vary widely, depending on the terms of the GSA. These costs can include outright fines and potential disgorgement and restitution, if any is required, but can also include the costs of conducting internal investigations, making necessary compliance reforms, and paying for monitors, among others.

Given these downsides, organizations may be tempted to make superficial or perhaps subversive efforts to cooperate in the hopes of favorable treatment at minimum cost. The DOJ, however, is generally accustomed to this probability. In the Thompson Memo, issued in 2003 by Deputy Attorney General Larry Thompson, the DOJ recognized that some organizations, "while purporting to cooperate with a Department investigation, in fact take steps to impede the quick and effective exposure of the complete scope of wrongdoing under investigation."[9] The DOJ and other regulators are likely to have a keen sense for the difference between real cooperation and superficial efforts, and the difference in their responses can be dramatic.

In fact, once an organization agrees to cooperate, it is unlikely to be able to turn back without incurring substantial damage. As Larry Finder and Ryan McConnell put it, "Once a company got on the cooperation bus, they were either on or off, there was no middle ground."[10] Organizations should understand that an offer to cooperate is not the end of a process, but only the beginning of a potentially long endeavor throughout which regulators are likely to make substantial demands to which the organization will be expected to acquiesce.

What this effectively means for an organization's leaders is that decisions may have to be made early, and quickly, on extremely complicated issues such as whether and when to self-disclose, how to handle the findings of internal investigations, and how likely regulators will be to offer a GSA as an alternative to trial.

Taxonomy of GSAs

No two GSAs are identical, and they are used differently by different enforcement agencies. While there are many agencies employing GSAs, this chapter focuses on three: the DOJ, the SEC, and the Office of Inspector General (OIG) of the U.S. Department of Health and Human Services (HHS), the primary watchdog for health-care providers and suppliers. Together, these organizations are responsible for a majority of GSAs.

Under these organizations, however, GSAs have evolved differently. While the DOJ and SEC have tended to employ pretrial agreements such as DPAs and NPAs, OIG has evolved the CIA and other similar agreements. The details of these types of GSAs are typically crafted to reflect the nature of the underlying misconduct, the organization and its operating environment, and sometimes even the tenor of the enforcement team.

Major Types of GSAs and Common Elements

Three major types of GSAs are available for use by the government: the Deferred Prosecution Agreement, the Non-Prosecution Agreement, and the Corporate Integrity Agreement.

Deferred Prosecution Agreements. As its name implies, a deferred prosecution agreement postpones and potentially averts prosecution. When instituting a DPA, the government files charges against an entity, but agrees to dismiss those charges after a set period of time if the entity abides by the terms of the agreement. Typically, the entity will accept responsibility for the underlying wrongdoing and admit to a statement of facts that can be used in a subsequent prosecution should the enforcement body determine that the DPA has been violated. In this worst-case scenario, the organization makes what it believes to be all efforts to comply, sinks its energies and resources into meeting government demands, and yet finds itself as a defendant in an extremely challenging case where it has admitted to the underlying crime. In DPAs, organizations also typically pay a combination of a criminal fine, civil penalty, and restitution. In addition to these features, DPAs commonly include stipulations that the organization reform its internal controls and agree to host (and pay for) a corporate monitor to oversee the implementation of the DPA's terms.

Nonprosecution Agreements. NPAs differ from DPAs in a few respects. First, no criminal charging instrument is filed, and the entity is not required to make an admission of guilt. Moreover, NPAs are generally less detailed than DPAs and are less likely to include provisions for corporate monitors. Despite that, the entity agrees to cooperate with an ongoing investigation, which may mean helping to build a case against one or more of its employees suspected of wrongdoing. Further, the company will typically agree to reform its operations to remedy risk-specific internal control weaknesses. After a designated time period, the matter will be resolved if the government determines the company has complied with the terms of the agreement.

Corporate Integrity Agreements. The third settlement arrangement covered in this chapter is a CIA, which often takes the form of a negotiated compliance obligation agreed to by companies doing business with certain federal agencies, such as the HHS. CIAs generally come in two parts: first, there is a settlement agreement that recites the wrongdoing, contains an admission of culpability, and establishes fines, etc.; second, the corporate integrity agreement discusses agreed-upon changes to internal controls, training, monitoring, and reporting. Settlement agreements are generally not made public, while the CIAs are. If it is determined that the obligations of the CIA are not being met, the OIG can refer the matter to the DOJ for criminal prosecution. Criminal prosecution would also have the effect of barring the organization from future participation in federal health-care programs such as Medicare and Medicaid. Failure to comply with a CIA may also result in administrative exclusion from those programs, which would likely threaten the existence of most health-care organizations.

Although CIAs are generally tailored to the entity, its existing compliance infrastructure, and the underlying misconduct, CIAs have some common elements. For example, CIAs generally require organizations to adopt internal controls and a written code of ethics, to conduct compliance training, to implement internal monitoring of controls, and to retain an independent review organization to monitor adherence with the CIA. Other common requirements include creating a compliance officer position, establishing anonymous whistleblower mechanisms, agreeing to voluntarily disclose "reportable events" as defined in the CIA, and providing annual reports to the OIG on the status of compliance activities. CIAs typically bind the subject for three- to five-year terms.

Evolution of GSAs

GSAs evolved from various organizations such as The Defense Industry Initiative, the Department of Justice, the Securities and Exchange Commission, and the Department of Health and Human Services.

The Defense Industry Initiative

Traces of the modern-day approach to GSAs can be found as far back as 1986, when then-President Reagan formed the Packard Commission, a blue-ribbon panel to investigate scandals around procurement fraud among defense contractors. One of the Packard Commission's major recommendations was for defense contractors to adopt internal controls to mitigate the likelihood of fraud and other misconduct. The Defense Industry Initiative (DII) emerged out of these recommendations as a voluntary effort by defense contractors, who agreed to adopt core principles of ethical behavior.[11]

The Defense Industry Initiative's Five Core Principles, Updated March 2010

The principles include:

1. We shall act honestly in all business dealings with the U.S. government, protect taxpayer resources and provide high-quality products and services for the men and women of the U.S. Armed Forces.
2. We shall promote the highest ethical values as expressed in our written codes of business conduct, nurture an ethical culture through communications, training, and other means, and comply with and honor all governing laws and regulations.

3. We shall establish and sustain effective business ethics and compliance programs that reflect our commitment to self-governance, and shall encourage employees to report suspected misconduct, forbid retaliation for such reporting, and ensure the existence of a process for mandatory and voluntary disclosures of violations of relevant laws and regulations.
4. We shall share best practices with respect to business ethics and compliance, and participate in the annual DII Best Practices Forum.
5. We shall be accountable to the public, through regular reporting by DII to Congress and the public. These reports will describe members' efforts to build and sustain a strong culture of business ethics and compliance.

This is a summary only. The full text is available at www.dii.org/about-us/dii-principles.

Further, in 1986, the Department of Defense (DOD) developed the Voluntary Disclosure Program (VDP), which offered to defer suspension or debarment from defense contracting if the subject organization complied with the VDP's terms. Under the VDP, defense contractors had to demonstrate that they were behaving in good faith by surrendering all documents as requested by the government, providing technical assistance to the government if needed, and allowing employees to be interviewed by government investigators. The DOJ backed the VDP, offering leniency for organizations that showed good faith and took certain remedial compliance measures. By leveraging the contracting communities' long-term interests in maintaining contracting relationships, the government was able to draw organizations into voluntary arrangements, making a sharp break from the status quo of command-and-control-style regulation.

Ultimately, the VDP and DII were successful in driving change in the defense contracting community. By mid-1988, contractors participating in the DII made 96 voluntary disclosures and returned $43 million to the government.[12] By the end of the 1980s, more than half of the DOD contractors had signed the DII.[13]

GSAs under the DOJ and SEC

The DII also had effects outside of the defense contracting community. In 1994, the U.S. Sentencing Commission established the Sentencing Guidelines, which aimed to produce appropriate and uniform sentencing procedures for organizations, including reducing a corporation's liability if it disclosed fraud on its own initiative. The Sentencing Guidelines' guidance on compliance programs built a framework on some of the now-ubiquitous compliance elements introduced in the DII. These include, among others, having an organization establish a code of conduct, conduct training for employees on compliance and ethics, set up whistleblowing mechanisms, effectively monitor its compliance program, and implement industry leading practices.

The Sentencing Guidelines influenced early GSAs. In 1992, Salomon Brothers, the investment bank, agreed to pay $290 million in sanctions, forfeitures, and restitution to resolve charges arising out of an alleged misconduct in Treasury auctions and government securities trading. In addition to the monetary penalties, the GSA required that the investment bank continue cooperating in various government investigations and institute procedures to prevent the reoccurrence of such violations.[14] Salomon's settlement also required it to implement a compliance program with policies to prevent future fraud. The following year, the DOJ struck a DPA with Prudential Securities that incorporated elements of the Sentencing Guidelines, including making efforts to evaluate the organizations' compliance programs and other remedial measures.[15] Despite this, the DOJ employed GSAs relatively rarely throughout most of the 1990s.

Another milestone came in 1999, when then-DOJ Deputy Attorney General Eric Holder issued a memorandum filling a void of official guidance about how prosecutors should bring criminal charges against an organization. The "Holder Memo" laid out a series of factors for federal prosecutors to weigh when considering whether to prosecute a corporate entity versus only the individuals responsible for the misconduct.[16]

Holder Memo Factors to Consider

- The nature and seriousness of the offense
- The pervasiveness of the wrongdoing
- Prior conduct of the company
- Voluntary disclosure by the company of the wrongdoing and the company's willingness to cooperate in the investigation of its agents
- The adequacy of the company's compliance program
- The remedial actions taken by the company to deal with the wrongdoing
- The impact a prosecution might have on innocent third parties
- The alternative mechanisms prosecutors might choose to punish the company.

Source: Eric H. Holder, Deputy Attorney General, memorandum to Heads of Department Components and United States Attorneys regarding "Principles of Federal Prosecution of Business Organizations," U.S. Department of Justice, June 1999.

The Holder Memo was significant to the development of GSAs in that it shed some light on what DOJ attorneys would look for in organizational efforts to mitigate fraud and misconduct. Still, throughout the 1990s and early 2000s, these agreements remained rare. From 1992 to 2001, only 11 GSAs were entered into—with, at most, 2 agreements entered in any given year.[17]

Then in 2002, the indictment of Arthur Andersen and its resulting collapse gave prosecutors a clear reason to seek an alternative to charging for suspected crimes. Arthur Andersen was generating roughly $9 billion globally per year prior to its collapse, but by the end of the prosecution, its value had all but evaporated after millions of dollars in settlements, the loss of virtually all its clients, and an exodus of leading partners.[18] Approximately 28,000 employees lost their jobs in the United States (86,000 worldwide) as a result of the prosecution (never mind that the U.S. Supreme Court eventually reversed its conviction).[19]

The collateral damage that ensued from Andersen's prosecution illuminated the need for an alternative—and GSAs provided an appealing middle ground where the government could pursue its interests while avoiding many unwanted repercussions. The use of GSAs increased dramatically: From 2002 to 2005, the DOJ entered into twice as many NPAs and DPAs as it had over the previous decade (1992–2002).[20] Whereas there were 5 corporate pretrial agreements in 2003, during the course of the next four years, 76 agreements were reached, with 35 in 2007 alone.[21]

As the number of GSAs increased, so did calls for greater clarity around government expectations for organizational cooperation in exchange for leniency, viewed as lacking in the DOJ's Holder Memo. In 2003, Deputy U.S. Attorney Larry Thompson filled this gap with a corporate charging policy called "Principles of Federal Prosecutions of Business Organizations."[22] This "Thompson Memo" emphasized cooperation as a factor in evaluating whether to prosecute. Such factors included whether the subject organization assisted prosecutors in investigating and prosecuting individuals suspected of the wrongdoing, waived attorney-client and work product protections with respect to conversations with certain individuals, and paid legal fees for employees that were the targets of the investigations. These became highly controversial requirements and were followed with additional guidance from Deputy Attorney General Paul McNulty in 2006 (the "McNulty Memo").[23] Thereafter, GSAs became longer and more sophisticated, and they typically included requirements for attorney-client privilege and work product protection waivers, admissions of responsibility, and promises not to contradict the agreement.

GSAs under the HHS

Parallel with the development of DPAs and NPAs in the 1990s, HHS was embroiled in its own regulatory scandal: Medicare and Medicaid fraud. Though

Medicare and Medicaid had been around since the 1960s, complex and incon-sistent reimbursement rules created an environment rich in fraud opportunities. For instance, in 1992 the Government Accountability Office provided an estimate that approximately 10 percent of all health-care spending potentially could be lost to fraud and abuse. In fiscal year 1996, comprehensive audits of Medicare financial statements by the OIG found $23 billion in overpayments of Medicare claims. Building on the experience of the DII and borrowing from the Sentencing Guidelines, the OIG launched its own voluntary disclosure program in March 1995 as part of an initiative called "Operations Restore Trust," which later evolved into the "Provider Self-Disclosure Protocol." Pursuant to the Self-Disclosure Protocol, entities can voluntarily report violations of federal law and are expected to conduct an internal investigation and a self-assessment.[24] Under the protocol, once an organization came forward, it would typically negotiate a settlement, which often included a combination of fines and a CIA.

Large, publicly traded health-care corporations, such as National Medical Enterprises, Inc., and Caremark, Inc., were the subjects of some of the first CIAs in 1994 and 1995. These early CIAs were relatively unsophisticated when stacked next to modern CIAs. These early CIAs basically required the entities to hold compliance training for key individuals, have these individuals certify their understanding, and then report this to the HHS.[25] However, as health-care abuse became a larger public issue, the HHS extended its enforcement efforts to all types of providers, large and small and in various health-related industries. The OIG entered into 4 CIAs in 1994, but the number ballooned to 233 in 1998.[26]

During this period, CIAs also grew in sophistication to address fraud schemes that were coming to the fore, particularly with the improper usage of Medicare billing codes and the provision of substandard quality of care. CIAs addressed these and other issues by incorporating requirements for internal con-trols and other preventive measures to address these specific issues.[27] Some exam-ples of these terms include, among others, hiring a compliance officer or appointing a compliance committee, developing written standards and policies, implementing a comprehensive employee training program, retaining an inde-pendent review organization to review claims submitted to federal health-care programs, establishing a confidential disclosure program, and restricting employ-ment of ineligible persons.[28]

Then in 2001, the newly appointed inspector general for HHS, Janet Rehnquist, reevaluated the OIG's use of CIAs and, particularly, the burden they were placing on industry. Thereafter, CIAs changed in important ways; for exam-ple, Rehnquist revealed that for CIA purposes, OIG will now divide civil false claims cases into three categories: (1) cases that can be settled without a CIA; (2) cases where OIG and DOJ will wait to decide whether a CIA is necessary, separating the civil settlement process from the CIA process; and (3) cases that will require a CIA because the provider's internal controls are inadequate to prevent and detect fraud.[29]

As the requirements of CIAs changed over time, so did the targets of CIAs. The DOJ pursued large pharmaceutical manufacturers (including Pfizer, GlaxoSmithKline, and AstraZeneca), and each enforcement action produced complex and lengthy CIAs aimed at addressing sales, marketing, and drug pricing schemes.[30]

More recently, compliance agreements have focused on medical device manufacturers. For example, in 2007, a wave of investigations targeted five major knee and hip manufacturers. Biomet Orthopedics, Depuy Orthopaedics, Smith & Nephew, Stryker Corp., and Zimmer Holdings allegedly provided kickbacks to surgeons in exchange for consulting contracts and exclusive use of their products. Stryker was the first to come forward and entered into an NPA. The others were subjected to DPAs.[31]

Additionally, the OIG has been employing a new type of agreement with more frequency—the certification of compliance agreement (CCA). This agreement is similar to a CIA, except that it does not require a monitor, instead requiring only annual reporting on progress toward the CCA's goals. This marks yet another development in the HHS OIG's palette of tools to manage compliance violations under its purview, allowing it to respond in a more nuanced manner as situations arise. For example, organizations that self-disclose misconduct are more likely to get a CCA than organizations that try to conceal their misconduct. Moreover, CIAs are now requiring the subject's board to pass resolutions certifying the effectiveness of its compliance program, ensuring compliance is prioritized at the highest levels of the organization.

In April 2008, the OIG again refined the Self-Disclosure Protocol to further limit the use of CIAs. In an open letter, the OIG explicitly stated that providers who voluntarily disclose potential fraud in good faith and cooperate with the OIG in a timely manner would generally not be required to enter into CIAs. The new disclosure and settlement process is designed to expedite the resolution of instances of fraud, whereby providers have 90 days from self-disclosure to conduct their own internal investigations and submit complete disclosures to the OIG.[32] While it may be too early to draw concrete conclusions on the impact of this release, there have been early signs of a slowdown in CIAs, CCAs, and other settlement arrangements, with only 77 entered into in 2008, 66 in 2009, and 26 in 2010.[33]

Responding to Practical Challenges

Having described the background on the taxonomy and history of GSAs, this chapter now turns to providing practical guidance for key considerations at various stages along the life of a GSA. The first stage covers considerations in the run-up to negotiating a GSA, including issues surrounding self-disclosure and cooperation in regulatory inquiries. The second stage looks more deeply at negotiating the terms of a GSA, including understanding the government's interests, assessing the organization's strengths and weaknesses, and presenting a compelling case for minimal government involvement in remediation. The third stage handles some critical issues in implementing and living under a GSA, including getting compliance efforts right and understanding the rules around selecting and employing corporate monitors. The final stage looks at the often-uneventful closing out of a GSA.

Before a GSA Is Reached

Before a GSA is reached, there are actions an organization can take that may impact negotiations. These actions can include self-reporting of known or suspected misconduct and cooperating with regulators.

Self-Reporting of Known or Suspected Misconduct

A GSA always begins with an event—an alleged or suspected illegal act. The alleged illegal conduct may be a one-off occurrence or may have been happening for an extended period of time. Regardless of the length of time, at some point, an organization faces the question of whether and how to inform regulators of the known or suspected misconduct. This is an inherently difficult question involving judgment calls about whether the misconduct rises to the level of something reportable. This may vary widely depending on the seriousness of the misconduct and the sensitivity of the regulatory environment, among other factors. Leaders should also consider the timing of disclosure, such as whether to report the misconduct immediately or to fully investigate it before reporting it.

While self-disclosure may seem irrational to some, a well-executed disclosure, done freely, gives an organization a chance to take control over a potentially unpredictable situation. An organization that hides violations from regulators, only to be discovered later, is less likely to garner the benefit of regulatory leniency. Conversely, an organization that comes forward not only is more likely to be viewed benevolently, but may be better able to frame the government's understanding and potentially impact its response to the issue. In making this and subsidiary decisions, it is useful to view the organization's behavior from the regulator's perspective before, during, and after the voluntary disclosure process.

Organizations face the threshold question of whether a known or suspected violation rises to the level of being reportable. Such an assessment should be based on both a reasonable understanding of the scale and scope of the violation and on some form of an investigation. The organization should also consider the potential impact of the matter on the organization itself and its stakeholders, the government's likely interest in prosecution, and the amount of money that might be involved in potential government fines and disgorgement, if any. In summary, the organization should consider whether the violation is likely to be considered material in the eyes of relevant regulators. Examples of material violations in the context of securities law may include misconduct that would require a restatement of financial information and misconduct by senior management and directors. Materiality may be different in the FCPA space, for example, where there are no official *de minimis* (i.e., negligible) considerations by the DOJ.

An initial investigation into potentially material misconduct should be thorough enough to identify the major issues at play. The goal is to win the trust of regulators by demonstrating that the investigation was thorough and, in so doing, render external (government) investigation unnecessary. The government is likely to inquire into the details of the organization's internal investigative efforts, and the organization's handling of the initial inquiry will likely influence the government's comfort in giving the organization latitude in resolving the matter independently. In this respect, conducting a poorly executed investigation may be worse than conducting no investigation because it may weaken the regulators' confidence in the organization's ability to manage the violation on its own. In addition to the steps noted above, the organization should make efforts to document the investigation adequately, giving special attention to preserving evidence likely to be of interest to regulators.[34]

It is a good idea to consider possible remedial actions from the very beginning of the process. Organizations should identify any control weaknesses that may have given rise to the wrongdoing, and they should review their compliance program and governance structures against prevailing authoritative guidance, including the Sentencing Guidelines. By conducting such an internal compliance program assessment, organizations could be better positioned to anticipate remedial measures the government might expect and to begin to address material deficiencies in advance of government inquiries.

When an organization is ready to disclose, it should consider what channels are available to do so. The DOJ Antitrust Division's Corporate Amnesty Program is an example of a highly nuanced and active program. This program provides amnesty from prosecution for the first entity to report anticompetitive activity (e.g., by a cartel). This has a double benefit for the DOJ. It provides a strong incentive for organizations to self-report and, in so doing, increases the volume of potential prosecutions. It also creates a rich source of evidence on the anticompetitive behavior of other members involved in a particular anticompetitive conspiracy. Moreover, the program often ends up creating a race to self-disclose since, in the case of cartel-type violations, only the first reporter gets amnesty. Acceptance into the Corporate Amnesty Program can result in a complete pass from criminal prosecution if the organization cooperates in the DOJ's investigation. In addition, all officers, directors, and employees who cooperate may be shielded from prosecution.

Regardless of the channel selected, predisclosure activities should be carried out with all deliberate speed; every day counts where self-disclosure is concerned. Even if the organization is not racing to disclose under an amnesty program, the government is likely to scrutinize the organization's behavior in the time leading up to self-disclosure (particularly for evidence of stalling or an attempted cover-up). Therefore, organizations should not spend months investigating and developing remedial measures before reporting. Instead, assuming the organization determines that self-disclosure is appropriate, it should self-disclose at the earliest reasonable time.

Among the factors to consider in deciding the timing of self-disclosure are:

- The existence of an amnesty program, where the benefits of self-disclosure may be lost if another party discloses first
- The likelihood of losing control of an investigation through, for example, a whistleblower reporting the issue or regulators discovering the violation independently
- The organization's comfort that it grasps the full nature and extent of the suspected misconduct

Undue delay may increase the skepticism of regulators as well as the likelihood that regulators will learn of the issue through other means, which not only eliminates the advantage of self-disclosure, but also puts the organization in the uncomfortable position of having to explain why it did not disclose earlier.

In addition to when to disclose, organizations should consider what to disclose—or perhaps more to the point, how much to disclose. An organization's disclosure should be as thorough as is reasonably possible under the circumstances, providing all known and pertinent facts. A prime test of whether the organization has disclosed all pertinent information is whether the information is sufficient for law enforcement personnel to identify the nature and extent of the offense and the individual(s) responsible for the criminal conduct.[35]

Looking at regulatory guidance in the area of self-disclosure, the SEC provides 13 factors it considers when weighing the value of self-policing and self-reporting in its so-called Seaboard report, which outlines why there was an absence of charges against Seaboard Corporation for its cooperation with the SEC's investigation. These include:

- What was the nature of the misconduct involved
- How the misconduct arose
- How high up the chain of command the misconduct was known or perpetrated

- How long the misconduct lasted
- How much harm the misconduct caused to investors and other constituencies
- How the misconduct was detected
- How long after the discovery of misconduct it took to implement an effective response
- What steps the company took upon learning of the misconduct
- What processes the company followed to resolve the issues
- Whether the company is committed to learning the truth, fully and expeditiously
- Whether the company promptly made available to the SEC the results of its internal review staff and provided sufficient documentation of its response
- What assurances exist that the conduct is unlikely to reoccur
- What changes may have occurred to the company since the misconduct occurred, e.g., merger or bankruptcy[36]

These SEC factors provide useful insight into what regulators may be looking for in a self-disclosure. Both the nature of the misconduct and the manner in which it was handled are likely to be important considerations in the regulator's mind.

The incentives for thorough disclosure can be substantial. For example, under recent HHS OIG policy, a health-care provider's "submission of a complete and informative disclosure, quick response to OIG's requests for further information, and performance of an accurate audit" create a presumption that the organization has adopted effective compliance measures.[37] Hence, if the organization pays an "appropriate" fine, the provider may not be required to enter into a CIA.[38] This creates an even larger incentive for organizations to work proactively with government by self-disclosing.

In 2010, the SEC announced an expansion of its enforcement cooperation initiative to individuals as well as corporations. According to the SEC release, "the Commission has set out, for the first time, the way in which it will evaluate whether, how much, and in what manner to credit cooperation by individuals to ensure that potential cooperation arrangements maximize the Commission's law enforcement interests . . . It is similar to the so-called 'Seaboard Report' that was issued in 2001 and detailed the factors the SEC considers when evaluating cooperation by companies."[39]

In the 2010 announcement, the SEC outlined four general considerations for individuals:

- The assistance provided by the cooperating individual
- The importance of the underlying matter in which the individual cooperated

- The societal interest in ensuring the individual is held accountable for his or her misconduct
- The appropriateness of cooperation credit based upon the risk profile of the cooperating individual[40]

Cooperating with Regulators in the Run-up to Negotiations

Once regulators become aware of a potential violation, whether self-disclosed or otherwise, the organization should have a strategy for cooperating with the likely government requests for information and cooperation. This strategy should incorporate how the organization will deal with requests the government is likely to make. Two issues of particular relevance here are the waiver of attorney-client and work product protections in relation to potentially culpable individuals, as well as the organization's decision (and, sometimes, obligation) to provide legal counsel to individuals subject to government investigation. These issues have been at the center of substantial controversy in recent years.

In 1998, the DOJ's Holder Memo instructed U.S. attorneys to consider "the corporation's timely and voluntary disclosure of wrongdoing and its willingness to cooperate in the investigation of its agents, including if necessary, the waiver of corporate attorney-client and work product privileges . . ." when making charging decisions.[41] This issue is given greater weight since a majority of U.S. jurisdictions hold that once a privilege is waived, it is waived for all purposes, including future litigation. Any request for waiver of privilege should be weighed seriously and negotiated in light of recent developments in the field.

In 2006, the McNulty Memo required prosecutors to get written authorization from the deputy attorney general before requesting waiver. The McNulty Memo also instructs prosecutors not to consider a corporation's payment of legal fees of employees when deciding whether to charge a corporation with a criminal violation.[42]

On August 28, 2008, Deputy Attorney General Mark Filip published revisions to the McNulty Memo that altered the way the DOJ defines cooperation in an investigation. Specifically, the Filip Memo states that "eligibility for cooperation credit is not predicated upon the waiver of attorney-client privilege or work product protection"[43] and that prosecutors should not ask for such waivers and are directed not to do so. Prosecutors are also instructed not to consider whether a corporation advances legal fees for its employees or whether the organization retained or punished an employee in evaluating cooperation.[44]

Still, despite these restrictions, the government can consider whether an employee was disciplined as part of remedial measures to the compliance program, that is, whether the organization found the individuals had committed wrongdoing. Further, under the Filip Memo, organizations may need to provide information obtained in the course of an internal investigation. While this may not affect privilege in the immediate investigation, if such information would be used in subsequent litigation, production of the information may constitute waiver of attorney-client or work product privilege in that latter litigation. In any event, organizations should endeavor to strike a balance between protecting the rights of its employees while not appearing to be protecting individuals who have committed wrongdoing.

Since the issuance of the Thompson Memo, waivers in GSAs have been on the decline. Whereas between 2003 and 2006, 26 of 47 agreements had waivers, in 2007, only 3 GSAs contained them. In 2008, only 2 GSAs[45] contained waivers, and even those were restrictively worded, requiring, for example, only a "limited waiver of attorney-client privilege with respect to certain subject matters important to DOJ's understanding of the internal investigation."[46] Thus, while organizations should be prepared if regulators should "request" waiver of attorney-client or other privileges, such requests are much less likely, and organizations have stronger leverage to push back if the request seems to overreach DOJ's current guidelines.

Negotiating a GSA

Organizations should consider several issues when preparing for negotiations with government officials. First, the organization should try to understand the government's interests in resolving the matter and respond accordingly, with the end goal of demonstrating a genuine willingness to cooperate and an ability to adequately handle the issue in question.

When deciding who will negotiate with the government, the organization should consider selecting individuals who were not directly involved in internal investigations. Regulators may prejudice internal parties who appear to have a vested interest in the credibility and results of internal investigations or internal control remediation, which may in turn weaken the negotiating credibility of the organization's case. In this respect, organizations might consider retaining a reputable third party, such as legal counsel, to conduct negotiations on its behalf.

An organization should take a critical look at itself when developing a negotiation strategy. Attempting to embellish weaknesses and hide unfavorable facts can undermine the government's confidence that the organization is presenting a full and fair representation of the matter. The less confidence regulators have, the more likely they are to insist on their own investigation. Instead, the organization should clearly describe the nature and scope of the issue, explain how it happened, recount in detail its response to the issue, and paint a clear picture of why the organization is capable of stemming similar violations in the future. Further, the organization should not seek to "spin" the information provided to the government and, instead, focus on making factual disclosures on the incident and explaining the evidence provided.[47] Overt couching and posturing may give regulators the impression that the information presented is biased. Essentially, the organization should be prepared to educate regulators on the organization and its operations, internal controls, and capability to tackle misconduct internally.

The organization should also prepare realistic alternatives to prosecution that may address the government's concerns. One example would be to propose a comprehensive remediation plan with an established probationary period for government oversight. This could have the added benefit of enhancing the organization's control over negotiations and demonstrating a determination and capacity to act independently. An organization may also enhance its case by proposing, for example, a corporate monitor's duties during the GSA. In such disclosures, the organization can detail what information a monitor would have access to, how often and to whom the monitor would report, and what form the reports might take. By working proactively to set out suggested parameters, the organization may further its case that it is capable of dealing with the issues independently and thereby is more likely to negotiate a GSA with favorable terms.

Operating under a GSA

Components of an organization's response to operating under a GSA may include crafting a compliance program response and selecting and employing a corporate monitor, depending on the terms of the respective GSA.

Crafting an Organization's Compliance Program Response

Organizations should respond to serious misconduct by creating or enhancing internal controls in order to prevent, detect, and respond to further violations. This is advisable when any substantial breaches arise. However, when regulatory self-disclosure is in the picture, enhancing internal controls takes on an added importance because remedial actions, and their effectiveness, are likely to be scrutinized. Indeed, this may be the ideal circumstance to build a model compliance program. Taking a minimalist approach in this effort is usually the wrong tack. First, superficial efforts are unlikely to impress regulators—they will be able to distinguish between genuine and bare minimum efforts. But more to the point, perfunctory compliance efforts are less likely to be effective in forging real improvements in compliance, and recurring misconduct in the context of a GSA can cost dearly. In 2008, one organization earned the unpleasant distinction of becoming the first to have its DPA revoked by the DOJ for noncompliance. The organization failed in its efforts to stop ongoing FCPA violations and was required to pay $4.2 million in fines and serve two years of organizational probation.[48] This was a relatively light punishment in light of what the DOJ could have levied.

Conversely, however, organizations may not have infinite resources to throw at compliance challenges. After spending for fines and disgorgements, organizations may find themselves with very few resources to implement a "best-in-class" compliance program. Whatever the situation, organizations seeking to allocate resources efficiently may find themselves confronting the question of how much energy and resources to devote to compliance reforms.

While important, this question should not be the organizing principle for the entity's compliance reforms. While regulatory lenience may be an organization's endgame, the real focus should be on understanding the compliance risks an organization faces and building effective internal controls to drive real improvements in preventing, detecting, and responding to fraud and misconduct. In other words, the effectiveness of the compliance program should be the organization's primary goal. By creating truly effective compliance controls that comport with what the government expects to see, an organization stands a much better chance of satisfying its regulators and, hence, receiving lenience.

Organizations may also be tempted to take a narrowly tailored approach to compliance remediation, focusing only on the risks under regulatory scrutiny in lieu of conducting a broader "head-to-toe" organizational risk assessment and response. There are strong reasons to choose the latter approach. For example, violations in one subject area may indicate a weak control environment across the organization. Where the problems are due to a weak culture of compliance in a region or business unit, process-level controls alone are unlikely to be effective. In short, the compliance response should match the depth and gravity of the compliance risks. Attempts to shortcut may do a disservice to the organization in the long run. Where a risk assessment shows deeper and broader problems than are the subject of the GSA, the organization should consider remedial efforts that are responsive to these more systemic risks.

The vast majority of GSAs reached in the last few years required compliance program enhancements or overhauls. Between 2006 and 2008, three-quarters of DPAs and NPAs had compliance program requirements. In 2008, every DPA and NPA had compliance provisions.[49] An analysis of compliance features required in DPAs and NPAs in 2007 and 2008, conducted by Lawrence Finder et al., found that there were some elements common to each GSA that had compliance elements. These included:

- "A corporate compliance officer with dedicated resources who reports to the Board or the CEO, not the general counsel;
- "A code of conduct (ethics) and training programs designed to teach employees about the code of conduct, including certification by employees that they've received training;

- "A system of internal controls and procedures monitored by the corporate compliance officer and designed to ensure wrongdoing is discovered;
- "A hotline or email system, monitored by the corporate compliance officer, that ensures accurate and timely reporting of compliance issues without retribution by the employers."[50]

These are only a few programmatic elements in the broader set of compliance program elements generally contemplated by the Sentencing Guidelines and other leading sources of guidance. Organizations should consider the full spectrum of compliance program options when crafting a response to assessed organizational risk.

By keeping the organization's focus on effectiveness and tailoring a remediation plan to risks that have been objectively assessed, not only is the organization more likely to get an approving nod from regulators, but it is also likely to see real improvements in its compliance record and culture. In the end, that is a goal of regulators as well.

Selecting and Employing a Corporate Monitor

Organizations that enter into a GSA with the government (as opposed to being subjected to formal proceedings) are likely to find themselves hosting a corporate monitor for the duration of their agreement. Typically, corporate monitors are appointed by or with the approval of the government and are paid for by the business to supervise the business while it operates under the terms of its GSA. If a monitor concludes that the business is not abiding by the terms of the agreement, the monitor can recommend that a prosecution be initiated.

At the outset, it should be noted that the role of the monitor can evolve differently among the various enforcement agencies. For example, under the OIG agreements, monitors may tend to engage in transactional monitoring by testing internal controls through continuous auditing and monitoring. In addition, under the OIG, this monitoring role could be performed within the organization, instead of using external parties to "check the checker." With the DOJ, on the other hand, monitors focus on principles and behavioral monitoring, and the DOJ can rely on monitors to fulfill more monitoring activities.[51]

In a memorandum written in May 2008, Acting Deputy Attorney General Craig S. Morford provided a series of principles pertaining to the use of corporate monitors in NPAs and DPAs.[52] The "Morford Memo" addresses, among other things, the criteria for selecting a monitor, the need for a monitor's independence, restrictions on the scope of a monitor's duties, and procedures for resolving potential disputes over selected monitors. The memorandum is applicable only to criminal matters and does not apply to agencies other than the

DOJ. Attorneys are restricted from accepting monitors that have real or apparent conflicts of interest in the corporation or the DOJ. The Morford Memo requires that the monitor be "an independent third-party, not an employee or agent of the corporation or of the Government." Monitors are also prohibited from affiliation or employment with the subject of the GSA for one year from the end of the monitorship.

Since, by definition, GSAs occur prior to any legal action, lack of judicial oversight has exacerbated this latitude, in some instances leading to apparent conflicts of interest.[53]

The monitor's primary responsibility is to monitor and assess an organization's compliance with a GSA. The monitor may provide recommendations on the design and implementation of the organization's compliance program. While an organization is not technically mandated to enact all the monitor's recommendations, if the organization decides not to abide or does not respond within a reasonable time, either the organization or the monitor must notify the government, and the organization must provide an explanation. Depending on the requirements in the CIA, a monitor may have to report previously undisclosed or new misconduct directly to the government.

Exiting a GSA

There are a number of considerations in successfully transitioning from life under a GSA to operating completely independently again. An important question in this transition period is whether the organization will embrace the changes it forged during the life of the GSA or whether it will return to business as usual once the government's eye turns elsewhere.

Leaders of many organizations note that their time living under a GSA was actually a positive development for the organization, at least from the perspective of correcting underlying compliance issues. Compliance and ethics personnel have a powerful argument for the importance of their work when it is mandated by regulators. Under a GSA, compliance functions may receive resources and attention that otherwise might not have materialized. When the GSA is lifted, compliance personnel should continue the work of fostering a culture of compliance and maintaining effective internal controls, and be prepared to make the transition without significantly weakening the effectiveness of their compliance programs.

Moreover, compliance challenges are likely to see a bump at the time of the transition to post-GSA life. GSAs have a tendency to draw an organization's resources to a particular risk area, be it FCPA compliance, antitrust, or the like. During the term of the GSA—usually three to five or, sometimes, seven years—an organization's risk environment is likely to have changed. While organizations will ideally be keeping abreast of such changes during the course of their GSA, organizations may consider conducting a thorough compliance risk assessment before the end of the GSA's term. This will likely help the organization understand how its risk landscape may have migrated. This can ultimately be a good thing, as it can allow the organization to shift its resources and attention to higher-risk areas. Moreover, taking these steps gives regulators one more reason to be confident that the organization is prepared to move on from the GSA.

In summary, an organization should understand that a GSA is intended to set it on a right course to compliance. This course should be maintained beyond the life of the GSA, through the transition and after.

Conclusion

GSAs have grown in importance over the last two decades and are now a significant tool supporting government enforcement efforts. The increase in usage, particularly in the FCPA area, and the spike in fines being levied under GSAs have brought them front and center on the radar of many organizations. Any organization experiencing serious fraud or misconduct could potentially find itself as a candidate for a GSA. When serious fraud or other misconduct occurs, an organization is confronted with myriad challenges. The biggest question an organization will likely face will be whether or not to cooperate and seek government leniency. Corporations can rarely afford to risk a criminal charge and conviction. Thus, the choice here is often clear—if the misconduct is serious enough to warrant government interest, the incentives to cooperate can be substantial.

Chapter 14

Response: Recovery, Presentation, and Analysis of Electronically Stored Information

Adam M. Beschloss

Throughout the previous chapters of this book, we have discussed the various challenges to managing the risk of fraud and misconduct in today's increasingly global and regulated environment. However, perhaps the greatest challenges to the management of fraud and misconduct have been the ascendancy of the information age and the increasing digitalization of information. Whether developing systems to help prevent and detect fraud through various data-mining and analysis techniques and tools, responding to subpoenas or discovery requests, or uncovering information critical to the success of an investigation, the ability to know what data exist, in what form they exist, and how to access and use the data is an increasing imperative to the effective management of fraud and misconduct in a digital world.

Digital information in all its forms, including, for example, customer databases, finance systems, regulatory archives, word documents, image files, or e-mail, is collectively referred to as electronically stored information (ESI). Beyond just

Mr. Beschloss is a director in KPMG LLP's Forensic Technology practice in New York, NY. He delivers Evidence and Discovery Management services to corporate clients.
Additional contributors are Bernard A. Boit, Kelli J. Brooks, Edward L. Goings, Thomas P. Keegan, Kenneth C. Koch, Charles S. Meier, and Chris H. Paskach.

paper in digital form, ESI is a new paradigm for storing information that presents a set of difficult technical and operational challenges that do not exist in the world of paper.

This chapter discusses the role of technology in conducting investigations and responding to electronic discovery for litigation. It describes proactive measures to improve the identification, preservation, and collection of electronic data in the event such evidence is needed for litigation or internal investigations.

The Records Management Environment and the Impact on Investigations

The amount of digital information, along with the formats in which it is stored, continues to increase at an amazing rate. To put this in perspective, consider that a portable thumb drive that can fit in your shirt pocket and costs only $30 may hold as much as 20 gigabytes of data—the equivalent of 1 million pages. A small physical piece of digital media can translate into an overwhelming amount of information. Organizations create literally billions of stored documents every year and run the risk of their employees being able to leave the office with the equivalent of millions of pages of information in their pockets, including such sensitive data as intellectual property, client information, and competitive intelligence.

The conventional wisdom that "storage is cheap" shares responsibility for the digital information explosion and its attendant inefficiencies,[*] including vast amounts of duplicative and non-business-critical data that organizations ultimately store. Just imagine how many fantasy football and out-of-office e-mails are taking up space on data storage systems.

Compounding the volume challenge, ESI is disparate in nature, often broadly distributed, and it is maintained in varied and complex systems, some of which may be legacy systems that no longer even exist at the time the ESI becomes relevant to an investigation or litigation. Additionally, ESI contains information that is not always apparent to the user (e.g., metadata[†]) but can be crucial to proving issues in an investigation or the improper handling (spoliation[‡]) of which can result in courtroom sanctions.

---

[*] While noncritical storage, such as the hard drive in your home PC, may indeed be "cheap," storage of your organizational data is not, when considered in the context of the total cost inclusive of power consumption, security, disaster recovery and business continuity, data availability, etc.

[†] "Metadata" is typically defined as "data about data." Examples of metadata include "create date," "last modified date," "time stamp" on an e-mail, and other bibliographic information.

[‡] "Spoliation" is the intentional or unintentional destruction, altering, or withholding of evidence. Metadata, which can be a critical piece of evidence, can be easily altered or destroyed if handled incorrectly. The simple act of opening a file to review it changes significant amounts of metadata.

While paper is a fairly uniform medium and often more easily categorized and classified—certainly in the way it is read—ESI can take many forms. It is often system-dependent and may require proprietary technologies to access. In a typical business day, for instance, correspondence is created on computers and distributed through an e-mail system. Telephone messages are taken by digital voice mail systems. Faxes are sent and received digitally. Proximity card readers authenticate and log employees as they pass through restricted areas. Digital surveillance cameras monitor physical plants. Automobile-fleet GPS systems log vehicle locations and routes. Transaction logs capture corporate-controlled credit card usage. Document management systems track the authors, revisions, retention, and remediation of documents. Financial application databases store accounts payable, accounts receivable, general ledger, and other financial data and maintain transactional logs. All this information may be pertinent to an investigation, and any of it may contain evidence of improper behavior.

Disparate Technology Operating across Multiple Jurisdictions Increases Complexity

The disparate technology environments common to many organizations compound the challenge of managing electronic records. How do you classify an e-mail, for instance? The e-mail's content might be construed as a contract subject to a regulatory-prescribed retention schedule, a brokerage communication that must be archived, privileged communication or attorney work product, or perhaps data covered by the Health Insurance Portability and Accountability Act of 1996. Or the e-mail content may simply be the most recent fantasy football update. It fast becomes apparent that controlling data for such a wide variety of e-mail content in a records management architecture is a difficult task. Many organizations have no methodology, protocols, or system to identify and classify e-mail and, instead, take a "save-it-all" approach that, arguably, wastes resources and actually might *create* risk.

Technology innovations add to the complexity and risk. For example, voice messages delivered by e-mail are an illustration of new *convergent* technologies that can speed the pace of business and support the free flow of information, yet may increase risk. Consider the reaction of an organization's general counsel who learns that a company salesperson has made extraordinary claims about a product's capabilities in one of these voice messages. An organization that does not normally save voice mail, but does save e-mail, now has, de facto, voice mail being saved. The message could later be used as evidence in a claim against the company.

What if a record containing personally identifiable information (PII)* is attached to an e-mail correspondence and stored on a corporate computer server in Germany and is then used by a satellite office in China to aggregate customer data? To which jurisdiction does the PII belong? If counsel subsequently produces this document in response to a request by the U.S. Department of Justice, have privacy rights or sovereignties been violated? Have data privacy laws been broken?† The answers to questions regarding cross-border discovery are not necessarily clear and can be contentious.

In their article "'Blocking' Statutes Bring Discovery Woes,"[1] Marc J. Gottridge and Thomas Rouhette pose this question: "When should American litigators care about a judgment of the French Cour de Cassation (Supreme Court) requiring a French lawyer to pay a 10,000 euro fine?"‡ The authors note that in this decision (a case involving the French insurance company MAAF and the California Insurance Department[2]) a French lawyer working with an American law firm representing the California Insurance Department made a telephone call intending to obtain information informally from MAAF. The Cour de Cassation upheld a finding that the lawyer violated the blocking statute and affirmed a sentence of a 10,000 euro fine. This conflict highlights not only the legal implications of jurisdictional differences in the handling of data, but also the potentially costly deadlock that can occur between the local law governing a company division or subsidiary's place of business and the U.S. judge requiring discovery production.

In many organizations, records management policies and procedures have not been implemented in a manner that takes into consideration the complexity of the digital world overlaid on the requirements of investigations. Companies struggle with regulatory compliance as it relates to data preservation and destruction. For those organizations that have not devoted sufficient attention to this area, the potential for duplicative efforts, risk of spoliation, and inadvertent violation of data privacy laws looms large. It is in this environment that an organization's in-house counsel executes against the "duty to preserve" or adequately respond to a subpoena, and begins the investigatory process.

---

* Depending on the type of industry and situation, the protection of PII may be governed by various regulatory bodies. The HIPAA addresses the "Wrongful Disclosure of Individually Identifiable Health Information," and the Gramm-Leach Bliley Act (GLBA) governs financial institutions and addresses "limits on disclosure of nonpublic personal information to nonaffiliated third parties." These are only two examples of regulatory compliance issues that corporations should consider related to control and protection of PII.

† The European Union Privacy Directive and French Blocking Statute are just two examples of laws that may prohibit the collection and transportation of data.

‡ The 1980 Blocking Statute, French Penal Code Law No. 80-538, prohibits the disclosure of information to foreign public authorities when that disclosure may affect France's interests.

The Electronic Discovery Process

The associate general counsel of a Fortune 50 company once exclaimed, "I don't lose on facts, I lose on discovery!" Yet, despite the importance of e-discovery, organizations typically leave the job to outside counsel. And unfortunately, the vagaries of this arcane process are often made even more incomprehensible by the "techno speak" favored by IT departments and litigation support specialists.

Given the significant expense and risk involved in e-discovery, organizations should not allow their service providers (both outside law firms and e-discovery service providers) to operate carte blanche. Today's in-house counsel could benefit from better understanding the e-discovery process, not only within the context of regulatory and compliance requirements, but also in the context of business requirements. In short, e-discovery should be understood as a business process (operationally and financially), and organizations should demand the same accountability, efficiency, and effectiveness that they demand of any critical business process.

Rule 34: Producing Documents, Electronically Stored Information, and Tangible Things or Entering onto Land for Inspection and Other Purposes

(a) In General.

A party may serve on any other party a request within the scope of Rule 26(b):

(1) To produce and permit the requesting party or its representative to inspect, copy, test, or sample the following items in the responding party's possession, custody, or control:

(A) Any designated documents or electronically stored information—including writings, drawings, graphs, charts, photographs, sound recordings, images, and other data or data compilations—stored in any medium from which information can be obtained either directly or, if necessary, after translation by the responding party into a reasonably usable form; or

(B) Any designated tangible things; or

(2) To permit entry onto designated land or other property possessed or controlled by the responding party, so that the requesting party may inspect, measure, survey, photograph, test, or sample the property or any designated object or operation on it.

Source: Rule 34(a) of the Federal Rules of Civil Procedure, December 2009, p. 52, www.uscourts.gov/uscourts/RulesAndPolicies/rules/CV2009.pdf.

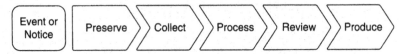

Figure 14.1. Traditional investigatory discovery workflow
Source: KPMG LLP, 2009.

The Operational View

Every investigation, while unique, has certain commonalities. Mapping the activities of a traditional investigatory discovery workflow from "anticipation," or the expectation of an investigation, through to "production to the requesting party" is represented in Figure 14.1.

The Duty to Preserve and Litigation Hold

The "duty to preserve" for litigation or in the context of a government investigation is a contentious area of the law since it does not have a clearly defined mandate. There are a handful of judicial opinions that are often used as benchmarks. For example, in *Zubulake v. UBS Warburg LLC*,[3] the court held that once a party "reasonably anticipates litigation," it must suspend its routine document retention policy and put a litigation hold in place. Organizations need to consider the implication of a "suspension of a document retention policy," which can be quite burdensome if the entity's records management policy has been to save everything.

What, then, is the scope of the duty to preserve? Must a corporation, upon learning of or recognizing the threat of litigation, preserve every piece of paper, every e-mail or electronic document, every backup tape? The *Zubulake* court's answer was a firm no, since doing so "would cripple large corporations . . . that are almost always involved in litigation."[*]

However, when it comes to the deletion of ESI, even seemingly innocent acts or acts that have no malicious intent may result in sanctions. Consider the impact of an IT professional deleting an old system to make room on the network while a lawsuit was pending. Because the deleted system may have contained relevant discoverable data, the actions of the IT professional could result in sanctions. Seemingly deliberate acts can result in much worse.

---

[*] *Zubulake I: Zubulake v. UBS Warburg LLC*, 217 F.R.D. 309 (S.D.N.Y. 2003). These issues were revisited by Judge Scheindlin (the presiding judge in *Zubulake*) in an Opinion and Order in *The Pension Committee of the University of Montreal Pension Plan, et al., v. Banc of America Securities, LLC, CITCO Fund Services (Curacao) N.V., The CITCO Group Limited International Fund Limited Services (Ireland) Limited, PricewaterhouseCoopers (Netherland Antilles), John W. Bendall, Jr., Richard Geist, Anthony Stocks, Kieran Conroy, and Declan Quilligan*, No. 05-CV-09016 (SAS) (S.D.N.Y 2010).

In a *National Law Journal* publication, Karen Willenken, counsel for Skadden, Arps, Slate, Meagher, and Flom LLP, writes, "In *U.S. v. Ganier, 68 F.3d 920* (6th Cir. 2006), the government investigated a company and its chief executive officer for improprieties in bidding for government contracts. When the CEO responded to news of the government's inquiry by implementing a new 'email retention policy' and deleting electronic documents from his desktop and laptop computers, the government indicted and convicted him based solely on obstruction of justice." Willenken continues, "Alternatively, the failure to preserve information and alleged improper handling of electronic evidence may be offered by the government as evidence of the employee's 'consciousness of guilt' concerning the indicted offense."[4]

It must be remembered, however, that document preservation is not just about maintaining or deleting records. An organization is expected to be able to effectively search this body of information and produce relevant documents. Furthermore, courts typically expect a high level of competency in the discovery process and require that if a relevant document exists in the organization's system, it will be found, preserved, and ultimately produced. Unfortunately, on occasion, both judges and litigants, who may have little technical expertise, have difficulty understanding just how daunting such requirements can be.

The amended Federal Rules of Civil Procedure (December 2006) address spoliation "absent bad faith" in Rule 37(f) (as amended) and offers a "safe-harbor" provision. Rule 37(f) provides that a court may not impose sanctions on a party that deletes or otherwise destroys ESI "as a result of the routine, good-faith operation of an electronic information system." However, as organizations and their counsel are expected to have a high level of competency in these matters, safe harbor in these cases does not provide a cover for negligence or poor performance. While litigants may be forgiven for minor failures, the courts do not turn a blind eye to litigants' obligations to locate and preserve potential evidence. Organizations with a lack of clear or enforceable policies and controls relating to litigation holds may not be able to avail themselves of the safe-harbor provision.

While the duty to preserve may be perceived as broad, this does not necessarily equate to broad collection, processing, and storage of data. For those organizations that have taken a save-it-all approach, the tendency is often to simply collect, process, and review all the data during the e-discovery process. This type of approach, however, significantly drives up the cost of discovery and can bury the reviewers under a high volume of nonrelevant documents in the collection—a hallmark of the traditional discovery process.

The traditional model of e-discovery, illustrated in Figure 14.2, is much like a lumber mill. The process begins with the massive tree trunk that is then chipped away as it goes through various processes to produce the required wood products. The lumber mill's process is linear, noniterative, and rigid. The traditional e-discovery process is much the same, allowing for very little in-process adjustment as massive amounts of data are brought in, and filters (e.g., keyword searches, date ranges, etc.) are applied to chip away at the collection with the remaining data reviewed. Of course, the more data that go into this process, the more likely it is that large amounts of data will come out, unnecessarily increasing review costs.

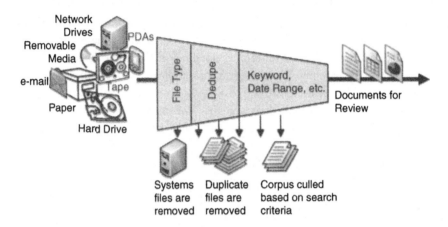

Figure 14.2. Traditional e-discovery model
Source: KPMG LLP, 2009.

The review stage is expensive—in terms of not just hourly rates, but also the number of hours devoted to the review of irrelevant material. As armies of contract attorneys and others are deployed for the review of these documents, the goal often becomes feeding as much data as possible, as fast as possible, so that review teams are not idle. Such a process, which often can be defined by silos, hand-offs, and suboptimization, has been discredited by widely accepted process efficiency and effectiveness disciplines.*

The New E-Discovery Process

The costly and inefficient models for processing digital evidence clearly highlight the need for a fundamental shift in the way e-discovery is executed. Such a shift requires a new look at how technology is positioned and deployed. This newer

---

* One such discipline is known as "Lean." Lean is a manufacturing and training process developed by the Department of Defense with roots dating to World War I and made famous by Toyota in demonstrating efficiency and removal of waste in a process (John Huntzinger, "The Roots of Lean, Training Within Industry: The Origin of Japanese Management and Kaizen," The Lean Institute, http://www.leaninstituut.nl/publications/Roots_of_Lean_TWI.pdf). "Six Sigma," developed at Motorola and made ubiquitous by General Electric, focuses on process effectiveness. Many organizations are adopting a hybrid of these two processes called "Lean Six Sigma," which recognizes that processes can be both *effective* and *efficient*.

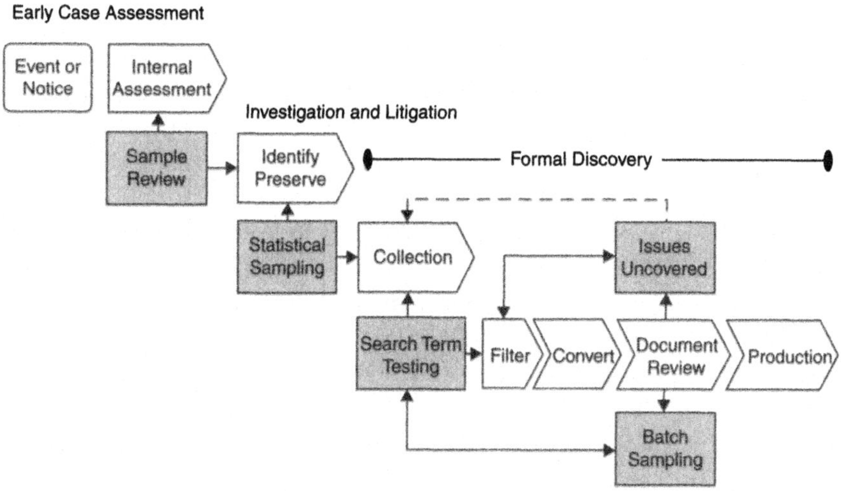

Early Case Assessment

Figure 14.3. Smarter e-discovery
Source: KPMG LLP, 2009.

approach is a managed workflow that seeks to drive down costs, and the approach demands the sort of efficiency and forethought that manages e-discovery holistically (from early case assessment to production), as illustrated in Figure 14.3. This e-discovery approach has roots in disciplines like Lean Six Sigma, and the establishment of project controls at an early stage of data management is critical to success.

Several factors are driving this shift in e-discovery; chief among them:

- The new Federal Rules of Civil Procedure, which require each party to agree to an e-discovery protocol and demonstrate preparedness and competency
- An acceptance of methods such as concept searching, data sampling, and testing that enable the corporate respondent to document and defend preservation and collection decisions that narrow the scope of collection and production
- Court opinions such as *Zubulake* and *Victor Stanley**
- The passage of Federal Rule of Evidence 502,[†] attempting to reduce the burden on the respondent and address the inadvertent waiver of privilege, while demanding accountability and defensibility

---

* *Victor Stanley, Inc. v. Creative Pipe, Inc., et al.,* No. MJG-06-2662 (D. Md. 2008) addresses waiver of privilege and speaks to search protocols and concepts like quality control and sampling.
[†]Rule 502 addresses the inadvertent disclosure of privileged documents in a production and provides that as long as reasonable steps were taken to prevent such a disclosure, there will be no waiver of privilege. (This speaks directly to sound and defensible processes and competency.)

- Massive data volumes (more specifically, very low relevancy rates), which tend to drive up costs significantly
- The fact that litigation generally, and e-discovery specifically, can no longer operate outside the purview of cost control without risking the potential economic ruin of the responding organization

And while market forces—which have been building over the last several years—have driven costs downward, little has been done to address the root cause of cost overruns, which is the volume of data being handled. In other words, while per-unit costs for collection, processing, and hosting electronic data may have gone down significantly, the number of units continues to go up. Therefore, the value of this new e-discovery workflow model is its potential to reduce data volume and improve targeting of document relevancy. In Lean manufacturing parlance, this translates to "less waste."

In this new e-discovery workflow model, rather than employing broad and untested data collections, data acquisition is sampled at the outset to test the efficacy of search terms and the relevance of targeted custodians (witnesses or involved parties) and systems. For example, low relevancy rates result in the recalibration of search terms or the reconsideration of relevant custodians, as well as the value of data collected from certain systems. An important corollary to this iterative deployment of technology is the creation of well-documented processes with a higher level of control—and an effective and perhaps more defensible process. If implemented well, organizations should anticipate cost savings resulting from the smart use of technology that focuses on a deceptively simple measure for cost control: processing less data.

Of course, the opposition in an investigation or litigation may have different ideas in mind. However, a sound and defensible strategy, evidenced in a workflow that is repeatable, reproducible, and well documented, can be effective in managing this tension and, consequently, managing the costs.

While there is now much authority and guidance relating to e-discovery in civil matters, as U.S. Magistrate John M. Facciola notes in *United States v. O'Keefe*, "In criminal cases, there is unfortunately no rule to which the courts can look for guidance . . . Be that as it may, Rule 34 of the *Federal Rules of Civil Procedure* speak[s] specifically to the form of production [and it would be] foolish to disregard them [in a criminal case, as] it is far better to use these rules than to reinvent the wheel when the production of documents in criminal and civil cases raises the same problems."[5]

Furthermore, it is important to note that "in the civil context, parties are encouraged to meet, confer, and cooperate in [aspects of e-discovery such as] the selection of key words or other search methodologies [necessary to adequate document productions]. In a criminal investigation, however, no parallel system exists."[6]

In this context, while Rules 34 and 17(c)* of the Federal Rules of Criminal Procedures fundamentally differ in how they view the scope of document collections, it would seem that the more than 70 years of authority in civil discovery, and the expertise gained in e-discovery in particular, can provide very useful guidance for criminal or internal investigations. *And not to apply the tenets of e-discovery espoused herein may be,* to quote Magistrate Facciola, *"foolish."* We further posit here that application of these processes to criminal matters may improve the ability to respond to a subpoena and document that the organization properly and adequately searched and produced relevant documents without being overly narrow, while guarding against the burdens of being overly broad.

Who, What, and Where Are the Data?

The protocols used to identify relevant data for preservation should be different from those used to identify data for collection. While preservation may be broadly applied to guard against claims of spoliation, or simply because there is uncertainty regarding relevance early in the case, this does not make the case for forensically collecting *all* the preserved data.† There are key considerations for determining an appropriate identification, preservation, and collection plan for ESI.

Identification

The identification stage involves discovery of fact and, in the case of ESI, the discovery of IT systems. The latter involves, among other things, mapping key witnesses to the systems they access in the context of the time frame being investigated. The task may be complicated if witnesses (or custodians) have changed physical locations or job positions or have left the organization altogether.

Understanding which electronic data systems are relevant to the matter at hand is as important as understanding what is considered relevant to an effective legal hold order. First, the legal hold order must preserve data broadly enough to ensure compliance, but not so broadly as to incur inappropriate costs and disruption to the organization. Second, the legal hold order must identify the most

---

* Rule 17(c) of the Federal Rules of Criminal Procedures, "Producing Documents and Objects," states:
  (1) In General. A subpoena may order the witness to produce any books, papers, documents, data, or other objects the subpoena designates. The court may direct the witness to produce the designated items in court before trial or before they are to be offered in evidence. When the items arrive, the court may permit the parties and their attorneys to inspect all or part of them.
  (2) Quashing or Modifying the Subpoena. On motion made promptly, the court may quash or modify the subpoena if compliance would be unreasonable or oppressive.
† Forensic collection means that the integrity of the data (including metadata) can be verified.

relevant data for collection and take into consideration how the data are to be collected. This identification process can benefit from preplanning and actions taken prior to any litigation or investigatory response.

At this point, potentially relevant (but perhaps not responsive) data have been identified in accordance with preservation requirements. The organization must preserve the records, documents, and correspondence that relate to a particular event (e.g., a suspected fraud, product, contract, merger, etc.) during a particular time span. Identified data should be mapped to the individuals involved with the matter. At this juncture, interviews may be undertaken with key witnesses who can provide direct confirmation of what data they may have in their possession and what systems may be pertinent to the matter.

Preservation and Collection

Policies and procedures that govern data collection should be established prior to the actual data collection, and those policies and procedures should guide the collection effort. This approach provides an organization and relevant third parties with documented assurance that the collected data have not been compromised and supports findings should there be a need to testify or provide affidavits regarding the methods of collection—particularly in matters of spoliation.

Admissibility of evidence in U.S. federal courts requires adherence to the strict guidelines found in the Federal Rules of Evidence (FRE). These rules govern the introduction of evidence in both civil and criminal proceedings. While they do not apply to matters in state courts, the rules of many states have been closely modeled on these provisions. Even though the FRE were never originally intended to deal with electronic evidence, they are used as the litmus test for admissibility into the courts. Under the FRE, electronic evidence is required to be relevant, legally permissible, reliable, properly identified, and properly preserved.

Source: The Federal Rules of Evidence, 2010, www.uscourts.gov/uscourts/RulesAndPolicies/rules/EV2009.pdf.

The methodologies and tools discussed in the following paragraphs can help achieve significant cost savings, not only in this phase of e-discovery, but also downstream as the ESI moves through the remainder of the discovery process.

Imaging versus Targeted Preservations

Traditionally, exact images (not copies) of entire data sources are made. This means that if a laptop contains a 60-gigabyte hard drive, the entire 60 gigabytes is preserved (including empty space, file fragments, systems files, programs, etc.).

The forensic image preserves everything on the hard drive, including metadata. Merely copying the drive or individual files may alter metadata such as "last access date," "edit dates," and other information. Simply opening a file to copy it can spoliate the evidence in situations where the date of a memo or who accessed it last is central to a claim. In other words, the evidence is destroyed.

However, procedures such as bit-level data imaging and subsequent forensic analysis can be performed selectively. The challenge is to obtain *only* potentially relevant files in a forensically sound manner. Until recently, tools that could perform this targeted forensic preservation and collection were not available. Today, however, some forensic technology service providers and software tools have the ability to acquire select files in a forensically sound manner, establish the required chain of custody, and document the origination of acquired data. The cost savings involved with data imaging can be significant and the efficacy of the subsequent document review procedures greatly enhanced.

In this regard, the dynamic in a criminal investigation, while different from civil discovery, will likely benefit from this broad preservation-targeted collection methodology. As noted in *U.S. v. Reyes*, "Rule 17(c) is not as broad as its plain language suggests, however, and it is narrower in scope than the corollary rules of civil procedure, which permit broad discovery." In short, the discovery requests that begin with the phrase "any and all," so common to e-discovery requests in civil litigation, are not tolerated in criminal matters. Rule 17(c) requires not only relevancy and admissibility, but *specificity* as well. [Emphasis added.] Judge Breyer, in *U.S. v. Reyes*, cites *Nixon 418 U.S. at 700* in noting that "Rule 17(c) requires a party to provide details sufficient to establish that the subpoena's proponent has made a good-faith effort to obtain evidentiary material and is not engaged in the proverbial 'fishing expedition.'" The request, in other words, should not be overly broad or vague.[7]

The countervailing tension for the respondent is demonstrating that your search has not been overly narrow. Again, the lessons from civil discovery and the methods described herein provide for the management of this tension, namely, well-documented, auditable, and reasoned approaches to how the search was conducted; what search terms and methodologies were used to identify responsive materials; and the procedures utilized in collecting and reviewing the potentially relevant evidence, buttressed by a preservation strategy that supports additional sampling should the scope broaden.

Once identified, preserved, and collected, the data must be processed. Data processing is perhaps the most purely technical aspect of managing ESI for discovery and is a sphere of commonality across discovery whether it is being done in support of civil litigation, criminal investigation, or Hart Scott Rodino second request.*

Processing

There can be a tendency to move through the phases of e-discovery in a lockstep fashion, leaving little room for adjustments. The approach advocated here, as illustrated in Figure 14.3, allows for a more dynamic, iterative process—a controlled process that offers the opportunity for continual improvement. The use of data sampling techniques is an example of this approach and marks a significant departure from the "collect-all, process-all, review-all" approach of the traditional e-discovery workflow.†

The term "processing" in e-discovery refers first to the culling of data based on criteria developed by counsel. The culling or filtering of ESI will likely include "deduplication" (the removal of exact duplicates),‡ as well as other filtering techniques such as the use of keywords, file size, file type, date, and metadata. This stage of the processing presents further opportunities for analysis and adjustments before documents are loaded to a document management system for review.

Review and Production

The document review in an investigation and the potential subsequent document production are the most costly components in e-discovery. The significant interest in "concept search" engines, which automate review using sophisticated computer analytics rather than the human decision-making process, is fueled in

---

* The Hart Scott Rodino Act (1976) subjects certain mergers and acquisitions to antitrust review by the DOJ and FTC. In some instances, a *second request* is made for additional information and documentation (U.S. Code 15, 18a, Premerger Notification and Waiting Period).

† This cycle of continuous analysis and adjustment is central to the Six Sigma methodology-*DMAIC: define, measure, analyze, improve,* and *control.* Six Sigma leverages the concept that each step in a process can create constraints or opportunities for the step that follows as the work flows forward. In this iterative cycle of the DMAIC, constraints can be removed and opportunities uncovered through sampling and analysis. And it does so without the cost and waste associated with rework as the improvements happen proactively *in process.*

‡ Deduplication is the suppression of exact duplicates so that only one instance of the document or e-mail is presented for review. Exact duplicates are typically defined as documents having the same MD5 hash value (a 32-digit number). This hash value is a digital fingerprint of the document. While it is not impossible that two different documents can have the same hash value, it is highly improbable. The hash value is also used in chain of custody to demonstrate that a file has not been altered during processing.

part by the combination of high data volumes, short review time frames, and the need to reduce spiraling review costs.*

One value of concept-based e-discovery tools is their ability to group similar documents into conceptual patterns or themes, such as recognizing that 1,000 e-mails are all about fantasy football pools. A reviewer can then tag† such e-mails as nonresponsive in a matter of seconds, saving time and cost. The use of concept-based tools, linguistic analysis, and other automated efforts can be an effective method for dealing with large volumes of ESI.

The managed, iterative processes illustrated in this chapter, as well as the proactive steps that can be taken during early case assessments (such as data sampling) and records management initiatives, all focus on reducing the volume of ESI to a point where something useful can be done with the data. These methods address the root cause of the problem by helping to narrow the scope of document collection from the outset. In this way, the body of documents made available for review, while in many cases far from small, will be as focused and relevant as possible.

Still it is likely a document population requiring review will be large even after aggressive culling has occurred. This can be as true for criminal investigations as it is for civil litigation. In particular, shared drives (used by departments to store and share data related to their work) and corporate reporting systems can produce huge volumes of data, even when utilizing a targeted approach. Again, when one begins with hundreds of millions of documents, reviewing even only 5 percent can be daunting and will require counsel to detail and certify actions related to how the search was conducted, why certain methods were chosen, why documents are considered privileged, and so forth. Failure to do so can trigger repercussions, including the waiver of affirmative defenses and even monetary sanctions. *Victor Stanley v. Creative Pipe* highlights these points.

After finding that the defendant indeed waived privilege when inadvertently producing the privileged documents, Judge Grimm writes in *Victor Stanley v. Creative Pipe*, "Defendants, who bear the burden of proving that their conduct [in conducting a privilege review] was reasonable . . . failed to provide the court with information regarding: the keywords used; the rationale for their selection; the qualifications of [the defendant] and his attorneys to design an effective and reliable search and information retrieval method . . . or whether they analyzed the results of the search to assess its reliability, appropriateness for the task, and the quality of its implementation."[8] In short, the production of the documents

---

* As of this writing, while not yet mainstream, offshore review is gaining credence with some law firms and other organizations as a way of mitigating document review costs.
† Tagging is the method of recording an attorney's decision for each document during review regarding relevance, privilege, or issue.

was not viewed as inadvertent or accidental, but rather the outcome of a process that was not reasonable, thoughtful, or defensible.

More recently, Judge Shira Scheindlin in a coda to *Zubulake* noted in *The Pension Committee of the University of Montreal Pension Plan, et al.* opinion and order, "While litigants are not required to execute document productions with absolute precision, at a minimum they must act diligently and search thoroughly at the time they reasonably anticipate litigations."[9]

Conclusion

There are several lessons to draw upon in improving the cost efficiency and operational effectiveness of e-discovery. First, organizations should deal with electronic data at the very early stages of discovery—even before formal discovery commences. The courts look to the Federal Rules of Civil Procedure (in criminal matters as well), and similar state court rules, and hold litigants to the requirements for locating documents, reviewing them, and making them available in a usable format for the opposition. Organizations must have a reliable and defensible means of identifying such information and preserving it when the legal obligation first arises. As discussed and illustrated in this chapter, failure to do so has significant impact on the rest of the e-discovery process and can result in serious sanctions if not conducted properly.

In earlier years, many organizations opted for what they believed to be the safest approach to electronic discovery—saving all documents. This method resulted in increased cost and risk to a company. Documents not deleted pursuant to regular document retention schedules are now potentially discoverable in litigation. Companies that saved everything later found themselves facing the high cost related to the processing and review of larger volumes of data. While there is no "one-size-fits-all" approach to e-discovery, in today's data-driven operating environment, proactive information and document management is a critical component of successful business management.

As Judge Grimm noted in *Victor Stanley*, "Common sense suggests that even a properly designed and executed keyword search may prove to be over-inclusive or under-inclusive, resulting in the identification of documents as privileged which are not, and not-privileged when, in fact, they are. The only prudent way to test the reliability of the keyword search is to perform some appropriate sampling of the documents determined to be privileged and those determined not to be in order to arrive at a comfort level that the categories are neither over-inclusive nor under-inclusive."[10]

While Judge Grimm's comments are aimed at a privilege review specifically, and search construction more broadly, we suggest that this approach is both "prudent" and perhaps even "common sense" throughout the e-discovery continuum.

Magistrate Judge Andrew J. Peck was even more strident: "This Opinion should serve as a wake-up call to the Bar in this District [S.D.N.Y.] about the need for careful thought, quality control, testing, and cooperation with opposing counsel in designing search terms or 'keywords' to be used to produce e-mails or other electronically stored information ('ESI') . . . It is time that the Bar—even those lawyers who did not come of age in the computer era—understand this."[11] Whether creating litigation hold and preservation protocols or devising collection and culling strategies, it is clear that to meet cost and procedural challenges, e-discovery methodologies must be properly designed, executed, and tested and involve appropriate sampling to verify the process. While the application of the right technologies to do the right job at each point in the continuum is required, those technologies are only truly effective when used in support of a defensible methodology. A successful methodology will be an iterative approach to e-discovery that controls cost while meeting judicial challenges.

Endnotes

Introduction

1. Richard H. Girgenti, "Compliance Programs' New Mantra: Value Preservation and Value Creation," *The Metropolitan Corporate Counsel,* Northeast Edition 16, no. 5, May 2008, cover page and p. 62.
2. Jaclyn Jaeger, "Maturity of Compliance Systems, Program Lags," *Compliance Week,* December 2009.
3. Jaeger, "Maturity of Compliance Systems, Program Lags."
4. Jaeger, "Maturity of Compliance Systems, Program Lags."
5. Corporate Executive Board, *Executive Guidance for 2010: Confronting Six Enemies of Post-recession Performance,* Washington, DC, 2009, p. 21.
6. Corporate Executive Board, *Executive Guidance for 2010,* pp. 21–22.

Part I

1. Alex Berenson, *The Number: How the Drive for Quarterly Earnings Corrupted Wall Street and Corporate America,* New York: Random House, 2003.
2. American Institute of Certified Public Accountants, *Management Override of Internal Controls: The Achilles' Heel of Fraud Prevention—The Audit Committee and Oversight of Financial Reporting,* New York, 2005.

Chapter I

1. Association of Certified Fraud Examiners, Inc. (ACFE), *2008 Report to the Nation on Occupational Fraud and Abuse,* Austin, TX, 2008, pp. 4, 12, www.acfe.com/documents/2008-rttn.pdf.

2. Sameer T. Mustafa and Heidi H. Meier, "Audit Committees and Misappropriation of Assets: Publicly Held Companies in the United States," *Canadian Accounting Perspectives,* vol. 5, no. 2, 2006, www.caaa.ca/AccountingperspectivesCAP/BackIssues/vol5num2/exeartpzzStCtbvY.html.

3. ACFE, *2008 Report to the Nation,* pp. 4, 12.

4. U.S. Department of Justice, "Former Fast Food Managing Director and District Manager Plead Guilty to Tax Evasion and Bank Fraud," press release, February 23, 2003, www.justice.gov/tax/usaopress/2003/txdv03ohs30224_1.html.

5. U.S. Department of Justice, "Nevada Man Sentenced to 18 Months in Prison in Scheme to Steal Customer Payments from Business in Savage, Maryland," press release, May 3, 2006, www.justice.gov/usao/md/Public-Affairs/press_releases/press06/Nevada%20Man%20Sentenced%20to%2018%20Months%20in%20Prison%20in%20Scheme%20To%20Steal%20Customer%20Payments%20from%20Business%20in%20Savage,%20Maryland.html.

6. Peter Shinkle, "Scam Gets Ex-Boeing Official Year in Prison," *St. Louis Post-Dispatch,* June 24, 2006, www.stltoday.com.

7. Mary Flood, "Accountant Admits Embezzling $3.6 from Pasadena Firm," *Houston Chronicle,* October 19, 2009, www.chron.com/disp/story.mpl/hot-stories/6674910.html.

8. Matt Gryta, "Canisius Embezzler Pleads Guilty," *The Buffalo News,* October 10, 2009, www.buffalonews.com/cityregion/story/823567.html#.

9. GateHouse News Service, "Latest Conviction Concludes Massport Payroll and Benefits Fraud Case," October 31, 2008, www.wickedlocal.com/wakefield/town_info/government/x199482284/Latest-conviction-concludes-Massport-payroll-and-benefits-fraud-case.

10. U.S. Department of Justice, "General Manager and Financial Controller of Silver Spring Country Club Sentenced for Stealing Over $1.3 Million from Club Accounts," press release, October 19, 2009, www.justice.gov/usao/md/Public-Affairs/press_releases/press08/GeneralManagerandFinancialControllerCountryClubSentencedforStealingFromClubAccounts.html.

11. James McAndrews and William Roberds, "The Economics of Check Float," Federal Reserve Bank of Atlanta *Economic Review,* Fourth Quarter 2000, p. 17, www.frbatlanta.org/filelegacydocs/roberds.pdf; Suzanne Mahadeo, "Check Fraud: Separating Money from Worthless Paper," *Fraud Magazine,* September/October 2005, www.acfe.com/resources/view.asp?ArticleID=463.

12. Richard Verrier, "Proper Controls Can Deter Employee Theft," *Los Angeles Times,* May 22, 2007, articles.latimes.com/2007/may/22/business/fi-smallembezzle22.

13. Stephen Taub, "'Mr. John' Pleads Guilty in Tishman Toilet Scam," *CFO.com*, August 5, 2008, www.cfo.com/article.cfm/11877496/ c_11876318?f=TodayInFinance_Inside.

14. U.S. Department of Justice, "Former Accountant of Dundalk Law Firm Admits to Stealing Over $1 Million and Arson," press release, September 16, 2009, www.justice.gov/usao/md/Public-Affairs/press_releases/press08/ FormerAccountantofDundalkLawFirmAdmitstoStealingover1MillionandAr son.html.

15. Sarah Antonacci, "Treasurer's Employee Admits to Embezzlement," *State Journal-Register,* August 20, 2008, www.treasurer.il.gov/news/in-the-news/ 2008/SJR20August2008.htm.

16. ACFE, *2008 Report to the Nation*, p. 13.

17. ACFE, *2008 Report to the Nation*, p. 50.

18. Vikki Ortiz, "Woman Indicted in the Theft of Business Secrets," *Chicago Tribune,* April 3, 2008.

19. U.S. Securities and Exchange Commission, "SEC Charges Bernard L. Madoff for Multi-billion Dollar Ponzi Scheme," press release 2008-293, December 11, 2008, sec.gov/news/press/2008/2008-293.htm; "SEC Charges R. Allen Stanford, Stanford International Bank for Multi-billion Dollar Investment Scheme," press release 2009-26, February 17, 2009, sec.gov/news/press/2009/2009-26.htm.

20. Curt Anderson, "AP: Ponzi Collapses Nearly Quadrupled in '09," Associated Press, December 28, 2009.

21. U.S. Department of Justice, "Statement of Lanny A. Breuer Assistant Attorney General before the Judiciary Committee United States Senate Entitled Mortgage Fraud, Securities Fraud and the Financial Meltdown: Prosecuting Those Responsible," December 9, 2009, p. 11.

22. Joseph T. Wells, *Encyclopedia of Fraud*, 3rd ed., Austin, TX: Association of Certified Fraud Examiners, 2007, p. 719.

23. Caribbean Net News, "Stanford Knighted by Antigua-Barbuda," *Caribbean Net News (Cayman Islands)*, November 2, 2006, www.caribbeannetnews.com/ cgi-script/csArticles/articles/000040/004049.htm.

24. Erin E. Arvedlund, "Don't Ask, Don't Tell," *The Wall Street Journal,* May 7, 2001, online.barrons.com/article/SB989019667829349012.html.

25. Anderson, "AP: Ponzi Collapses Nearly Quadrupled in '09."

Chapter 2

1. Mark S. Beasley, Joseph V. Carcello, Dana R. Hermanson, and Terry L. Neal, *Fraudulent Financial Reporting: 1998–2007: An Analysis of U.S. Public Companies*, Committee of Sponsoring Organizations of the

Treadway Commission, May 2010, p. 13, www.coso.org/documents/
COSOFRAUDSTUDY2010_000.pdf.

2. U.S. Securities and Exchange Commission, "SEC Charges Terex
Corporation with Accounting Fraud," press release, August 12, 2009,
www.sec.gov/news/press/2009/2009-183.htm.

3. Association of Certified Fraud Examiners, Inc., *2008 Report to the Nation
on Occupational Fraud and Abuse*, Austin, TX, 2008, p. 14,
www.acfe.com/documents/2008-rttn.pdf.

4. Moody's Analytics, *EDF Case Study: Enron*, New York, February 25, 2010,
www.moodyskmv.com/research/Enron.pdf.

5. Colin Barr, "Meet the Market's Biggest Losers: WorldCom," *CNNMoney*,
February 5, 2010, money.cnn.com/galleries/2010/fortune/
1002/gallery.biggest_losers.fortune/10.html.

6. Mark S. Beasley, Joseph V. Carcello, Dana R. Hermanson, and Terry L.
Neal, *Fraudulent Financial Reporting, 1998–2007: An Analysis of U.S.
Public Companies*, COSO. 2010, p. 17.

7. Stephen Taub, "SEC Charges Former CFO, Five Others at HBOC," *CFO*,
September 28, 2001, www.cfo.com/article.cfm/3001245?f=search.

8. Securities and Exchange Commission, "SEC Charges Terex Corporation."

9. U.S. Securities and Exchange Commission, "Final Judgment Entered
against Defendant Bristol-Myers Squibb Company," press release, August
6, 2004, www.sec.gov/litigation/litreleases/lr18822.htm.

10. U.S. Securities and Exchange Commission, *SEC Staff Accounting Bulletin:
No. 101—Revenue Recognition in Financial Statements*, Release No. SAB
101, December 3, 1999, www.sec.gov/interps/account/sab101.htm.

11. U.S. Securities and Exchange Commission, *In the Matter of Sunbeam
Corporation, Respondent, United States of America before the Securities and
Exchange Commission, Securities Act of 1933, Release No. 7976, Securities
Exchange Act of 1934, Release No. 44305, Accounting and Auditing
Enforcement, Release No. 1393, Administrative Proceeding*, File No.
3-10481, May 15, 2001, www.sec.gov/litigation/admin/33-7976.htm.
Jarden Corporation acquired the Sunbeam brand as part of its
purchase of American Household Inc. in 2005. Neither Jarden nor any
of its current management were affiliated with Sunbeam during
the 1990s.

12. U.S. Securities and Exchange Commission, *Securities and Exchange
Commission, Plaintiff, v. Neil R. Cole, Defendant* (U.S.D., S.D.N.Y., Civil
Action, April 30, 2003), www.sec.gov/litigation/complaints/comp18120b.htm.

13. U.S. Securities and Exchange Commission, *Report Pursuant to Section 704
of the Sarbanes-Oxley Act of 2002*, 25, 3, www.sec.gov/news/studies/
sox704report.pdf.

14. U.S. Securities and Exchange Commission, *Securities and Exchange Commission v. Collins & Aikman Corporation, David A. Stockman, J. Michael Stepp, Gerald E. Jones, David R. Cosgrove, Elkin B. McCallum, Paul C. Barnaba, John G. Galante, Christopher M. Williams, and Thomas V. Gougherty, Defendants,* Civil Action No. 07-CV-2419 (LAP) (U.S.D.C., S.D.N.Y., March 26, 2007), sec.gov/litigation/complaints/2007/ comp20055.pdf.

15. U.S. Securities and Exchange Commission, "Enforcement Proceedings: In the Matter of Krispy Kreme Doughnuts, Inc., SEC Charges Krispy Kreme Doughnuts, Inc.," *SEC News Digest,* no. 2009-41, March 4, 2009, www.sec.gov/news/digest/2009/dig030409.htm.

16. U.S. Securities and Exchange Commission, *United States Securities and Exchange Commission, Plaintiff, v. Frederick S. Schiff and Richard J. Lane, Defendants* (U.S.D.C., D.N.J., August 22, 2005), www.sec.gov/litigation/complaints/comp19343.pdf.

17. Securities and Exchange Commission, *SEC Staff Accounting Bulletin: No. 101—Revenue Recognition in Financial Statements.*

18. U.S. Securities and Exchange Commission, *Securities and Exchange Commission, Plaintiff, v. PowerLinx, Inc. (f/k/a Seaview Video Technology, Inc.), George S. Bernardich III, and James R. Cox, Defendants,* Civil Action, Case No. 1:06CV01172 (U.S.D.C. for the District of Columbia, June 27, 2006), www.sec.gov/litigation/complaints/2006/comp19740.pdf.

19. U.S. Securities and Exchange Commission, *Securities and Exchange Commission, Plaintiff, v. Tyco International Ltd., Defendant,* 06 CV 2942 (U.S.D.C., S.D.N.Y., April 13, 2006), www.sec.gov/litigation/complaints/2006/comp19657.pdf.

20. U.S. Securities and Exchange Commission, "SEC Charges Scott D. Sullivan, WorldCom's Former Chief Financial Officer, with Engaging in Multi-billion Dollar Financial Fraud," press release 2004-25, March 2, 2004, www.sec.gov/news/press/2004-25.htm.

21. The Associated Press, "Ex-WorldCom CEO Checks in for Prison Term: Bernard Ebbers Sentenced to 25 Years for Role in the Accounting Fraud," *MSNBC,* September 26, 2006, www.msnbc.msn.com/id/15011730.

22. U.S. Securities and Exchange Commission, *United States Securities and Exchange Commission, Plaintiff v. Bally Total Fitness Holding Corporation, Defendant,* Case: 1:08-CV-00348 (U.S.D.C. for the District of Columbia, February 28, 2008), www.sec.gov/litigation/complaints/2008/comp20470.pdf.

23. KPMG LLP, "Depreciation," *KPMG's Accounting and Reporting Guide—US,* Chapter 61.000, May 2007, workspaces.amr.kworld.kpmg.com/aro/AROWeb/DocumentWindow.aspx?ref=US_DPP_KARG_61000&sec=1&q=depreciation+expense.

24. U.S. Securities and Exchange Commission, *Securities and Exchange Commission, Plaintiff vs. Dean L. Buntrock, Phillip B. Rooney, James E. Koenig, Thomas C. Hau, Herbert A. Getz, and Bruce D. Tobecksen, Defendants*, Complaint No. 02C 2180 (U.S.D.C., N.D.IL, March 26, 2002), www.sec.gov/litigation/complaints/complr17435.htm.

25. Joseph T. Wells, "Ghost Goods: How to Spot Phantom Inventory, What Auditors Have to Know to Uncover Phony Figures," *Journal of Accountancy*, June 2001, www.acfe.com/resources/view.asp?ArticleID=18.

26. The United States Attorney's Office, "Top Corporate Officers of Allou Healthcare Plead Guilty to Massive Corporate Fraud, Insurance Fraud, and Bribery Schemes," Eastern District of New York, press release, November 22, 2005, www.justice.gov/usao/nye/pr/2005/2005nov22.html.

27. Charles F. Malone, "Detection of Inventory Fraud," *AllBusiness*, December 1, 1994, www.allbusiness.com/accounting-reporting/auditing/477762-1.html.

28. Financial Accounting Standards Board, *Summary of Statement No. 144: Accounting for the Impairment or Disposal of Long-Lived Assets*, August 2001, www.fasb.org/jsp/FASB/Pronouncement_C/SummaryPage&cid=90000001 0257.

29. U.S. Securities and Exchange Commission, *In the Matter of Dennis L. Hynson, CPA, Respondent, Order Instituting Cease-and-Desist Proceeding Pursuant to Section 21C of the Securities Exchange Act of 1934, Making Findings and Imposing a Cease-and-Desist Order, Administrative Proceeding, United States of America before the Securities and Exchange Commission,* Securities Exchange Act of 1934 Release No. 57891, Accounting and Auditing Enforcement Release No. 2834, Administrative Proceeding File No. 3-13049, May 30, 2008, www.sec.gov/litigation/admin/2008/34-57891.pdf.

30. U.S. Securities and Exchange Commission, *In the Matter of Platinum Software Corporation, John F. Keane and William B. Falk, Respondents, Order Instituting Public Proceeding and Opinion and Order Pursuant to Section 21C of the Securities Exchange Act of 1934, United States of America before the Securities and Exchange Commission,* Securities Exchange Act of 1934 Release No. 37185, Accounting and Auditing Enforcement Release No. 781, Administrative Proceeding File No. 3-8999, May 9, 1996, www.sec.gov/litigation/admin/3437185.txt.

31. U.S. Securities and Exchange Commission, *SEC Staff Accounting Bulletin: No. 100—Restructuring and Impairment Charges*, Release No. SAB 100, Staff Accounting Bulletin No. 100, November 24, 1999, www.sec.gov/interps/account/sab100.htm.

32. U.S. Securities and Exchange Commission, *In the Matter of Sunbeam Corporation, Respondent, Order Instituting Public Administrative Proceedings, Pursuant to Section 8A of the Securities Act of 1933 and Section 21C of the*

Securities Exchange Act of 1934, Making Findings and Imposing a Cease-and-Desist Order, United States of America before the Securities and Exchange Commission, Securities Act of 1933 Release No. 7976, Securities Exchange Act of 1934 Release No. 44305, Accounting and Auditing Enforcement Release No. 1393, Administrative Proceeding File No. 3-10481, May 15, 2001, www.sec.gov/litigation/admin/33-7976.htm.

33. American Institute of Certified Public Accountants, *Auditing Accounting Estimates,* AU Section 342, SAS No. 57; SAS No. 113, March 2006, www.aicpa.org/download/members/div/auditstd/au-00342.pdf.

34. U.S. Securities and Exchange Commission, *Securities and Exchange Commission v. Michael Strauss, Stephen Hozie and Robert Bernstein,* Civil Action No. 09-CV-4150 (RB) (S.D.N.Y., April 28, 2009), www.sec.gov/litigation/litreleases/2009/lr21014.htm.

35. Financial Accounting Standards Board, "Statement of Financial Accounting Standards No. 157: Fair Value Measurements," *Financial Accounting Series,* No. 284-A, September 2006, www.fasb.org/cs/BlobServer?blobcol=urldata&blobtable=MungoBlobs&blobkey=id&blobwhere=1175818754924&blobheader=application%2Fpdf.

36. American Institute of Certified Public Accountants, *Management Override of Internal Controls: The Achilles' Heel of Fraud Prevention,* New York, 2005, p. 4, www.aicpa.org/audcommctr/download/achilles_heel.pdf.

37. American Institute of Certified Public Accountants, *Accounting and Auditing for Related Parties and Related Parties Transaction: A Toolkit for Accountants and Auditors,* New York, December 2001, p. 5, ftp.aicpa.org/public/download/news/relpty_toolkit.pdf.

38. U.S. Securities and Exchange Commission, *United States Securities and Exchange Commission, Plaintiff, v. Escala Group, Inc., Gregory Manning, Larry Lee Crawford, CPA, Defendants,* Civ. No. 09-CIV (U.S.D.C., S.D.N.Y., March 23, 2009), www.sec.gov/litigation/complaints/2009/comp20965.pdf.

39. U.S. Securities and Exchange Commission, "SEC Settles with Former Raytheon Officers for Improper Disclosure and Accounting Practices: Former CFO, Controller, and Subsidiary CFO Agree to Pay Over $1.5 Million in Disgorgement and Penalties," press release, March 15, 2007, www.sec.gov/litigation/litreleases/2007/lr20041.htm.

40. U.S. Securities and Exchange Commission, *United States Securities and Exchange Commission, Plaintiff, v. Richard J. Miller, Gary S. Jensen, and Michael E. Beaulieu, Defendants,* Civ. No. 09-CIV-4945 (U.S.D.C., S.D.N.Y., May 22, 2009), www.sec.gov/litigation/complaints/2009/comp21058.pdf.

Chapter 3

1. Time.com, "SCANDALS: The Lockheed Mystery," *Time*, September 13, 1976, www.time.com/time/magazine/article/0,9171,914576-1,00.html.

2. *International Anti-bribery and Fair Competition Act of 1998*, 15 U.S.C. §§ 78dd-1, et seq., Public Law 105-366, 105th Cong. (November 10, 1998), section (h)2(A), www.justice.gov/criminal/fraud/fcpa/ docs/ fcpa-english.pdf.

3. *Securities Exchange Act of 1934 Section 30A(f)(3)(A)*, Public Law 111–72, 111th Cong. (October 13, 2009), www.sec.gov/about/laws/sea34.pdf.

4. U.S. Department of Justice Fraud Section, "*Lay-Person's Guide to FCPA*," Washington, DC, www.justice.gov/criminal/fraud/fcpa/docs/lay-persons-guide.pdf.

5. Hamid Davoodi and Vito Tanzi, *Roads to Nowhere: How Corruption in Public Investment Hurts Growth*, Washington, DC: International Monetary Fund, March 1998, www.imf.org/external/pubs/ft/issues12/index.htm.

6. Organisation for Economic Co-operation and Development (OECD), *Convention on Combating Bribery of Foreign Public Officials in International Business Transactions*, Paris, 2010, pp. 32–33, www.oecd.org/dataoecd/ 4/18/38028044.pdf.

7. Transparency International, "Corruption Threatens Global Economic Recovery, Greatly Challenges Countries in Conflict," press release, Berlin, November 17, 2009, www.transparency.org/news_room/latest_news/ press_releases/2009/2009_11_17_cpi2009_en.

8. OECD, *Convention on Combating Bribery of Foreign Public Officials in International Business Transactions and Related Documents*, Article 1, Paris, 2010, p. 6.

9. OECD, *Convention on Combating Bribery of Foreign Public Officials in International Business Transactions and Related Documents*, Article 3, Paris, 2010, p. 7.

10. OECD, *Convention on Combating Bribery of Foreign Public Officials in International Business Transactions and Related Documents*, Article 4, Paris, 2010, p. 7.

11. OECD, *Convention on Combating Bribery of Foreign Public Officials in International Business Transactions and Related Documents*, Article 8, Paris, 2010, p. 8.

12. Melissa Klein Aguilar, "OECD Anti-bribery Guide as Path to FCPA Compliance," *Compliance Week*, March 30, 2010, www.complianceweek.com/ article/5866.

13. U.K. Ministry of Justice Publications Section, "Bribery Act 2010," U.K. Ministry of Justice, www.justice.gov.uk/publications/bribery-bill.htm.

14. Benjamin W. Heineman, Jr., and Fritz Heimann, "Arrested Development," *The National Interest*, November/December 2007, p. 1.

15. Benjamin L. Liebman, "Legitimacy through Law in China?" *PBS WideAngle*, 2009, www-tc.pbs.org/wnet/wideangle/files/2009/04/legitimacy-through-law-in-china.pdf.

16. OECD, *Report on the Application of the Convention on Combating Bribery of Foreign Public Officials in International Business Transactions and the 2009 Revised Recommendation on Combating Bribery in International Business Transactions*, Paris, October 15, 2010, p. 11, http://www.oecd.org/dataoecd/10/49/46213841.pdf.

17. U.S. Department of Justice, "Three Vetco International Ltd. Subsidiaries Plead Guilty to Foreign Bribery and Agree to Pay $26 Million in Criminal Fines," press release, February 6, 2007, www.justice.gov/opa/pr/2007/February/07_crm_075.html.

18. U.S. Department of Justice, "Baker Hughes Subsidiary Pleads Guilty to Bribing Kazakh Official and Agrees to Pay $11 Million Criminal Fine as Part of Largest Combined Sanction Ever Imposed in FCPA Case," press release, April 26, 2007, www.justice.gov/opa/pr/2007/April/07_crm_296.html.

19. U.S. Department of Justice, "Siemens AG and Three Subsidiaries Plead Guilty to Foreign Corrupt Practices Act Violations and Agree to Pay $450 Million in Combined Criminal Fines," press release, December 15, 2008, www.justice.gov/opa/pr/2008/December/08-crm-1105.html.

20. U.S. Department of Justice, "Kellogg Brown & Root LLC Pleads Guilty to Foreign Bribery Charges and Agrees to Pay $402 Million Criminal Fine," press release, February 11, 2009, www.justice.gov/opa/pr/2009/February/09-crm-112.html.

21. KPMG LLP, *2008 Anti-bribery and Anti-corruption Survey*, New York, 2008, p. 7.

22. Shearman & Sterling LLP, *Latin Node Inc.: Undiscovered FCPA Violations Wipe Out an Investment*, New York: Shearman & Sterling LLP Client Publication, April 15, 2009.

23. Alvaro Cuervo-Cazurra, "The Effectiveness of Laws against Bribery Abroad," *Journal of International Business Studies*, vol. 39, no. 4, 2008.

24. Dow Jones Risk & Compliance, *Dow Jones State of Anti-corruption Compliance Survey*, New York: Dow Jones Financial Information Services, December 2009.

25. U.S. Department of Justice Fraud Section, "Opinion Procedure Release 04-01," U.S. Department of Justice, www.justice.gov/criminal/fraud/fcpa/opinion/2004/0402.pdf.

26. KPMG LLP, *2008 Anti-bribery and Anti-corruption Survey*, p. 6.

27. KPMG LLP, *2008 Anti-bribery and Anti-corruption Survey*, p. 6.

28. U.S. Department of Justice Fraud Section, "Foreign Corrupt Practices Act Review Opinion Procedure Release No. 08-01," U.S. Department of Justice, www.justice.gov/criminal/fraud/fcpa/opinion/2008/0801.pdf.

29. KPMG LLP, *2008 Anti-bribery and Anti-corruption Survey*, p. 8.

Chapter 4

1. Peter Reuter and Edwin M. Truman, *Chasing Dirty Money: The Fight against Money Laundering*, Washington, DC: Institute for International Economics, 2004, p. 13.

2. U.S. Department of Justice, *Money Laundering Offenders, 1994–2001*, Washington, DC, July 2003, p. 1.

3. Financial Industry Regulatory Authority, "E*Trade Units Fined $1 Million for Inadequate Anti–Money Laundering Program," news release, January 2, 2009, www.finra.org/newsroom/newsreleases/2009/p117667.

4. U.S. Sentencing Commission, *Guidelines Manual*, §8B2.1, November 2009, www.ussc.gov/2009guid/GL2009.pdf.

5. Financial Action Task Force, *An Introduction to FATF and Its Work*, Paris, 2010, p. 3, www.fatf-gafi.org/dataoecd/48/11/45139480.pdf.

6. *U.S. v. $4,255,625.39*, 551 F Supp.314 (S.D. Fla. 1982), aff'd. 762 F.2d 895 (11 Cir. 1985).

7. *USA PATRIOT Act of 2001*, Public Law 107-56, 107th Cong. (October 26, 2001), §314 (a) and (b), 326, 312, and 352.

8. *USA PATRIOT Act*, § 352.

9. Federal Financial Institutions Examination Council (FFIEC), *Bank Secrecy Act/Anti–Money Laundering Examination Manual*, 2010, p. 147.

10. James H. Freis, Jr., "The Objectives and Conduct of Bank Secrecy Act Enforcement" ABA/ABA Money Laundering Enforcement Conference, October 20, 2008, www.fincen.gov/news_room/speech/pdf/20081020.pdf; Financial Action Task Force Groupe d'action financiére, *Guidance on the Risk-Based Approach to Combating Money Laundering and Terrorist Financing*, Paris, June 2007; the Wolfsberg Group, "Wolfsberg Statement—Guidance on a Risk Based Approach for Managing Money Laundering Risks," Wolfsberg AML Principles, www.wolfsberg-principles.com/risk-based-approach.html.

11. KPMG International, *Global Anti–Money Laundering Survey 2007*, Switzerland, July 2007, p. 19.

12. FFIEC, *Bank Secrecy Act/Anti-Money Laundering Examination Manual 2010*, p. 22.

13. KPMG International, *Global Anti–Money Laundering Survey 2007*, p. 29.

14. U.S. Department of Immigration, Customs and Enforcement, "Money Remitter Sentenced to Over 9 Years for Money Laundering Conspiracy and Concealing Terrorist Financing," press release, November 4, 2008, www.ice.gov/pi/nr/0811/081104baltimore.htm.

15. Financial Industry Regulatory Authority, "E*Trade Units Fined $1 Million for Inadequate Anti–Money Laundering Program."

16. U.S. Department of the Treasury, Financial Crimes Enforcement Network, *U.S. v. Sigue Corporation and Sigue LLC*, dpa No: 4:13CRLCC5HRWS (E.D. MO, January 28, 2008).

17. KPMG International, *Global Anti–Money Laundering Survey 2007*, p. 39.

18. KPMG International, *Global Anti–Money Laundering Survey 2007*, p. 11.

19. Network Branded Prepaid Card Association, *Recommended Practices for Anti–Money Laundering Compliance for U.S.-Based Prepaid Card Programs*, Washington, DC, February 22, 2008, www.nbpca.org.

20. KPMG International, *Global Anti–Money Laundering Survey 2007*, p. 33.

21. KPMG International, *Global Anti–Money Laundering Survey 2007*, p. 16.

22. Freis, "The Objectives and Conduct of Bank Secrecy Act Enforcement."

23. FFIEC, *Bank Secrecy Act/Anti—Money Laundering Examination Manual*, p. 78.

Chapter 5

1. *False Claims, U.S. Code 31* (2009), §§ 3729-33 et seq.

2. *Federal Acquisition Regulation*, Subpart 52.203-13 (December 2008); *Federal Acquisition Regulation*, Subpart 9.406-2 (August 1995); *Federal Acquisition Regulation*, Subpart 9.407-2 (August 1995).

3. *Allison Engine Co., Inc. v. United States ex rel. Sanders*, 128 S.Ct. 2123 (2008).

4. Gibson, Dunn & Crutcher LLP, *President Obama Signs Legislation Significantly Expanding the Scope of the False Claims Act*, New York: Gibson, Dunn & Crutcher LLP Client Alert, May 26, 2009, www.gibsondunn.com/publications/pages/PresidentObamaLegislationExpandsScope-False ClaimsAct.aspx.

5. U.S. Department of Justice, "Justice Department Recovers $2.4 Billion in False Claims Cases in Fiscal Year 2009; More Than $24 Billion Since 1986," press release, November 19, 2009, www.justice.gov/opa/pr/2009/November/09-civ-1253.html; U.S. Department of Justice, "More Than $1 Billion Recovered by Justice Department in Fraud and False Claims in Fiscal Year 2008," press release, November 10, 2008, www.justice.gov/opa/pr/2008/November/08-civ-992.html.

6. U.S. Department of Justice, Civil Division, "Fraud Statistics—Health & Human Services," October 1, 1986–September 30, 2008, www.justice.gov/opa/pr/2008/November/fraud-statistics1986-2008.htm.

7. Department of Justice, "Justice Department Recovers $2.4 Billion in False Claims Cases in Fiscal Year 2009"; Department of Justice, "More Than $1 Billion Recovered by Justice Department in Fraud and False Claims in Fiscal Year 2008."

8. Department of Justice, "Justice Department Recovers $2.4 Billion in False Claims Cases in Fiscal Year 2009"; Department of Justice, "More Than $1 Billion Recovered by Justice Department in Fraud and False Claims in Fiscal Year 2008."

9. "Stimulus Overseer: Waste 'Inevitable,'" *The Washington Times*, March 13, 2009, www.washingtontimes.com/news/2009/mar/13/stimulus-funds-over-seer-says-waste-inevitable.

10. "Neil Barofsky: Bringing Transparency to TARP," *The Metropolitan Corporate Counsel*, October 4, 2009, www.metrocorpcounsel.com/current.php?artType=view&EntryNo=10222.

11. Office of the Special Inspector General for the Troubled Asset Relief Program, *Advancing Economic Stability through Transparency, Coordinated Oversight and Robust Enforcement*, Quarterly Report to Congress, Washington, DC, October 21, 2009, www.sigtarp.gov/reports/congress/2009/October2009_Quarterly_Report_to_Congress.pdf.

12. U.S. Department of Justice, "Manhattan U.S. Attorney Charges Hedge Fund Managers, Fortune 500 Executives, and Management Consulting Director in $20 Million Insider Trading Case," press release, October 16 2009.

13. U.S. Securities and Exchange Commission Selective Disclosure and Insider Trading Act, Exchange Act Release Nos. 33-7881, 34-43154, IC-24599, www.sec.gov/rules/final/33-7881.htm.

14. U.S. Securities and Exchange Commission, "SEC Charges Vice Chairman of ISE Holdings and Business Partners with Insider Trading," press release 2008-042, March 13, 2008.

15. U.S. Securities and Exchange Commission, "SEC Obtains $2.1 Million Emergency Asset Freeze and Charges Rome Resident within Days of His Alleged Insider Trading," press release 2008-091, May 16, 2008.

16. U.S. Securities and Exchange Commission, "SEC Charges Wall Street Professionals and Others with Widespread Insider Trading," press release 2008-301, December 18, 2008.

17. Remarks by Robert Khuzami, Director, SEC Division of Enforcement, U.S. Securities and Exchange Commission, at a press conference, New York, November 5, 2009, sec.gov/news/speech/2009/spch110509rk.htm.

Chapter 6

1. U.S. Sentencing Commission (USSC), *Guidelines Manual,* §8B2.1, November 2009, pp. 503–505, www.ussc.gov/2009guid/GL2009.pdf.

2. U.S. Sentencing Commission, Amendments to the Sentencing Guidelines, pp. 33, 38, www.ussc.gov/2010guid/20100503_Reader_Friendly_ Proposed_Amendments.pdf.

3. USSC, *Guidelines Manual,* §8B2.1, pp. 503–505.

4. Michael Siconolfi and Laurie P. Cohen, "The Treasury Auction Scandal at Salomon—Sullied Solly: How Salomon's Hubris and a U.S. Trap Led to Leaders' Downfall—Board Accepts Resignations; Treasury Levels Sanction; Firm Still Faces Problems—Gutfreund 'Not Apologizing,'" *The Wall Street Journal,* August 19, 1991, p. A1.

5. Michael Siconolfi, Laurie P. Cohen, and Kevin G. Salwen, "SEC Probes Collusion by Trader—Subpoenas Will Seek Price Fixing Evidence in Treasury Market," *The Wall Street Journal,* August 27, 1991, p. C1.

6. Ronald R. Sims, "Changing an Organization's Culture under New Leadership," *Journal of Business Ethics,* vol. 25, 2000, p. 67.

7. USSC, *Guidelines Manual,* §8B2.1, pp. 503–505.

8. USSC, *Guidelines Manual,* §8A1.2, p. 498.

9. USSC, *Guidelines Manual,* §8B2.1, pp. 503–505.

10. Sims, "Changing an Organization's Culture under New Leadership," p. 67.

11. Thomas Donaldson, "Dangerous Currents," *Directors & Boards,* 2004, p. 2, lgst.wharton.upenn.edu/donaldst/Documents/Dangerous%20Currents.pdf.

12. USSC, *Guidelines Manual,* §8B2.1, pp. 503–505.

13. Ethics and Compliance Officer Association (ECOA) Foundation, *The Ethics and Compliance Handbook, a Practical Guide from Leading Organizations,* Waltham, MA, 2008, p. 29.

14. Ethics Resource Center (ERC), *Leading Corporate Integrity: Defining the Role of the Chief Ethics & Compliance Officer (CECO),* August 2007, p. 18, www.ethics.org/files/u5/CECO_Paper_UPDATED.pdf.

15. ECOA Foundation, *The Ethics and Compliance Handbook,* p. 34.

16. ERC, *Leading Corporate Integrity,* p. 25.

17. ERC, *Leading Corporate Integrity,* p. 27.

18. USSC, *Guidelines Manual,* §8B2.1, pp. 503–505.

19. ECOA Foundation, *The Ethics and Compliance Handbook,* p. 39.

20. ERC, *Leading Corporate Integrity,* p. 23.

21. USSC, *Guidelines Manual,* §8B2.1, pp. 503–505.

22. USSC, *Guidelines Manual,* §8B2.1, pp. 503–505.

23. *In re Caremark Int'l Inc. Derivative Litig.,* 698 A.2d 959 (Del. Ch. 1996).

24. Ben W. Heineman, Jr., "Avoiding Integrity Land Mines," *Harvard Business Review*, April 2007, p. 1, www.law.harvard.edu/programs/olin_center/corporate_governance/articles/Heineman-HBR-Avoiding-Integrity-Landmines-April07.pdf.
25. Alan Rappeport, "Clawbacks Claw Their Way into Corporate Strategy," CFO.com, June 4, 2008, www.cfo.com/article.cfm/11488592/c_11485705?f=home_todayinfinance.

Part IV

1. KPMG International Cooperative, *Fraud Risk Management: Developing a Strategy for Prevention, Detection, and Response,* New York, 2006, p. 20.

Chapter 7

1. Harvey L. Pitt, "Risky Business: Assessing and Managing Risk," *Compliance Week,* June 2, 2004.
2. Transparency International, Corruption Perceptions Index (2009), www.transparency.org/policy_research/surveys_indices/cpi/2009/cpi_2009_table.
3. KPMG LLP, *Integrity Survey 2008–2009,* New York, KPMG LLP, 2009, p. 11.
4. Rick Romell, "Koss Embezzlement May Exceed $20 Million," *Milwaukee Journal Sentinel,* December 24 2009, www.jsonline.com/business/80085207.html.
5. KPMG LLP, *Integrity Survey 2008–2009,* p. 11.
6. Chris Hamilton, *HealthSouth: A Case Study in Corporate Fraud,* Simi Valley: Arxis Financial, Inc., April 2009, www.arxisfinancial.com/images/pdfs/Fraud-Health_South_Case.pdf.

Chapter 8

1. KPMG LLP, *Integrity Survey 2008–2009 white paper*, New York, 2009, p. 14, us.kpmg.com/news/index.asp?cid=2954.
2. KPMG LLP, *Integrity Survey 2008–2009 white paper*, p. 14.
3. Mission statement, Johnson & Johnson, 1943, "Our Credo," www.jnj.com/wps/wcm/connect/c7933f004f5563df9e22be1bb31559c7/our-credo.pdf?MOD=AJPERES.
4. American Express Company, *American Express Company Code of Conduct*, New York, June 1, 2007, p. 22, media.corporate-ir.net/media_files/irol/64/64467/2007_AXP_COC.pdf.
5. FedEx Corporation, *Code of Business Conduct and Ethics*, Memphis, adopted June 2, 2003, last amended July 13, 2009, p. 29, files.shareholder.com/downloads/FDX/0x0x138778/6b957b1f-ac83-4b37-835b-8b24e63b338f/code.pdf.

6. *Sarbanes-Oxley Act of 2002*, Public Law 107-204, 107th Cong., 15 USC 7264, (July 30, 2002), www.gpo.gov/fdsys/pkg/PLAW-107publ204/pdf/PLAW-107publ204.pdf.
7. U.S. Securities and Exchange Commission, Form 20F, Washington, DC, www.sec.gov/about/forms/form20-f.pdf.
8. KPMG LLP, *Integrity Survey 2008–2009 white paper*, p. 6.
9. KPMG LLP, *Integrity Survey 2008–2009* (Data gathered during survey data collection phase; however, it was not published in white paper.).
10. KPMG LLP, *Integrity Survey 2008–2009 white paper*, p. 11.
11. Committee of Sponsoring Organizations, "Internal Control—Integrated Framework," COSO Web site, 1992, www.coso.org.
12. KPMG LLP, *Integrity Survey 2008–2009 white paper*, p. 8.
13. KPMG LLP, *Integrity Survey 2008–2009 white paper*, p. 12.

Chapter 9

1. U.S. Sentencing Commission, *Guidelines Manual*, §8B2.1(a)(1), November 2008.
2. U.S. Department of the Treasury, Mission of the Office of Foreign Assets Control, www.treas.gov/offices/enforcement/ofac.
3. U.S. Government Accountability Office (GAO), *Report to the Permanent Subcommittee on Investigations, Committee on Homeland Security and Governmental Affairs, U.S. Senate. Company Formations: Minimal Ownership Information Is Collected and Available*, Washington, DC, April 2006.
4. GAO, *Report to the Permanent Subcommittee on Investigations, Committee on Homeland Security and Governmental Affairs*.
5. FinCEN, "The Role of Domestic Shell Companies in Financial Crime and Money Laundering: Limited Liability Companies," Department of the Treasury Financial Crimes Enforcement Network, November 2006.
6. Jacques Steinberg, "Fact-Checking the Resume of a Student Accused of Lying," *The Choice*, May 20, 2010.
7. Directorate for Financial and Enterprise Affairs, "Convention on Combating Bribery of Foreign Public Officials in International Business Transactions," OECD, www.oecd.org/document/21/0,3343,en_2649_34859_2017813_1_1_1_1,00.html.
8. Peter Elkind, "A Merger Made in Hell: The Inside Story of the Decade's Dumbest Deal. One Man Ran His Company like Boot Camp, the Other like Summer Camp," *Fortune*, November 9, 1998.
9. KPMG LLP, *2008 Anti-bribery and Anti-corruption Survey*, New York, 2008, p. 9.
10. Associated Press, "US Justice Department Probing Oil Operations in Nigeria," July 25, 2007.

11. The Panalpina Group, "News from Panalpina: Panalpina Commenced Settlement Discussions with the US Department of Justice," Panalpina on 6 Continents, www.panalpina.com/www/global/en/media_news/news/news_archiv_2/09_12_09.html.

12. FinCEN, "The Role of Domestic Shell Companies in Financial Crime and Money Laundering: Limited Liability Companies."

13. Federal Trade Commission (FTC), *Fair Credit Reporting Act*, 15 U.S.C. §1681b(a)(3)(B) (July 2004).

14. FTC, *Fair Credit Reporting Act*, §1681a(d)(1)(B).

15. FTC, *Fair Credit Reporting Act*, §1681b(b)(1)(A)(ii).

16. FTC, *Fair Credit Reporting Act*, §1681b(b)(2)(A)(i).

17. FTC, *Fair Credit Reporting Act*, §1681b(b)(3)(A).

Chapter 10

1. Association of Certified Fraud Examiners (ACFE), *2008 Report to the Nation on Occupational Fraud & Abuse*, Austin, TX, 2008, p. 20, www.acfe.com/documents/2008-rttn.pdf.

2. ACFE, *2008 Report to the Nation on Occupational Fraud & Abuse*.

3. Shaheen Pasha, "Enron's Whistle Blower Details Sinking Ship," CNNMoney.com, March 16, 2006, money.cnn.com/2006/03/15/news/newsmakers/enron/index.htm.

4. Lilanthi Ravishankar, *Encouraging Internal Whistleblowing in Organizations*, Silicon Valley, CA: Markkula Center for Applied Ethics, Santa Clara University, 2003, www.scu.edu/ethics/publications/submitted/whistleblowing.html.

5. Alexander Dyck et al., *Who Blows the Whistle on Corporate Fraud?* Chicago: University of Chicago, October 2008, p. 5, cerl.wustl.edu/media/workshop/werl_20090526.pdf.

6. The Wall Street Reform and Consumer Protection Act of 2009, HR 4173, 111th Cong., 1st sess. (December 2, 2009), Sec. 922.

7. Corporate Executive Board, "Enhancing Compliance Risk Detection Unlocking Information Traps, Risk Management in Crisis?" Presentation at the 2009 ECOA Sponsoring Partner Forum, Compliance and Ethics Leadership Council, facilitated by Ronnie Kann, managing partner, 2009.

8. U.S. Sentencing Commission, *Organizational Sentencing Guidelines*, www.ussc.gov/2004guid/2004cong.pdf.

9. *U.S. Sarbanes-Oxley Act of 2002*, Section 806, Public Law 107-204, 107th Cong. (July 30, 2002), pp. 58–60, www.sec.gov/about/laws/soa2002.pdf.

10. *Sarbanes-Oxley Act of 2002*, Section 301.

11. 2007 Corpedia, Inc., and Association of Corporate Counsel, *2007 Compliance Program and Risk Assessment Benchmarking Survey*, Washington, DC: Association of Corporate Counsel, 2007, p. 50, available by subscription at www.acc.com.

12. KPMG LLP, *Integrity Survey 2008–2009*, New York, 2009, p. 14, us.kpmg.com/news/index.asp?cid=2954.

13. Security Executive Council, *2007 Corporate Governance and Compliance Hotline Benchmarking Report*, Washington, DC, 2007, www.tnwinc.com/downloads/2007ComplianceBenchmarkReport.pdf.

14. Security Executive Council, *2007 Corporate Governance and Compliance Hotline Benchmarking Report*.

15. The Network, *Best Practices in Ethics Hotlines, a Framework for Creating an Effective Anonymous Reporting Program*, Norcross, GA, 2006, www.tnwinc.com/downloads/bestpractices_ethicshotlines.pdf.

16. 2007 Corpedia, Inc., and Association of Corporate Counsel, *2007 Compliance Program and Risk Assessment Benchmarking Survey*, p. 50.

17. The Network, *Best Practices in Ethics Hotlines*.

18. "'Staged' Calls to Compliance Hotlines Can Help Separate Effective Operators from Bad Performers," *Health Business Daily*, September 18, 2008, reprinted from *Report on Medicare Compliance*, www.aishealth.com/Compliance/ResearchTools/RMC_Staged_Calls.html.

19. SpeakUp®: A European Approach to Whistleblowing—22 May 2009.

20. Global Integrity, "Global Integrity Report," 2007, report.globalintegrity.org.

21. Global Integrity, "Global Integrity Report."

Chapter 11

1. Committee of Sponsoring Organizations of the Treadway Commission (COSO), *Internal Control—Integrated Framework: Guidance on Monitoring Internal Control Systems Volume II—Guidance* (Altamonte Springs, FL, June 2008), p. 1, www.coso.org/documents/VolumeII-Guidance.pdf.

2. U.S. Securities and Exchange Commission, "Final Rule: Management's Report on Internal Control Over Financial Reporting and Certification of Disclosure in Exchange Act Periodic Reports," www.sec.gov/rules/final/33-8238.htm#P209_53297.

3. COSO, *Internal Control—Integrated Framework Volume II—Guidance*, www.coso.org/documents/VolumeII-Guidance.pdf.

4. U.S. Sentencing Commission (USSC), *Guidelines Manual*, §8B 2.1, November 2004, p. 476, www.ussc.gov/2004guid/CHAP8.pdf.

5. USSC, *Guidelines Manual*, §8B 2.1, p. 477.

6. COSO, *Internal Control—Integrated Framework Guidance on Monitoring. Internal Control Systems Volume III—Application Techniques*, Altamonte Springs, FL, June 2008, p. 16, www.coso.org/documents/VolumeIII-ApplicationTechniques.pdf.

Chapter 12

1. Steven Walker, "The Attorney Client Privilege and Work Product—Navigating Recent Changes and How They Affect Your Technology Company," p. 5, www.abanet.org/litigation/committees/intellectual/roundtables/0308_outline.pdf.
2. *Upjohn Co. et al. v. United States et al.,* 449 U.S. 383 (1981) (4th Cir. January 13, 1981).
3. Directors & Boards, Boardroom Briefing, *Corporate Internal Investigations,* 2005, p. 18, www.directorsandboards.com/BoardroomBriefing3.pdf.

Chapter 13

1. Mike Koehler, "Breuer—Siemens Investigation (As to Individuals) Remains Open," *Corporate Compliance Insights*, May 10, 2010, www.corporatecomplianceinsights.com/2010/breuer-siemens-investigation-as-to-individuals-remains-open.
2. U.S. Department of Justice, *United States of America v. Siemens Aktiengesellschaft et al.*, Department's Sentencing Memorandum, D.D.C., December 18, 2008, p. 3, www.usdoj.gov/opa/documents/siemens-sentencing-memo.pdf.
3. Koehler, "Breuer—Siemens Investigation (As to Individuals) Remains Open."
4. Sarah Streicker and Z. Scott, "Siemens Agrees to Pay Record-Breaking US$800 Million for FCPA Violations," *White Collar Defense & Compliance, Securities Enforcement & Investigations Update,* Chicago: Mayer Brown, December 16, 2008, pp. 2–3, www.mayerbrown.com/publications/article.asp?id=5951.
5. John Wilke, Nathan Koppel, and Peter Sanders, "Milberg Indicted on Charges Firm Paid Kickbacks: Class-Action Giant Accused of Spending Over $11 Million to Secure Lead Plaintiffs," *The Wall Street Journal,* May 19, 2006.
6. Gina Keating, "Last Two Milberg Defendants Sentenced," *Thompson Financial News,* November 3, 2008, www.forbes.com/feeds/afx/2008/11/03/afx5641936.html.
7. Washington Legal Foundation, "Deferred Prosecution and Non-Prosecution Agreements," Chap. 6, p. 6-2, General Dick Thornburgh

(March 17, 2007), in *Federal Erosion of Business Civil Liberties*, Washington, DC, 2008, lawprofessors.typepad.com/whitecollarcrime_blog/files/wlf_timeline.pdf.

8. Larry Thompson, Deputy Attorney General, memorandum to Heads of Department Components and United States Attorneys regarding "Principles of Federal Prosecution of Business Organizations," U.S. Department of Justice, January 20, 2003, §IX, www.usDOJ.gov/dag/cftf/corporate_guidelines.htm.

9. Thompson, memorandum regarding "Principles of Federal Prosecution of Business Organizations."

10. Lawrence D. Finder and Ryan D. McConnell, "Devolution of Authority: The DOJ's Corporate Charging Policies," *St. Louis University Law Journal*, vol. 51, no. 1, December 5, 2006, p. 16, www.haynesboone.com/files/Publication/f425114a-53ed-472e-af5f-034b94a8c19d/Presentation/PublicationAttachment/0c4489ee-9f9d-4bff-b90a-12f37349b821/Finder%20and%20McConnell%20article—St.%20Louis%20U%20Law%20Journal—Dec.%202006.pdf.

11. Defense Industry Initiative on Business Ethics and Conduct. "Origins of DII," Defense Industry Initiative, www.dii.org/about-us/history.

12. David Morrison, "Tinkering with Defense," *The National Journal*, vol. 20, no. 36, p. 2178, September 3, 1988.

13. Charles Walsh and Alissa Pyrich, "Corporate Compliance Programs as a Defense to Criminal Liability: Can a Corporation Save Its Soul?" *Rutgers Law Review*, vol. 47, p. 605, January Session 1995.

14. Department of Justice, "Department of Justice and SEC Enter $290 Million Settlement with Salomon Brothers in Treasury Securities Case," May 20, 1992, www.justice.gov/atr/public/press_releases/1992/211182.htm.

15. Finder and McConnell, "Devolution of Authority," p. 13.

16. Eric H. Holder, Deputy Attorney General, memorandum to All Component Heads and United States Attorneys regarding "Bringing Criminal Charges against Corporations," U.S. Department of Justice, June 16, 1999, federalevidence.com/pdf/Corp_Prosec/Holder_Memo_6_16_99.pdf.

17. National Press Club, "Crime without Conviction: The Rise of Deferred and Non Prosecution Agreements," a Report Released by *Corporate Crime Reporter*, Washington, DC, December 28, 2005, www.corporatecrimereporter.com/deferredreport.htm.

18. Kit R. Roane, "Andersen Clients Bolt—and Legal Risks Mount," *U.S. News & World Report*, vol. 132, no. 8, March 10, 2002, www.usnews.com/usnews/news/articles/020318/archive_020343.htm.

19. "Arthur Andersen Conviction Overturned: Jury Instructions Too Vague in Enron Document-Shredding Case," CNN.com, May 31, 2005, www.cnn.com/2005/LAW/05/31/scotus.arthur.andersen; *Arthur Andersen, A Case Study by the Tuck School of Business at Dartmouth*, no. 1-0026, 2001, p. 5, mba.tuck.dartmouth.edu/pdf/2001-1-0026.pdf.

20. Finder and McConnell, "Devolution of Authority," p. 13.

21. Lawrence Finder and Ryan McConnell, *Annual Corporate Pre-Trial Agreement Update—2007*, prepared for the ABA White Collar Conference, March 2008, p. 2, www.haynesboone.com/files/Publication/db8ca5c2-5f7 c-4d9b-8ca7-31cd23b2e130/Presentation/PublicationAttachment/3c6dfcf6-422f-4f33-9539-c142811f6d1b/Annual-Corporate-Pre-Trial-Agreement-Update—2007.pdf.

22. Thompson, memorandum regarding "Principles of Federal Prosecution of Business Organizations."

23. Paul J. McNulty, Deputy Attorney General, memorandum to Heads of Department Components and United States Attorneys regarding "Principles of Federal Prosecution of Business Organizations," U.S. Department of Justice, December 12, 2006, www.justice.gov/dag/speeches/2006/mcnulty_memo.pdf.

24. Lewis Morris and Gary W. Thompson, "Reflections on the Government's Stick and Carrot Approach to Fighting Health Care Fraud," *Alabama Law Review*, vol. 51, no. 1, Fall 1999, pp. 319–373, www.law.ua.edu/pubs/lawreview/articles/Volume%2051/Issue%201/Morris.pdf.

25. Morris and Thompson, "Reflections on the Government's Stick and Carrot Approach to Fighting Health Care Fraud."

26. Washington Legal Foundation, *Federal Erosion of Business Civil Liberties*, p. 6-4.

27. Office of Inspector General, "Building a Partnership for Effective Compliance: A Report on the Government Industry Roundtable," April 2, 1999, U.S. Department of Health & Human Services, oig.hhs.gov/fraud/docs/complianceguidance/roundtable.htm.

28. Office of Inspector General, "Corporate Integrity Agreements," U.S. Department of Health & Human Services, oig.hhs.gov/fraud/cias.asp.

29. Pepper Hamilton LLP, "Corporate Integrity Agreements: A Kinder, Gentler OIG," Health Care Law Alert, December 10, 2001, www.pepperlaw.com/publications_update.aspx?ArticleKey=113.

30. Department of Health and Human Services and the Department of Justice, *Health Care Fraud and Abuse Control Program Annual Report for FY 2003*, Washington, DC, December 2004, www.durrelllaw.com/2003HCFAC-Durrell-fraud-lawyer-boston.pdf.

31. John Reiss et al., "Your Business in Court 2007–2008," *Food and Drug Law Journal*, vol. 63, no. 4, 2008, p. 761, www.saul.com/common/publications/pdf_1773.pdf.

32. Daniel R. Levinson, "An Open Letter to Health Care Providers," Department of Health & Human Services, Office of Inspector General, April 15, 2008, www.oig.hhs.gov/fraud/docs/openletters/OpenLetter4-15-08.pdf.

33. Office of Inspector General, *Corporate Integrity Agreements Document List*, U.S. Department of Health & Human Services, oig.hhs.gov/fraud/cia/cia_list.asp.

34. Joshua Hochberg, "Compliance Programs, Voluntary Disclosure and Internal Investigations: Making Sure the Government Gives You Maximum Credit for 'Doing the Right Thing,'" *The Metropolitan Corporate Counsel*, November 2005, p. 4, www.metrocorpcounsel.com/pdf/2005/November/04.pdf.

35. U.S. Sentencing Commission (USSC), *Guidelines Manual*, §8C2.5 Commentary 12, November 2009, www.ussc.gov/2009guid/8c2_5.htm.

36. U.S. Securities and Exchange Commission, *Report of Investigation Pursuant to Section 21(a) of the Securities Exchange Act of 1934 and Commission Statement on the Relationship of Cooperation to Agency Enforcement Decisions*, Release No. 44969/1470, October 23, 2001, www.sec.gov/litigation/investreport/34-44969.htm.

37. Levinson, "An Open Letter to Health Care Providers, p. 2."

38. Levinson, "An Open Letter to Health Care Providers, p. 2."

39. U.S. Securities and Exchange Commission, "SEC Announces Initiative to Encourage Individuals and Companies to Cooperate and Assist in Investigations," press release, January 13, 2010, sec.gov/news/press/2010/2010-6.htm.

40. U.S. Securities and Exchange Commission, "SEC Announces Initiative to Encourage Individuals and Companies to Cooperate and Assist in Investigations."

41. Holder, memorandum regarding "Bringing Criminal Charges against Corporations."

42. Paul J. McNulty, Deputy Attorney General, memorandum to Heads of Department Components and United States Attorneys regarding "Principles of Federal Prosecution of Business Organizations." U.S. Department of Justice, December 12, 2006, http://www.justice.gov/dag/speeches/2006/mcnulty_memo.pdf.

43. Mark R. Filip, Deputy Attorney General, memorandum to Heads of Department Components and United States Attorneys regarding "Principles of Federal Prosecution of Business Organizations," U.S.

Department of Justice, August 28, 2008, §9-28.720, www.usDOJ.gov/
opa/documents/corp-charging-guidelines.pdf.

44. Filip, memorandum regarding "Principles of Federal Prosecution of
    Business Organizations."
45. Lawrence D. Finder, Ryan D. McConnell, and Scott L. Mitchell,, "Betting
    the Corporation: Compliance or Defiance? Compliance Programs in the
    Context of Deferred and Non-Prosecution Agreements: Corporate Pre-trial
    Agreement Update—2008," p. 15, www.haynesboone.com/files/
    Publication/95fb72e1-4087-4fb0-bcf4-f1129357979f/Presentation/
    PublicationAttachment/635a5a13-1c91-41b2-bc74-f1f38d5eb326/
    Betting_the_Corporation.pdf.
46. Finder, McConnell, and Mitchell, "Betting the Corporation," p. 12.
47. Hochberg, "Compliance Programs, Voluntary Disclosure and Internal
    Investigations," p. 4.
48. U.S. Department of Justice, "Aibel Group Ltd. Pleads Guilty to Foreign
    Bribery and Agrees to Pay $4.2 Million in Criminal Fines," press release,
    November 18, 2008, www.usDOJ.gov/opa/pr/2008/November/08-crm-
    1041.html.
49. Finder, McConnell, and Mitchell, "Betting the Corporation," p. 12.
50. Finder, McConnell, and Mitchell, "Betting the Corporation," p. 23.
51. Vincent L. DiCianni, "New Principles Can Help Independent Corporate
    Monitoring," American Health Lawyers Association, www.affiliatedmoni-
    tors.com/articles/HLW_article.pdf.
52. Craig S. Morford, Acting Deputy Attorney General, memorandum to
    Heads of Department Components and United States Attorneys regarding
    "Selection and Use of Monitors in Deferred Prosecution Agreements and
    Non-Prosecution Agreements with Corporations," U.S. Department of
    Justice, March 7, 2008, www.usDOJ.gov/dag/morford-useofmoni-
    torsmemo-03072008.pdf.
53. John Martin, "$52M-plus Payday for Christie's Old Boss," *The Star-Ledger,*
    January 10, 2008, blog.nj.com/ledgerarchives/2008/01/52mplus_payday_
    for_christies_o.html.

Chapter 14

1. Marc J. Gottridge and Thomas Rouhette, "'Blocking' Statutes Bring
   Discovery Woes," *New York Law Journal,* April 30, 2008.
2. Cour de Cassation Chambre Criminelle, Paris, December 12, 2007,
   Juris-Data No. 2007-332254.
3. *Zubulake v. UBS Warburg LLC,* 217 F.R.D. 309 (S.D.N.Y. 2003).
4. Karen E. Willenken, "Hard Drives: Critical in Government
   Investigations," *National Law Journal,* March 22, 2010.

5. *U.S. v. Michael John O'Keefe, Sr. Sunil Agrawal, Defendants,* 537 F. Supp.2d 14 (U.S. Dist. 2008) LEXIS 12220: 4.

6. Daniel R. Margolis, Mark R. Hellerer, and Wayne C. Matus, "The Electronic Turn in Criminal Subpoenas," *New York Law Journal,* March 23, 2010, www.law.com/jsp/lawtechnologynews/PubArticleLTN.jsp?id=1202446647500.

7. *U.S. v. Gregory L. Reyes and Stephanie Jensen,* No. CR 06-0556 CRB (N.D. Ca. 2006), 6–7.

8. *Victor Stanley, Inc. v. Creative Pipe, Inc., et al.,* No. MJG-06-2662 (D. Md. 2008), 18.

9. *The Pension Committee of the University of Montreal Pension Plan, et al, v. Banc of America Securities, LLC, Citco Fund Services (Curacao) N.V., The Citco Group Limited, International Fund Services (Ireland) Limited, PricewaterhouseCoopers (Netherland Antilles), John W. Bendall, Jr., Richard Geist, Anthony Stocks, Kieran Conroy, and Declan Quilligan,* No. 05-CV-09016 (SAS) (S.D.N.Y. 2010), 84–85.

10. *Victor Stanley, Inc. v. Creative Pipe, Inc., et al.,* No. MJG-06-2662 (D. Md. 2008), 11–12.

11. *William A. Gross Construction Associates, Inc., Plaintiff, v. American Manufacturers Mutual Insurance Company, Defendant,* No. 07-CV-10639 (S.D.N.Y. 2009), 1, 5.

Index

CPSIA information can be obtained at www.ICGtesting.com
Printed in the USA
BVOW06*1432200815

414309BV00013B/107/P